ENDORSEMENTS

Read what songwriters say about *88 Songwriting Wrongs & How to Right Them* (the first edition of this book).

"Having made every one of these mistakes in the actual order that they were written, this book could have saved me *years* of wasted time."

—Rick Carnes, president, Songwriters Guild of America and hit songwriter of songs recorded by Garth Brooks, Alabama, Reba McEntire, Conway Twitty, Pam Tillis, and more

"*88 Songwriting Wrongs & How to Right Them* was the first songwriting book I ever purchased. I had a dream of being a performing songwriter ... Your book helped me to understand how to organize, structure and market my songs. I refer to your book all the time and feel that it has helped me become the songwriter I am today! Thank you!"

—Denise Vasquez, Los Angeles, California. Four-time winner of the ASCAP Performing Songwriters Award, Nominated by the L.A. Music Awards for Best Indie Female Vocalist and Best Indie Album of the Year

"So far I have gotten eighty-two independent artist cuts on my songs, and hope to hit the one hundred mark soon! Your book *88 Songwriting Wrongs & How to Right Them* helped me to reach that goal. This is an amazing book and I highly recommend it to any songwriter who wants to write songs that other artists will want to cut."

—Jeff Moxcey, Waterville, Maine

"Two years ago, I purchased your book, *88 Songwriting Wrongs & How to Right Them*. I have read it three times. Every time I do, I have a breakthrough. As with many songwriters, music is my life and my life is so much more rewarding now. I want to thank you both for such an incredible book. Knowing now how much of a difference it has made in my life, I have purchased many copies as presents for friends."

—Paul Maher, Bronx, New York

"Just wanted to let you know, that as a professional songwriter and musician, I've worn out my first edition of your book. Cover to cover, it not only helped fix what I was doing wrong as a beginner, but prepared me for troubles I would encounter down the road with my career. Without it, I don't think I would have had the know-how and straightforward honesty that was necessary for me to fine-tune my songs into not only something that sells, but really rocks!"

—Dennis Fallon, Pennsylvania

"Pat and Pete Luboff have maintained their commitment to developing and educating songwriters since I met them more than thirty years ago. Their own songwriting and teaching skills and experiences, along with their dedication to the craft, is abundantly clear in this book—accessible, clear, keenly observant, innovative and delivered with love, humor, and utter practicality."

—John Braheny, Author of *The Craft and Business of Songwriting*

"*88 Songwriting Wrongs & How to Right Them* is the distilled wisdom of folks who have watched songwriters struggle for years. Once I admitted I was making mistakes, I was open to solutions. This book has provided many."

—Mark Lee, Tempe, Arizona

"I got a copy of your *88 Songwriting Wrongs & How to Right Them* when it was hot off the press and I can offer a bunch of specific ways in which it has helped guide me in my search to improve my own writing. To this day when folks ask me for advice on how to improve their songwriting, it is a book I definitely recommend. There is an incredible amount of very specific terrific advice in your book. I am delighted that I read it when I did as it saved me a lot of rewriting time!"

—Bobbie Gallup, Nashville, Tennessee

"This book was the first book I ever bought on songwriting. It was also the most important. Until I owned this book, I was in the B.C. (as in 'Before a Clue') phase of my songwriting education and development. Pat and Pete Luboff's considerable gifts gently led me onto the path of discovering my own abilities and potential. This book is still a valuable reference and resource in my musical arsenal."

—Charles Alexander, Nashville, Tennessee

"I believe the 'dream' chases *you*. And it finally caught up with me at Luboffs' 'Songwriting Wrongs' number seventy. Therein bespeaks a wake-up call to anyone creating anything who, for whatever reason, has kept their gift(s) under a rock. If this is you, the fact that you're reading this now is no accident—it's time! Pore over the book's entirety, utilize the knowledge, and keep it within reach as a desk reference throughout your development. It will serve in providing the tools necessary to construct and perfect your craft. And answer some questions you may not have even thought of asking. So what are you waiting for?"

—Phil John de Anguera, Scipio Center, New York

"I just finished reading your book *88 Songwriting Wrongs & How to Right Them* and felt I had to send you a thank-you note! I am a fairly new songwriter and your book was easy to read and provided me with a wealth of information! Information can be obtained in many ways, but what makes your book special is the positive way you word things. I felt like you were right there supporting me while I was reading! I will continue to use your book as a wonderful reference and refer it to others."

—Diane Kopin, Nashville, Tennessee

"I am a songwriter and performer and proud owner of *88 Songwriting Wrongs and How to Right Them*! First I want to say how helpful your book has been; I have read through it several times and find myself constantly returning to it for inspiration and direction. Thank you both for writing such an informative and motivating book!"

—James Thacker, Nashville, Tennessee

"I finished reading your book *88 Songwriting Wrongs and How to Right Them* and wanted to let you know that it truly inspired me. It was very beneficial in providing me some direction to pursue my writing ability. The great info you provided mixed with humor was great. ('Collaborator breath' was too funny!) I have written poetry for many years and only after a friend suggested that I try writing songs did I purchase your book and begin to learn about lyric writing. Great job!"

—Ben Kuznicki II, Rogers City, Michigan

"When it came time for me to begin to take my songwriting seriously and become a student of the craft, I often used Pete and Pat's book as a reference guide to make sure my work was on track. I could always find something within its pages that helped to shed light on any problems I might be having. It was an invaluable resource."

—Jon Ims, BMI Song-of-the-Year songwriter for "She's In Love With the Boy," a number-one hit for Trisha Yearwood; "Falling In Love," a hit for Reba McIntyre; and songs for the Dixie Chicks and Confederate Railroad

"*88 Songwriting Wrongs & How to Right Them* was one of the very first songwriting and music business books that I read cover to cover. It covered about eighty-eight things that I did not even know I had to think about to be successful with songwriting. The chapters were short, so I was always looking forward to the next one."

—Geoff Kern, Carrollton, Texas

"I bought your book *88 Songwriting Wrongs & How to Right Them* because I was doing eighty-seven of the wrongs and needed help!! Your book really turned around my way of thinking and I now have five songs published. Thanks for writing the book."

—John Wesley Coutts, Dundee, Scotland

"*88 Songwriting Wrongs & How to Right Them* was the first book I purchased on songwriting thirteen years ago. It provided great insight into the craft and business of songwriting, lessons that helped me to develop common sense about this unique business, which few of us are born with."

—Donna M. Opfer, Dream Power Music, St. Louis, Missouri

"The two books available by Pat and Pete Luboff are essential to any aspiring or established songwriter. The tips help keep the focus on the title of the song and help prevent making some of the common mistakes. With these two books you will never experience writer's block, because they give you the skills necessary to explore all options and to allow yourself to always have a new idea. I teach guitar and help students with songwriting. I use the *12 Steps to Building Better Songs* as my model and the *88 Songwriting Wrongs & How to Right Them* as my reference manual. I don't know how I could get by without these two incredibly valuable resources!"

—Lee Johnson, Boulder, Colorado

"I have to tell you, your book is absolutely the best. I wish every songwriter out there could read it. It just amazes me how many people are so arrogant about what they write, and yet almost every one of their songs has eighty-seven out of eighty-eight wrongs in it. I have learned so much about songwriting from your book, yet the thing I learned the most was that my inner voice about songwriting has been right."

—Greg Stephens, Denver, Colorado

101 SONGWRITING WRONGS AND HOW TO RIGHT THEM

How to Craft and Sell Your Songs

101

SONGWRITING WRONGS AND HOW TO RIGHT THEM

How to Craft and Sell Your Songs

PAT and PETE LUBOFF

WRITER'S DIGEST BOOKS

Cincinnati, Ohio
www.writersdigest.com

Visit our Web sites at www.writersdigest.com and www.wdeditors.com for information on more resources for writers. For more fine books from Writer's Digest Books, visit www.fwbookstore.com.

To receive a free weekly e-mail newsletter delivering tips and updates about writing and about Writer's Digest products, register directly at our Web site at http://newsletters.fwpublications.com.

11 10 09 08 07   5 4 3 2 1

Distributed in Canada by Fraser Direct, 100 Armstrong Avenue, Georgetown, ON, Canada L7G 5S4, Tel: (905) 877-4411; Distributed in the U.K. and Europe by David & Charles, Brunel House, Newton Abbot, Devon, Q12 4PU, England, Tel: (+44) 1626 323200, Fax: (+44) 1626 323319, E-mail: postmaster@davidandcharles.co.uk; Distributed in Australia by Capricorn Link, P.O. Box 704, Windsor, NSW 2756 Australia, Tel: (02) 4577-3555

Library of Congress Cataloging-in-Publication Data

Luboff, Pat, 1946-

101 songwriting wrongs and how to right them : how to craft and sell your songs / By Pat and Pete Luboff. -- 2nd ed.

p. cm.

Includes index.

Previous ed.: 88 songwriting wrongs & how to right them, 1992.

ISBN 978-1-58297-480-4 (pbk. : alk. paper)

1. Popular music--Writing and publishing. 2. Music trade. I. Luboff, Pete, 1945- II. Title. III. Title: One hundred one songwriting wrongs and how to right them. IV. Title: One hundred and one songwriting wrongs and how to right them.

MT67.L8 2007

782.4216413--dc22   2007020130

Edited by Michelle Ehrhard
Designed by Eric West
Cover: Ibanez AW40NT Acoustic Guitar; for more information
    go to www.ibanez.com
Cover photography by Damian Hevia (www.dhevia.com)
Production coordinated by Mark Griffin

DEDICATION

This book is dedicated to all songwriters for their courage to create the mirrors of our lives.

ABOUT THE AUTHORS

Pat and Pete Luboff are platinum-selling hit songwriters with recordings by Patti LaBelle, Bobby Womack, Snoop Dogg, Michael Peterson, and the Norman Luboff Choir (that's Pete's dad), among others. "Body Language," a song they co-wrote with Harold Payne, is the title song of the musical written by Emmy-winning producer Michael Ajakwe, Jr. The Luboffs publish their own songs through Pea Pod Music.

They lived in Los Angeles for twenty-seven years, during which time they were deeply involved in the National Academy of Songwriters (Pat as president and Pete as vice chairman) and the Los Angeles Chapter of the Recording Academy (as editors of their newsletter, the *L.A. Record*, and Pete as first vice president and national trustee). As music business photojournalists, they created the national magazine of the Recording Academy, then known as *Grammy Pulse*. They also served as editors of *Songwriter Magazine* and the newsletter of the California Copyright Conference and contributed numerous articles to many music business publications.

The Luboffs began to teach songwriting in 1979 with the creation of the Monday night workshops at the National Academy of Songwriters. Pete taught an advanced songwriting course at UCLA Extension for thirteen years. When TAXI opened its doors in 1992, Pete became one of the first screeners and Pat joined him later. They have taught songwriting workshops from coast to coast.

At the suggestion of a songwriter in one of their workshops, they visited Nashville in the fall of 1999. It was love at first hearing! By spring of 2000 they had made the move to Music City, USA. They continue to lead a Monday night workshop, now called the Sounding Board, near Music Row. The Luboffs also teach workshops for Nashville Songwriters Association International (NSAI) and have participated in NSAI's Songposium and Tin Pan South events. When they're not teaching, you'll find them collaborating with artists, staff writers, publishers, and producers, or singing in clubs around Nashville, including the world-famous Bluebird Café.

Pat and Pete Luboff are available for workshops in your area and for individual songwriting consultations in person, via phone and e-mail. For more information, visit their Web site at www.writesongs.com or call (615) 596-3482.

ACKNOWLEDGMENTS

Every day is Thanksgiving for us. We are grateful for our lives as songwriters and for the people in our lives who inspire us to write songs. There are too many to mention here, but we will list a few.

We owe special thanks to Rich Wiseman for his help with this book. And thanks to our editor at Writer's Digest Books, Michelle Ehrhard, who showed us what we could not see. Others who have shared their expertise include:

Richard Aberdeen, Freedom Train Music; Chris Baptiste, TAXI; Rick Carnes, the Songwriters Guild; Barbara Cloyd; Debi Cochran, Nashville Songwriters Association International (NSAI); Tamara Allegra Conniff, *Billboard*; Terri Fricon, Fricon Entertainment; Bart Herbison, NSAI; Tom Long, Artists & Repertoire, Inc.; Denny Martin, Denny Martin Music; Marjorie McIntosh; Nancy Moran, Azalea Music Group; Gilli Moon, Warrior Girl Music; John Mullins, SESAC; Ralph Murphy, the American Society of Composers, Authors and Publishers (ASCAP); Don Passman, Esq.; David Rivers; Madeleine Smith, Madeleine Smith Music Services; the Sounding Board Songwriters; Stephanie Thomson; Alicia Warwick, the Recording Academy; and Brian Austin Whitney, Just Plain Folks.

A big thank y'all to the Nashville songwriting community for welcoming us with open arms. We especially thank our wonderful collaborators: James Eubanks, Casey Kelly, Tim Mathews, Craig Monday, Harold Payne, Michael Peterson, Michael Puryear, Jon Robbin, Justin Spears, Bill Warrington, and Don Wayne.

To our family, Dot, Gunilla, Paladin, Pepper, and Tina, and to those who have passed on but are ever-present in our hearts, we give thanks for you every day.

Thanks to every songwriter who ever wrote a song, and to those whose songs have reached our ears and touched our hearts. And thanks to God for the miracles we receive daily.

TABLE OF CONTENTS

PART 1: IN THE BEGINNING
Wobbly Song Foundations

PART 2: WHAT IN THE WORD?

Watching What You Say in Your Lyrics

PART 3: MAKING THE MUSIC
Melodic Mistakes

PART 4: ONCE WRITTEN, LOOK TWICE
Rewriting Wrongs

PART 5: TWO HEADS, OR MORE, ARE BETTER
Collaboration Misconceptions

PART 6: GETTING IT RECORDED
Demo No-Nos

PART 7: ALLOW ME TO PRESENT MY SONG
Pitching Package Pratfalls

PART 8: MAKING DISCONNECTIONS
How Not to Get Your Songs Heard

PART 9: THE CD RELEASE PARTY'S OVER
Post-Record Release Problems

PART 10: WILD WEIRD WEB
Internet Entanglements

DEAR SONGWRITERS

Fifteen years have passed since this book originally appeared as *88 Songwriting Wrongs & How to Right Them*. In that time, the Internet has changed the world. Back then, you could make a taped copy of a song, but it wouldn't be as good as the original. Now, you can make endless perfect digital copies and send them out over the Internet for the whole world to download.

Fifteen years ago, there were many major record labels. As we write, the majors are down to four conglomerates. They are adjusting to the new paradigm; waking up to the reality that digital downloading is the way music will be delivered in the future. CD sales are declining; record stores are going out of business. Devices smaller than lighters now hold five hundred songs. As the major record labels dwindle in numbers, a huge number of writers/artists are taking their creative lives in their own hands.

Corporations have bought up many of the traditional radio stations. One corporation can program over a thousand stations at once. Corporations mean business and that means selling: An hour of radio time is almost thirty minutes of commercials. Satellite radio and Internet radio are growing to meet listeners' needs for diversity.

What does all this mean for us as songwriters? Everything and nothing. Everything because technology is the means by which we bring our songs to the world and the way we get paid for our creations. Nothing because we still have to face the unknown and create something out of nothing. Without songwriters, there would be no songs. And what would the world be without songs? We don't even want to think about it!

Thanks to all the writers who have taken the time to let us know how much they've enjoyed our book. We especially love the writers who have shown us their copies—underlined and indexed and covered with notes in the margins. Our favorite comment: "Your book was the best songwriting investment I ever made." We are delighted and honored to know we've helped you.

Write on,

Pat & Pete Luboff
www.writesongs.com

FOREWORD

How do you write a hit song?

by Rick Carnes, President of the Songwriter's Guild of America

As president of the Songwriters Guild of America and a lifelong professional song-writer, I should be able to answer that question when people ask it. Alas, I have no idea. Or rather, I have an idea that probably won't work but once out of one hundred tries. But that one success is all it takes to be a professional songwriter!

For more than thirty years, I have written thousands of failed songs and a handful of hits. I have done the wrong thing with my music and my career 99 percent of the time. So I feel infinitely qualified to tell you this book you are holding in your hands is a virtual road map through the minefield of failure that is songwriting. And these aren't the little failures either. These are the great big, song-destroying, career-ending kind of failures that you cannot afford to make. If the book stopped with a simple list of those catastrophes it would be worth a fortune. But Pat and Pete have done so much more than merely point out the problems. They have rolled up their sleeves and worked for years in the industry and, with their students in their world renowned workshops, have come up with solid, workable answers.

In this book, there is a wealth of information to help you navigate around (and sometimes through) 101 heartbreaks. I suppose you could just learn the hard way, like I did, but then that would be mistake 102!

INTRODUCTION

"Everybody makes mistakes. That's part of trying."
—Fred Rogers on Mr. Rogers' Neighborhood

*"Forget about the consequences of failure.
Failure is only a temporary change in direction
to set you straight for your next success."*
—Denis Waitley

Songwriting is a lifelong learning process. It's more than a craft; it's a way of life. Songwriters speak for those who cannot express themselves. To do that, songwriters need to develop a keen sensitivity to the human condition. And we all know that to err is human!

This is a book about common mistakes songwriters make. We use the word *mistakes* even though we don't believe there are such things: There are no mistakes; there are only lessons learned.

Songwriting is like flying a plane. Pilots don't just stick the plane in the air, point it in the right direction, and sit back while it flies in a straight line to its destination. Their instruments constantly feed back information, and the pilots constantly correct the course. In one sense, they are constantly "making mistakes" that have to be corrected. The creative process in songwriting is the same: You take off in one direction with a song and the song feeds back information about whether you are on the right course.

We learned something wonderful years ago while we were homeschooling our children. We were teaching science by doing experiments. The assignment called for us to make a hypothesis about the outcome. We did so and conducted the experiment. Our hypothesis was incorrect, but we realized in a blinding flash that we had learned just as much from making an incorrect hypothesis as we would have from making the so-called correct one.

As songwriters, it's our job to check our egos at the door and leave them there. If we insist we can't make mistakes, that our creations spring from us in a perfect state, why would we ever want to change them? And if we don't want to change them, how will we grow as songwriters? Our choice is to follow Sir John Templeton's advice:

"If we become increasingly humble about how little we know, we may be more eager to search." Or to fit the definition of insanity, widely attributed to Albert Einstein, "… doing the same thing over and over and expecting different results."

And the mistakes don't stop when the song is finished. There are a lot more than 101 mistakes to be made and lessons to be learned in demoing, pitching, and doing business with the song.

So embrace your mistakes. Learn from them. Change and grow. That's the beauty of being a songwriter.

Write on,

Pat & Pete Luboff

PART 1

IN THE BEGINNING

Wobbly Song Foundations

THE ONES THAT GOT AWAY

*Be prepared to capture music
and lyric ideas when they come*

You're having dinner at a crowded restaurant and the couple at the next table is experiencing a challenge in their relationship. You can tell by the way they're discreetly yelling at each other, not loud enough to get thrown out but with sufficient volume for you to hear every word.

As a songwriter, you know it's in your job description to eavesdrop on conversations. The basic, real-life emotions people express in their everyday relationships are the building blocks of songs that tap into the lives of your listeners. So you listen, and sure enough, one of the combatant lovers comes up with a great title in the middle of a heated sentence. You smile as you slice your next bite of food. *Great title,* you think; *I'm going to remember that.*

But by the time you're ordering the dessert course, you're asking yourself, *What was that she said?* It's too late to ask that question. The phrase has escaped your mind completely. You feel empty in spite of your meal; maybe you let a great song get away.

The solution to this problem is simple. Never let the possibility of a great idea get past you. Scribble it on a napkin if you must, but put it in writing or record it in some way

when it first sparks your enthusiasm. Later, you may look at it and wonder what you saw in it. Then you can deliver your paper napkin to the local recycling center with a clear conscience, knowing you gave the idea a chance to be seriously considered.

Song titles and ideas are in the air. You'll hear them in phone conversations, see them in the newspaper, find them popping out of the depths of your mind as you're driving down the highway. As a songwriter, it's your job to be ready to catch these fleeting thoughts as they fly by. Ideally, you should be prepared in an organized way (see the next chapter). But if Boy or Girl Scouting is not in your history, it's up to you to improvise when a song title appears in a restaurant and finds you without a pencil or scrap of paper. Many great songs have been written on paper napkins with borrowed pens.

Plenty of songwriting goes on in moving vehicles. Since it's not easy to find someone to borrow a pencil or paper from at fifty-five or even twenty-five miles per hour, you should equip your car with these items. Some writers pull over to the side of the road when inspiration hits; others

4

speed on and scribble. Billy Steinberg, the lyricist in the Tom Kelly/Billy Steinberg collaborations of "Like a Virgin," "True Colors," and co-writer on "Eternal Flame" and "I Touch Myself," admitted to us that he's been known to swerve a bit when a hit has hit him on the road.

Technology can be your friend if you're writing on the run. When a bolt of inspiration strikes, many writers break out cassette tape recorders or tiny digital recorders to catch the spark.

This system was the favorite of Steve Allen who, with thousands of songs to his credit, has been cited in the *Guinness Book of World Records* as the world's most prolific songwriter. He was never without one or two mini-cassette recorders, and he filled up tapes rapidly because he was constantly open and receptive to the nonstop flow of ideas. He told us he couldn't tell whether he was creating them or remembering someone else's creations!

Use of a recorder, however, requires another step—you have to transcribe the recordings to have access to the ideas you've captured. Mr. Allen had that one licked, since his creativity paid off in the form of a pool of secretaries to do that job for him. He proved the value of catching ideas as they come to you.

In a dream, Mr. Allen wrote the tune most closely associated with him, "This Could Be the Start of Something Big." He woke up with the song still playing in his mind and quickly recorded it on tape. The moral of that story is: When you open up the channel, be ready to receive. Keep your notebook or your tape or digital recorder next to your bed. And may you dream a hit tonight!

Some people use their cell phones to call their home answering machines and leave a message. They can decide when they get home whether the message is inspirational. Laptop computers are now capable of recording fully produced demos, so catching that idea you just had is a snap for them. Pretty soon, we'll just push a button on our necks and what we say will be saved to our hard drives at home! In the meantime, pencil and paper still work, and always having those with you is the least you can do to honor your creative inspirations.

As in every songwriting rule, the exception has validity. Case in point: Willie Nelson told us that he never writes anything down in his writing process. He feels that if it can be forgotten, it wasn't strong enough. He wrote "Crazy" in his car. He was on his way home to Texas, retreating from Nashville where he had met with resounding rejection, and his house had just burned down. It was a rough ride home, but Willie used it to write one of our favorite songs in the world. If you haven't heard the Patsy Cline version of "Crazy," do yourself a favor. It's up there with one of the best recordings of all time.

Most songwriters, however, must catch the first inspiration, the seed of the song idea, to have the chance to see what it could grow into with some cultivation. A commitment to getting the idea into some tangible form for later consideration is a basic commitment to yourself as a songwriter.

2

IT'S HERE SOMEWHERE

Have an organized place to keep your song notes

Step number one is to catch the inspiration, the line or the melody, and record it somehow, no matter where or when it hits you. Caught with no pen or paper in the restaurant, you borrow the waiter's pen and scribble your inspiration on the paper napkin. You slip the napkin into your pocket and launch into your linguini, satisfied you have not let that one get away.

After dinner, you're off to the movies, and, by the time you get home, you have just enough energy to throw your clothes into the hamper and crawl between the sheets. One thing leads to another and your great idea goes through the wash and disappears with the rinse.

Getting it down in writing is not enough. Putting it someplace special, a place from which it can be retrieved and then reconsidered, is essential. If you're already prepared with a system for gathering your song seeds, you won't be left hunting for long-lost napkins in your lint filter.

A song-catching system can be as simple as a box or a drawer into which you throw all your scribbled-on scraps. Then you can pull out song ideas like raffle tickets and work on them at random for the fun of it. A more sophisticated system, but still easily within the reach of most of us, is a small bound notebook. Keep a pen clipped to the notebook and carry it with you at all times.

If categorizing appeals to you, a notebook with index tabs separating sections is a good organizing tool. Label the sections "Titles," "Songs in Progress," "Connections" (potential collaborators, people to pitch songs to), and "Tax-Deductible Expenditures" (mileage, CDs, cassettes, and so forth), or whatever suits your style of organizing. A list of titles is a wonderful starting point for a writing session, especially with a collaborator.

If you're serious about being a songwriter, you'll eventually have to set up a filing system for your copyrights and royalty statements. Why not start now? A section of a desk drawer or filing cabinet should be dedicated to your songwriting. Each completed song will need its own file folder, labeled with the title. The contents of the folder might be: the original scribbles of the early drafts of the song, a collaboration agreement among the writers of the song, a final lyric sheet, a chord sheet or number chart and a publishing contract for the song. If you bring your songs to a workshop where you get written responses from a circle of songwriters (as we do with all our songs), file those signed and dated lyric sheets. They can serve as proof of a date of creation. (For a complete explanation of changes in the copyright law, see chapter sixty-nine, "Copyright It, Right?") Other files can be set up to hold lists of titles and receipts for expenditures. As you develop a number of music business connections, you will need a filing system to keep track of names, addresses, phone numbers, and which songs were pitched to whom. If all this is Greek to you, read on. We'll explain later.

Almost everyone has a computer now and perhaps the bulk of your songwriting information will be stored on your hard drive. Please back up this information on a regular basis! We met a Canadian writer/artist whose laptop was stolen. All her song files were on it, including a lot of recording sessions. She had backed up some of it, but not recently. She could retrieve the lost recordings from the various studios she worked in, but not in time to have them for her already scheduled trip to Nashville. Computers are great except for when they crash or get lost or stolen—back them up!

No matter what your system, be sure you have some method for retrieving your great ideas.

3

THE TOO-EARLY EDITOR

*Don't stop the creative flow by
judging too early in the process*

You've managed to catch the inspiration on the fly and wrestle it down on paper, tape, or digital media; now you sit down and try to write the song. You face that blank page or computer screen. You write one lyric line, look at it, wrinkle your nose as if there were a skunk in the room, and cross the line out. You try another line. "That's bad, awful, stupid," you grumble at yourself as you scratch out line number two. After more than five or ten minutes of this, depending on your personal tolerance for pain, you become convinced that the original idea wasn't worth the paper napkin you scribbled it on. Maybe it's just that you're a lousy writer. Maybe you should never have been born. You've edited your song and yourself out of existence before either of you had a chance.

Part of the problem is you're trying to go from blank page to finished product. That's like having a pack of seeds on your desk and wondering why you can't pick the flowers. You haven't dug, planted, watered, weeded, or fertilized! Songs require some playing in the dirt before they can bloom.

If you're a writer who edits your ideas before they've had a chance to flow, take yourself to the nearest mirror and firmly tell yourself to *stop*. The crystal-clear ideas that flow in a song come from a deep well of human emotions. In order to tap into that source of ideas and let them flow through you, you have to prime the pump. Have you ever used an old-fashioned sink pump? Remember pumping the handle up and down, up and down? How many times did you pump before any water came? At first it was just a trickle. But after a while, a steady stream came easily with each push on the handle.

How do you prime your songwriting pump? One good way is to free-associate. Psychiatrists use free association as a way of revealing their patients' unconscious. Dr. Freud would say "mother" and the patient, instructed to reply with the first word that popped into her head, would usually say "father." If the patient screamed "butcher knife," Dr. Freud knew he had a guaranteed steady income.

Suppose the phrase that caught your ear in the restaurant was "What happened to the passion?" No wonder you liked that—*happened* and *passion* resonate with each other in a near rhyme (as opposed to a perfect rhyme, like *slow* and *go*). There's also a strong emotional tone to the line and a ring of universality. Every good relationship develops from an initial heated attraction to the subtler rosy glow of commitment—if the couple can hang in there.

Now it's time to free-associate. Let your mind spew out every word that comes into it without editing at all. Here's a sample of a free association on *happened*: lost, found, missing, missing in action, gone, faded, pale, cool, cold, frozen, ice, hard, easy, easy does it, don't do it, do you, will we, why not, why bother, hopeless, sad, sorry, it was an accident, slipped away, fell down, crashed, burned, explosion. Now let's try *passion*: heat, hot, fire, burning, yearning, desire, love, attraction, magnetism, electricity, lightning, thunder, rain, excitement, hunger, need, craving, thirst. Keep going until you feel you're done. You could also try looking up the words in a thesaurus, but only after you've free-associated them. Your connections will probably be more creative than those you will find listed there.

What you've done is similar to what an artist does before creating an oil painting: You've put your colors on the palette. Now you can see what you have to work with. A couple of these words may jump out at you from the page and say, "Use me, I'm unique. I call up a great image." You may be inspired to write lines around those words. Follow the urge but maintain the frame of mind you developed in the free-association exercise. Write everything that comes to your mind and do

not judge one bit of it. Remember where judging got you before, staring at a line of dark scribbles and contemplating nonexistence. Tomorrow will be soon enough to ask yourself if you like what you wrote today. Right now you're just getting out the raw materials. Don't try to rhyme. Don't try to write the finished lyric at all. Just pump, pump, pump out those ideas.

A writer friend of ours taught us a trick that has worked magic for us. First we decide who the singer is in the song, who he or she is singing to, and what the situation is. Then we pretend we are that singer, actually put ourselves in his or her shoes, and quickly write one hundred sentences that person would really say in that situation. Notice, we said *sentences*. We don't try to rhyme or fit in any meter. We don't try to be poetic. We just try to say something emotionally real in as many ways as we can. Surprise! Four of those sentences will stand out as interesting, unique, and just what we need. They often even rhyme! And the fact that they're sentences makes them, by definition, conversational. This process also yields interesting rhythms in the lyrics and keeps them from sounding boxy and sing-songy.

You can set your melodies free, too. Musical free association can be done with or without a tool in hand. A drum machine is fun to use to get your musical juices flowing. Start by creating a pattern on your machine (a.k.a. a "drum feel"). Drum feels in themselves suggest an attitude. If you just start singing over a feel that turns you on, unexpected inspiration can strike. Don't forget to have your recording device rolling to catch what comes to you.

If your tool is a guitar or piano, try practicing scales, chord inversions, difficult rhythmic combinations, anything that pushes the limits of your skills. You might find your fingers wandering in the middle of your F-sharp melodic minor scale because they want to "play hooky" from their studies. If they happen to hit upon a hot lick that could turn into the beginning of a song, follow that creative gust.

When creativity flows, it often digs channels. You find yourself always going to the same rhythms, the same chord changes. One way to break out of your rhythmic rut is to play the drum machine at the same time as either the guitar or piano. With the drum machine going, play chords with no real concern whether one follows the other. When and if they do come together, you will often find yourself in a musical place you wouldn't have gone on your own.

Another way to break away from the musical places your hands tend to go to by themselves is to create your music without that tool in your hand. Take your title or lyric ideas and sing them *a cappella* (without instrumental accompaniment). Make up lyrics as you go along. These can be silly or nonsense lyrics. You might even blurt out a really striking lyric line, especially if you keep your list of brainstormed phrases in front of you. The resulting gibberish is called a "dummy lyric." You'll be in good company; the Beatles' amazing song "Yesterday" started out as "Scrambled Eggs." Maybe the dummy words you mumble will create an interesting metric pattern or a catchy melodic phrase. Later you can put the dummy lyric in a musical setting with a drum pattern and guitar or piano arrangement. Then you can fine-tune the words on the melody.

The point of these techniques is to free yourself to create something new and fresh. You need to keep interested in your creation. Free exploration of unknown territories, taking creative risks, having fun with your writing—none of these are possible if you have a judge screaming in your head that you're wrong before you even begin.

For some people who want to write, the inner critic is so negative that the entire process gets frozen. If you have read this chapter and find you cannot stop the judge from pounding the gavel as soon as pencil approaches paper or fingers touch musical instruments, there is help. A self-help group called A.R.T.S. (Artists in Recovery through the Twelve Steps) uses a slightly amended version of the twelve steps of Alcoholics Anonymous to get beyond paralyzing self-criticism, writer's block, and invalidating attitudes. There are no dues or fees for membership. There may be a meeting in your area. If not, you can start one with help and literature from A.R.T.S. Check out their Web site at www.artsanonymous.org or call their hotline at (212) 873-7075.

4

DON'T MESS WITH MY MUSE
Don't think that discipline will hamper your creativity

Living on the other side of the looking glass from the songwriters who suffer from the too-early editor are the songwriters who refuse, on moral principle, to question anything they do. We've seen many of them in our workshops.

Their basic philosophy is that their creative process is a delicate flower that will wither if disturbed in any way. Discipline is a dirty word to them, as is any word having to do with the commonly accepted tools of the songwriting trade, including rhyming, structure, title, chorus, and clarity. They become angry in the workshop when we talk about these things and tell us in no uncertain terms that they want nothing to do with them. They see no value in learning about what goes into a song, and consider this a threat to their ability to connect with their mystical muse. Some say their songs must be perfect, because God delivered them in exactly that form.

We wonder why they come to the workshop at all if they feel this way. If they are convinced before they enter the room that they don't want to change their ways—that is, learn something new about songwriting—why are they there?

Thomas Edison said, "We don't know a millionth of one percent about anything." The more you know, the more you realize how little you know. Danny Dill, who wrote "Long Black Veil" and "Detroit City" and is now in his eighties, said to us, "You never *get* songwriting. And if you think you do, you're dead!" That's what we love about songwriting; it's a lifelong learning process.

Don't make the mistake of limiting your opportunities by pretending you know everything there is to know. Learning is fun and fuels the creative process. Knowing how songs are put together will not prevent you from putting yours together in your own way, force you to do it in a way you don't like, or dry up your creative well. Everything you learn can be used to help you grow as a songwriter.

A song is a particular kind of art form. It has a definite shape, just as an artist's canvas has measurable dimensions. The canvas can be tiny or huge. The tiny painting can fit in anyone's home. Only a mansion or a museum has a wall large enough for the huge painting. If your aim is to get your song recorded and played on the radio, there is a limit to the length of time you have to get your message across. There are many other variables that come into play if your song is to be chosen from the thousands upon thousands of others vying for the same two- to three-minute slot on the radio.

Maybe the idea of taking these things into consideration while you are writing makes you nuts. It could be that you don't really want to write mainstream commercial songs, that you seriously want to go where no songwriter has gone before and create an entirely new song art form.

We went to a concert of works written by contemporary composers several years ago. One young man sat down at the piano and proceeded to play something that sounded like he was just banging anywhere on the keyboard with his flat hand or his elbows—no regular rhythm, no melody, no chords we recognized. We thought, *This guy could be making a million mistakes and no one would ever know.* Five seconds later, he stopped dead, apologized to the audience, and said he had made a mistake and wanted to start from the beginning. When you're creating out where the buses don't run you can make your own rules, and who's to know if you break them, unless you tell them? There's a big, wide world of creativity that does not depend on the format-driven constraints of commercial radio. We are judges for the Just Plain Folks' annual contest and are constantly amazed at the level of creativity that songwriters display in unique niche categories. Visit www.jp folks.com to join this ever-growing, free online songwriting community.

The reality is, however, that many songwriters really do want to write songs that have commercial potential. It's just that some songwriters have swallowed the myth that the creative person can only function as some untamed force of nature, operating above the rules that govern everyday life. The rules of the songwriting craft are not there to stifle your creativity. Rather, they are there to give you a framework, to challenge you to fill that framework with such skill that those who hear your message will dance, cry, make love, and sing.

Songs express the full range of human experience: prayer, pride in country, the call to war, the joy of personal love or misery at its loss, rage at social injustice, teaching our children; storytelling, both serious and hilarious, dancing, and just plain having fun.

More than 150 years ago, Stephen Foster crystallized the form of the American popular song. A study of the structures in his songs will reveal the roots of the verse/chorus and verse/bridge forms we explain in chapter eleven, "No Bones About It." You probably can sing these songs without referring to sheet music: "Beautiful Dreamer," "Camptown Races," "(Way Down Upon the) Swanee River," "Oh! Susanna," "Jeannie With the Light Brown Hair," and "My Old Kentucky Home."

Those are the cream of the crop of over two hundred songs published before his death at the age of thirty-seven.

The fact that these forms are still in use today is a testimony to their value. There is something about the way our thoughts line up, the way music and words come together to express a reality more focused and pure than real life, the way rhymes satisfy our ears and repetition enchants us, that wants to fit itself into verse/chorus and verse/bridge song structures.

You wouldn't be a songwriter if you didn't love songs. But if you want to be a serious songwriter, there comes a time when the honeymoon is over, and you realize it doesn't happen by magic. Get on your work clothes, grab your mon-key wrench, and take apart any song you love until you understand why it is great. Buy the CD or pay for a download and transcribe the lyrics if they're not on the packaging. This scrutiny will fill you with information on structure, rhyme, imagery, and storytelling. You'll see that great songs are a highly disciplined art form. They are both 100 percent creativity and 100 percent structured, proof that structure and creativity are not mutually exclusive.

Fear not for your creativity. It is safe and can only be enhanced by learning what makes a great song great. You wouldn't try to read without knowing the alphabet first. Why try to write songs without a basic knowledge of the tools and structures of songwriting?

5

NOWHERESVILLE
Know what you're trying to say

Have you seen the great old Ernest Borgnine movie *Marty*? Marty asks his friend, "What do you want to do?" His friend replies, "I don't know, Marty. What do you want to do?" Marty answers, "I don't know. What do you want to do?" They do this quite a lot in the movie. Finally, Marty breaks away from his friends who can't decide what they want to do and takes the big risk of offering himself to a nice girl. He is rewarded with the happy ending of a promising relationship, while his friends are still hanging around the corner asking each other what they want to do. If you want a happy ending to your songwriting process, you will have to take the plunge. You must ask yourself, *What do I want to do with this song?* You need an idea of where you're going or you won't get there.

At a songwriting workshop we taught at Santa Fe Community College, Andy Lovato played a song for us, "Trouble Boy," that he had co-written with Tollis Pompeo. The demo was excellent. From the first note of the introduction, you got the feeling that the song was about something heavy. The atmosphere of the song was ominous.

Trouble Boy

Standing on a corner hanging out,
*   passing the time*
Not too hard to tell what's on his mind
He don't wanna play any games,
*   follow no rules*
He ain't gonna change and let down
*   his cool*
If you ask where he's going, he'll just
*   laugh and look away*
And say it don't matter, he just lives
*   day to day*

   Chorus:

   He's a trouble boy, trouble boy,
   trouble boy
   Take your trust and break it like
   it was a toy

Cruising down the street late at night,
*   he's never done*
Waiting for the chance to have his fun
Hiding out in back of his shades,
*   what does he care*
He ain't losing sleep, he's getting his share
Keeping wild, crazy hours with his crazy
*   bunch of friends*
Living in a dream where the party
*   never ends*

Chorus: repeat

You don't know what trouble is
Till you mess around with a trouble kid

Chorus: repeat

© Andrew Lovato/Tollis Pompeo

After we listened to the song and complimented Andy on his demo and the way the mood was communicated in the song, we asked him some questions: "What were you trying to make us feel? Are we supposed to feel sorry for the person in the song? Are we supposed to be moved to advocate for better social services for children so people won't grow up into this desperate state? What message did you want to get across?"

He answered, "Gee, I never thought about that."

His answer floored us. Here's a smart guy who has spent hours and hours crafting this song and hundreds of dollars producing a demo, and he didn't stop to think what he was trying to say in the first place!

In chapter three, we left you with your palette filled with lyrical and musical possibilities. You are like an artist who has put every color in the rainbow on the palette in preparation for a painting. Now you turn to the canvas and say, "I'm going to paint a still life of a bowl of fruit." Or, "I'm going to do a bold abstract painting that will express the joy I am feeling now." You have an intention, an idea you want to communicate.

The same is true for writing a song. Song is a powerful, emotional method of communication. What do you want to express, to communicate? Turn to your song canvas and tell it what you have in mind. You might say:

- I want this song to make people cry.
- I want people to jump up and dance when they hear this song.
- I want this song to be a number-one hit.
- I want to pitch this song to Celine Dion.
- I want to use this song to promote myself as an artist.
- I want a Christian artist to record this song.
- I want to change the world with this song.
- I want this song to be personal, to tell my husband I love him.

Let's go back to the song we were writing in chapter three, "What Happened to the Passion?" Suppose you decide to make people cry with this song. In that case, you would take the title in the direction of the end of a love affair. The singer could be extremely sad because he wants to continue in the relationship, but his lover isn't interested anymore. The tempo might be slow to medium, the range of the melody could be wide, rising and falling to emphasize the depth of emotion felt by the singer.

How about making people dance with the song? This time, the singer might be angry, ready to walk but getting in one last dig at the lover, something like, "You came on so strong, like you wanted me so much, but now that you have me where you wanted me, you don't want me anymore." The beat would be hard and fast. The melody might not have a very wide range, and the notes could fire rapidly.

Now consider the proposition that you want to write a number-one hit song. A study of the charts in *Billboard* (a major trade magazine of the music business) will show you that very few artists record *outside* songs (songs written by someone other than themselves, their producers, or their band members). It's up to you to identify the few artists who do record outside songs so you can aim the song you're about to write in their direction. All artists have an image, a look and sounds, that make them special. This image also includes the kinds of messages they will sing. Which artist might sing the message, "What Happened to the Passion?"

Patti LaBelle is an artist who records outside songs—a gold record on our living-room wall attests to that. She recorded "Body Language," a song we wrote with Harold Payne, on her *I'm in Love Again* album. Her image as a strong, independent woman could accommodate the demand "What Happened to the Passion?" So, you decide you want to write for Patti LaBelle. It will help to visualize her singing the song you are writing. (Don't forget to leave some room for her trademark vocal trips into the ionosphere.)

If your goal is to perform and record your song as well as write it, other factors have to be considered. Is this message im-portant to you? If it became a hit, could you sing it over and over again for years and still mean it? Does it communicate the image that you want to have as an artist?

How about trying to change the world with the song? "What Happened to the Passion?" could be a song that asks why there is so much apathy and self-doubt in America. Why are we suffering from one political scandal after another? Why doesn't everyone stand up and stop all the craziness? What happened to the energy, the coming together, that we had in the sixties? Could it be a country song? Asking yourself these questions in the beginning will help you focus on what you want to communicate and how you want to express it.

The decision to write a very personal song is a liberating one. You intimately know who you're writing to and you know, no matter what, the song will be a hit with that person. The details of your relationship will give you all the inspiration you need. In the end, this song may even be a number-one hit. That's what happened for Randy Goodrum when he wrote "You Needed Me" as a love song to his wife. Only one hundred-plus turn-downs later, Anne Murray recorded it. It's also possible that your personal song will remain just that, strictly personal. "What Happened to the Passion?" can become "I Love What Happened to the Passion" for your personal love song to your spouse. The lyrics could speak to your experience of a broader and deeper feeling than the first rush of attraction, and how great it is to experience that kind of growth in your relationship.

Now can you sense how each of these intentions affects the direction that the song takes? These big-picture decisions set the scene for the hundreds of other decisions that must follow as you choose each word of lyric, each chord, and each note of your melody. It's like making a decision to go to Los Angeles. L.A. is a big city! You still have to decide precisely where in L.A. you want to go. Having an idea of where you're going with your song will help you make choices along the way. Starting to write without your intention in mind is like taking a cross-country trip to an unknown destination. How will you know which way to turn when you come to a fork in the road? Without a clear intention, you wind up in Nowheresville.

6

HEARD BUT NOT SCENE

Have a clear idea of all the details of the song's setting

Songwriters come from far and wide to the workshop we started in 1979 in Hollywood and continue to facilitate in Nashville. John Oriettas from Quebec, Canada, brought in this song:

Somehow

Girl little did we know
How fast that love could grow
The time was short the time was sweet
Ooh girl I never will forget you

There's a place in my heart
It will never part
But now I have to leave
Ooh girl I will never forget you

> **Chorus:**
>
> *Somehow the moment that I met you*
> *Somehow I knew I never would*
> *   forget you girl*
> *You made a change in my life*
> *And somehow we've got to make*
> *   it last forever*

That look upon your face
I never will replace
You made me laugh you made me smile
Ooh girl I never will forget you

Bridge:

Me and you
Make our dreams come true
We're gonna make them last forever

© John Oriettas

This song left us wondering about many things. Who are the people involved? Where and when did this encounter happen? Is the relationship over or not? If it is over, why? Somehow, this song did not get across any hard information.

Have you ever noticed how the first few shots in a motion picture, those behind the title and the credits, tell you so much about where and when the story is taking place? That process in a motion picture takes about as long as you have to complete your whole song: three minutes. You don't have time to get into long shots of landscape. The listener must have a pretty good idea within the first few seconds of the where, when, who, what, and why of your song.

But how do you get all that into those few seconds? Try transcribing just the first one or two lines of the lyrics of your favorite songs and see how much information is communicated and how it's done. Hit writers may not literally put descriptive words into their opening lyrics, but they give a clear picture of who is singing, who is being sung to, why the singer wants to sing, what the message is, and where and when the singing is taking place.

When we write a song, answering these questions is one of the first activities in our process. We talk about who the people are. We call them the *singer* and the *singee*. The singer is the person doing the singing and the singee is the person being sung to. For instance, the singer in one song is a woman named Jean who can't stop thinking about her ex-husband. He has divorced her to marry another woman. She still lives in the home they shared together. It was a total shock to her; she had no idea there was anything wrong in their relationship. She is in pain and really wants to forget her ex-husband.

Jean is in her thirties. She has no children. She's a bank teller. She drives an old beat-up VW, and we could go on to hair and eye color, height, weight, and so on. We create a real person in our minds, a person with a lifestyle.

She has started a relationship with a new man, Richard. They met when he came into the bank to make a deposit. They have been on several dates and tonight she has invited him for dinner at her house. Even though she is not in love with Richard, she is willing to try being intimate with him. They have just finished eating dinner. What are they going to do next? Jean sings to Richard (the singee), asking him to make love to her to help her forget her pain. We don't have to show his reply to this request. We're just going to capture that dramatic instant in which she bares her heart and soul to him.

Jean is more important in this song than Richard, so we didn't describe him in so much detail. For some songs, we do a full characterization for both the singer and the singee.

Having all this background fleshed out builds a firm foundation for your song's unity. Picturing a specific person as the singer helps you choose the language the singer will use when he or she is speaking those one hundred sentences we talked about in chapter three. The little details may never find their way into the song, but they will be there in your mind, keeping the story of the song building in a realistic way. The reason we all love great stories is because we come to care about the people in the stories. We know about them. They become our friends. We identify with their feelings. The feelings don't exist without the people who feel them. That's why our songs have to be sung by characters who are real to us, because we have given them fully fleshed-out lives.

Without those details, "Somehow," from the beginning of this chapter, has nothing that reaches out and grabs us. We recommended that John go back to the drawing board with this one and work up a picture with many more details than he actually needs in the song.

How about this for a story line? The singer is a male. He is on a business trip to a distant city and he meets a beautiful woman who happens to be attending the same convention. She has long, thick, red hair that she keeps up in a bun at the business meeting. But, when they go out for dinner that night, she lets her hair down, symbolizing how relaxed they are with one another. They have a great time together. He wants to continue the relationship, but they live very far apart and both have to return to their hometowns in two days. On the last night they can be together they make love and it's wonderful. Now he's singing to her in the hotel room on that last night, desperately trying to think of a way to keep the relationship going, somehow. Phone calls, letters, trips, none of that would be enough because he wants her so much. Both of them have good jobs that would be difficult to give up. Both want the relationship, but at the same time both are fearful that they are moving too fast toward a big commitment that would uproot at least one of their lives.

Notice that the exact time and place of the singing of the song is mentioned. This is an extremely important bit of information. The writing technique of keeping the song *in the moment* of the emotion forces the lyrics to be immediate, highly charged with feeling, concrete, and direct. What kinds of things would this man actually say in this situation at this very moment? Answering that question, you'll "somehow" be inspired to write a strong melody and powerful lyrics.

For a wonderful example of lyrics that are right here, right now, full-on emotional and yet let you know exactly where the singer and singee are and how they're feeling, study "I Can't Make You Love Me." This song was written by Mike Reid and Allen Shamblin, inspired by a newspaper story about a divorce. The best-known version was a hit for Bonnie Raitt.

If you don't make the supreme effort to have your lyrics communicate your message with precise images, you can say along with William Safire, "Is sloppiness in speech caused by ignorance or apathy?

7

WHY BOTHER?

Make sure each song will motivate an artist to sing its message

One of our favorite possessions is an R. Crumb adult comic book entitled *Despair*. On the cover, the husband stares out the window and says to the wife, who sits rigidly in a chair staring off in the opposite direction, "See if there's anything good on …" In the balloon over her head is her reply, "Why bother?"

This scene never fails to amuse us. We've been there, in the doldrums of existence, where even television offers no hope. This is real-life pain, the stuff that makes for the best laughs. So even though the punch line is "Why bother?" there's a very sharp point being made by this image.

Why bother to write songs? Even though we love it and it's mostly great fun, it's definitely difficult and frustrating at times. Ultimately, we do it because we have something to say and we want others to hear it. We've covered the necessity of knowing what you want to write about in chapter five, and who and where you are writing about in chapter six. *Why?* is another important question you need to answer in your songs. Consider this song:

Letter to a Friend

Dear old friend
It's been a long time
How have you been?
I'm doing fine

I'm alone now
Mary is gone
Isn't it strange
How people move on?

Chorus:

Just wanted to keep in touch
To let you know I think of you
Especially when times are tough
But nothing much is new

I'm out of work
But that's okay
I watch the TV
Night and day

So say hello
To the old crowd
And drop on by
When you're in town

© James McCarthy

James wrote a lovely melody for this lyric and the song was a pleasure to hear. But after it was over, we asked ourselves and the workshop participants, "Why did the writer write this song?" Everyone was most interested in the lines about being out of work and still being okay. We all wanted to know how he accomplished that feat! But besides that, very little information was actually transmitted. Most important, there was no feeling of a burning reason that motivated the message.

Why did he write this letter to this person in particular? He tells us he's out of work and his wife is gone, and that is the sum of the information. A letter like this from a friend would leave us feeling confused. Why did he write if he wasn't going to tell us anything?

The message and the motivation for the message are like a two-headed snake. The reason we don't see more of them is that they can't agree on which way to go, and while they're deliberating, they get eaten. In your song, the motivation and the message have to be headed in the same direction for the song to be viable. And you are the one who has to make the decision about the direction they will take together.

You've heard actors talking about acting. When they prepare for a scene, they think long and hard about the character they are portraying. They make decisions about how that character would react to the situation presented by the drama. Before they act or speak, they ask themselves as the character, *What's my motivation?* To play the part convincingly, they need to know why they are saying this or doing that.

When you create a song, you're creating a movie in which the singer is the character, the actor, the star! If you get that person clearly focused in your mind and really work from the point of view of that character's intense need to express the chosen emotion, at that particular moment, to that particular listener, your song will automatically come from an authentic emotional stance.

Note that we said *intense need*. There have been eighty zillion songs that say, "I love you." If you want to write a song about that time-honored message, what will make your version special? What makes this love so intense that the singer feels the need to burst into song? In other words, why is your character singing this message? The better the reason, the better the song will be.

If James wants to tackle a rewrite of this song, we suggest he keep the pretty melody and go back to the drawing board with the lyrics. He might try choosing a situation that's less emotionally removed. Perhaps the singer could actually run into this old friend and be face-to-face with him, filling the listener in on some telling details of the changes that have occurred in his life.

Maybe the singer could actually cry and then get embarrassed. The desire to look good for very old friends that we haven't seen in a long time is universal. Perhaps this singer had the bad luck of running into an old friend when he was especially low and unable to put up a good front. What if it wasn't just an old friend, but an old lover, or even an ex-wife? You can see that these situations would be much more emotionally charged than James's current choice, which suffers from lack of focus and tension.

If you are writing a song for your sweetheart and you don't intend to take it further, you are free to sound like any greeting card on the shelf. But if your intention is to write a song that can be pitched to and recorded by a recording artist, you're up against a challenge.

Your song will be competing with thousands of other songs. You want to write one that will move someone to tears, make their heart stop or suddenly beat faster. Only a strong emotional motivation will inspire lyrics that cut to the bone and a melody that soars. That's what you will need to make your songs stand out from the crowd. That's why you need to know why your singer is singing.

8

SONGS FROM THE HEAD

Avoid writing songs that are too philosophical, emotionally removed, and cerebral

Songwriters will be songwriters. We love to play with words. We seek the universal truths. We sit up late at night and travel the uncharted seas of thought in our minds. Let's face it, we're bonkers.

An excellent lyricist who came to our workshop wrote a lyric that shows what happens when we indulge in philosophizing:

Visions of the Future

I'm seeing shadows
Outlines in my mind
They're soft and hazy
Obscure and undefined

They're like a memory
Of something yet to be
They're getting closer
Now my eyes can see

Chorus:

Visions of the future
Pictures in my head
Visions of the future
In shades of gold and red

The colors haunt me
Daring me to ask
"Is this the future
Or something from my past?"

I stand unmoving
Watching them draw near
My fascination
Struggles with my fear

Chorus: repeat

Lives I haven't lived yet
Sights I've yet to see
Mirrors of my soul
Of what I know will be

Chorus: repeat

© Tama Winograd

Tama wrote another lyric, entitled "Mother Earth," that inspired Bob Martinez and Pete to write a beautiful melody. Every time Pat hears that song, she cries because it is so moving. But "Visions of the Future" is another song entirely. It doesn't move us because it takes place entirely above our ears. You have to touch the heart or wrench the guts to move your listeners.

Tama brought "Visions of the Future" to the workshop and the consensus was that the subject matter was too philosophical to be entertaining. Tama knew when she wrote it that she wasn't trying to write a recordable song. She was feeling "spacey," so she wrote a "spacey" song. This is fine if you realize what you're doing and you do it to get it out of your system. Nobody can tell you not to write what you feel you need to write.

The trouble is that many newer songwriters are not as self-aware as Tama. They write songs that could be footnotes in the existential philosopher Martin Heidegger's *Being and Time*; then they make an investment of time and money to demo and pitch them. There's a big difference between writing anything you feel like writing and pitching anything you write. The first is something you do for yourself. The second requires an investment of money, presumably because you think the money will be recouped and additional income will be generated. If you're thinking you can get your philosophical treatise on the pop charts, you've got the wrong idea. The pop charts concern themselves with areas between the shoulders and the knees.

There is a market for songs of a philosophical nature, the New Age market. Anything goes in this field, from pure vocal sounds without words to poetic spiritual lyrics. Generally, New Age artists write and record their own material, and many have their own labels. There are also New Age record labels that sign artists and distribution companies that specialize in distributing New Age labels. Many of these artists start out by selling their own CDs on the Internet, through mail order, or by placing them in local stores. This is an alternative market that is worth looking into if you are of a spiritual or philosophical bent. An Internet search for "New Age music" yields over 250 million Web sites to explore.

It's up to you to distinguish the origin of the music you are writing. If your songs are strictly songs from the head, they may have a chance in the New Age genre, but only if you perform them yourself. They probably won't be suitable for pop, country, or R&B fields. If those are the fields you'd like to cultivate, you need to connect with your own emotions so your songs will connect with the listeners' emotions.

There's a fine point to be made here, because many songwriters write songs in which the singer is talking about being in love, but the emotions are once removed: The singer is talking about it instead of expressing it. For example:

From the head …
You say that you don't love me
You say you've had enough
I don't know what to say
I feel so out of touch

From the heart …
There's an empty place inside me
Where my heart used to be
And I'm filling it with tears
While you pack your bags to leave

Can you feel the difference in emotional intensity? The words that come from the heart are direct. They're not talking about what someone else is saying; they're saying what they want to say and using pictures to convey ideas. Writing from the heart means just that: *from* the heart, not *about* the heart. Next time your head tries to take over while you're writing a song, let your heart tell it who is boss. Songs that are visceral have more impact than songs that are cerebral.

REALITY ISN'T EVERYTHING

Don't force a song to fit your reality;
let it have its own integrity

Writers are told all the time to write from experience, to write about the things they know, the things they've seen, the things they feel, the places they've been. This is all true. But when it comes to writing songs, there's a saying in Nashville: "Don't let reality get in the way of a good song!" Here's a strong song that Gail Jennings brought to our Santa Fe workshop:

Queen of the Gypsies

You treated me like the Queen of the Gypsies
Something I could never be alone
You cast me as the star of the movie
I played the role of the bird that's flown

> *Would you believe I was lost in a forest*
> *I can't find my path through the trees*
> *If I said diamonds don't turn to rust*
> *Would you be there for me?*

You let me be the Queen of the Gypsies
But everything was better before
You made me feel like the star of the movie
Oh, oh, oh … I still wanted more

> *Should I say I was lost in the downpour*
> *Drowning in my silent screams*
> *You delivered me from the raingods*
> *Once more will you rescue me?*

You loved me like the Queen of the Gypsies
Like a perfect jewel you'd found
You worshipped me like the star
> *of the movie*
I don't know, I don't know, why I
> *let you down*

You let me be the Queen of Gypsies
But gypsies usually don't hang around

© Gail Jennings

This song is filled with terrific images. Let's summarize what the song is saying. The first verse says that his love made her feel very special, like the queen of the gypsies or a movie star. However, the last line says she left him. The second part, which is like a bridge, says she's lost and confused and makes a reference to a Joan Baez song that the listener may not understand and then asks the lover to be there for her. The second verse says he made her feel great, but she wasn't satisfied. The second bridge-type part says she was in big trouble and he saved her, and she wants him to save her again. The third verse says he was great, but she felt compelled to let him down. The tag says she left him.

How can she ask him to save her and leave him at the same time? When we asked Gail about these conflicting messages, she explained that the song was about one of her real relationships. Then we understood that this song is a very good example of how real life and art are like oil and water: You can shake them up, but they don't really mix.

Real life doesn't make a lot of sense most of the time. Art is a world that makes perfect sense within its own limits. We're drawn to art as an escape from the chaos of reality. (Maybe the whole impulse to create art comes from the urge to have some islands of perfection amid the imperfections of real life. Real life confronts us with diametrically opposed ideas that have to be held in our minds simultaneously, like reflections in a shattered mirror. Just as a magnifying glass focuses sunshine into a single, burning ray of light, art takes reality and concentrates it into purified ideas. Or, as Tom Clancy said, "The difference between fiction and reality? Fiction makes sense."

When you draw from your own life to write a song, there's a tendency to lose objectivity about whether the song makes sense. Gail is such a good writer that we don't wonder what she's saying, but we do wonder how she can say so many conflicting things at once. Conflict and drama are great in a song, especially when expressed in rich images, as Gail has done in this song. However, the combination of the messages, "You were great, you made me feel great, you saved me and I want you to save me again, and I left you," while entirely believable in real life, is confusing in a song. Perhaps the song would be stronger if Gail chose just two of these; for example, "You were great, you made me feel wild and free, so I left you." Life is not that simple, but we're talking about a work of art here, not life.

When you draw on your own experiences to write a song, remember that you are the creator here. You don't have to write down your experiences verbatim. In fact, you are much better off picking and choosing among them. Then you can put together a song that has a life of its own, one more orderly than real life can ever be.

I DID IT THEIR WAY

*Don't write to impress or please others;
write from your own passion*

We've all heard about writing songs from the heart, but whose heart? Songwriter Billy Steinberg made Tom Kelly realize that he had "meandered in a musical direction which didn't reflect his real passion for music." Tom tells the tale:

> I had slipped into this clique. I was singing background sessions and hanging out with a lot of really slick musicians. I lost my grounding, where I came from as far as where my real school of music is and what I love. Because I was a good singer and I got into this background scene, all of a sudden I was associating with a different type of people musically and my writing was being affected by that.
>
> When I met Billy, we discovered we shared a great common love of Buddy Holly, the Everly Brothers, Roy Orbison; it was truly uncanny how all of our favorite artists were the same. I really have to thank Billy because he encouraged me to use fewer chords and to unsophisticate myself. He said, "Let's write a really simple rock 'n' roll song." I had been going in the opposite direction.
>
> I was writing for the wrong people, writing to impress somebody of a certain

musical genre. Because they were the people I was around all the time, I wanted to write something that would turn their heads. In reality, it was not where my background was and not what eventually made a success for me.

Billy adds:

> I think a lesson people can learn from that is that some up-and-coming writers don't allow themselves to write freely from what they love about music. They look at the charts and they say, "Oh, dance music is making it now," or "Rap music is in now." Then they try to make themselves do those things. A good piece of advice would be to follow your instincts and write the best songs you can.

The question of whether a songwriter should try to write commercial-sounding songs to impress or write strictly from the heart without regard for commerciality ranks right up there with "To be or not to be." On one hand, if you write just to sound like a hit song and you don't believe in what you're doing, the song will be an empty shell. On the other hand, if your songs are out of touch with what's happening in the current music scene, it may be impossible to find a commercial outlet for them. On the *other* other hand, it is necessary, for your creative life, to be true to yourself as a songwriter, and there are more markets than the mainstream in which to get your songs heard. On yet *another* hand, there are lots of people out there making lots of money writing songs with no substance, a.k.a. records.

We could go on describing a millipede's worth of hands for the considerations are endless. But in the end, it comes down to you. *You* will have to decide what you intend to do with your songwriting and then go for it. Whether you choose to make music from the heart or music for the charts, you will have to live with the consequences. If you don't like the way your chosen path feels, you can always change course.

We think that the heart/charts dichotomy is a false one. We've met many great writers, both of the hits we were weaned on and of those on the charts today. It's obvious they're doing something they love. It's also obvious that they're writing with a keen awareness of great past and present songs and what makes them work. As with all other aspects of songwriting, here, too, we're called upon to achieve a delicate balance between concepts that appear to be in opposition.

The trick is to keep your heart connected while you plug into what currently sells. If you can do that, you may write a song that lasts forever and is recorded by everyone. These songs are called *standards*. Songs such as "The Wind Beneath My Wings," "Just the Way You Are," "Unchained Melody," "I Heard It Through the Grapevine," and "Yesterday" express universal emotions. Everyone wants to be valued and loved unconditionally and eternally. Everyone fears the loss of love and knows the pain of losing it. People never tire of hearing these songs and singers love to sing them. That's quite a standard to live up to.

NO BONES ABOUT IT

Give your songs structure

Can you picture how your body would look without any bones? What if the bones in one arm were a lot longer than those in the other? We take for granted the support and symmetry bones give our bodies because they are on the inside where they can't be seen, but we need them.

Songs need skeletons, too.

This idea seems to anger some young songwriters when we present it in our workshops. We'll never forget the young man in Minnesota who came up at the end of the day to argue with us that his favorite bands did not have structure in their songs. Since this was a two-week workshop, we had some time to work this out and asked him to bring in a few of his favorite albums the next day. He showed up with a stack of heavy metal albums under his arm the next morning and was shocked as we pointed to verses, bridges, hooks, and choruses. Every song had some kind of structure. Even rebels need a structure on which to hang their battle cries!

We can tell right away if a song presented in our workshops has structure because we ask the writers to hand out copies of their lyric sheets to everyone. Some lyrics wander all over the page with one very long section and another very short section, both labeled "Verse." Sometimes the "Chorus" section doesn't have the title in it. Or the lyrics are strung along in one long poem shape with each of the lines varying in length. When the structure is clean and clear, that's also obvious on the lyric sheet.

What is song structure? Please read "Common Song Structures" on pages 32–34 for an overview of this extremely important aspect of songwriting. There are two basic structures, verse/chorus and verse/bridge. Once you get a strong feeling for these, other combinations can be made. The best way to learn which song structures are being used today is to listen to the radio and identify the parts as you hear them. Then try writing songs in the various structures you hear. An extended explanation of this technique is included in chapter thirty-two, "The Long and Winding Melody."

You may notice that certain ideas tend toward a verse/chorus structure and others cry out to be in verse/bridge structure. When you play your song without singing the lyrics, or if you write the melody first, the structure should be obvious the first time you hear the song. It should also be obvious where the title will sit in the melody. The title must be in the most outstanding repeating notes of the melody. If you play your melody and no one spot really stands out, you have a problem. We will cover this in chapter thirty-six, "Don't Play It Again, Please."

Why do we need structure in songs? Songs are aural art, heard over a period of time. The listener wants to be interested in and excited by the song. If the listener feels lost and confused while listening to the song, he will tune out and turn the radio knob to another station. Radio stations know this, so they play songs they feel confident their listeners will love.

What makes you love a song? Don't you love it when the chorus comes around and the melody jumps out and grabs you and makes you want to sing along? At that same spot, the main idea of the song, the lyric you wish you had written because it's so true for you (and millions of others), fits on that melody like a glove. It's so

satisfying when that all comes together; you want it to happen more than once. As the emotional intensity in the song drops back during the verse, you can't wait for it to hit that high spot again. Never fear; the verse builds, perhaps a two-line lift (also called a pre-chorus) takes you even further up and then, bang, the chorus returns like emotional fireworks.

It's the regularity of the rise and fall in the structure that makes a listener feel satisfied. The verses are the setup, both in the information they contain and melodically, and the chorus (or the title in the verse/bridge form) is the payoff. In a song, the structure gives listeners several opportunities to experience this setup and payoff experience. It also gives you, the writer, the chance to get your point across with several new twists. If you can make the same words in the chorus mean something a little different each time by setting up the idea differently with each verse, that's called recoloring the chorus.

So don't let your songs lie there in a blob. Give them bones to dance with.

COMMON SONG STRUCTURES

The structure of a song is the skeleton that gives it shape. A clear structure is a must in a song, particularly if you intend to be commercial; i.e., you want to make money with your song.

There are two main types of song structures: the verse/chorus and the verse/bridge.

Verse/Chorus Structure

The verse/chorus structure is the one most prevalent on the radio. This song structure usually starts with a verse stating the problem, giving details of the situation, or in some way setting the stage for the coming title, which will solve the problem or sum up the situation. In order for the structure to stand, each lyric line must be strong enough to stand on its own. If you say the line out of the context of the song, it should express an understandable, complete thought or give the listener a complete visual picture. Each lyric line rests on the one before it, like a stack of child's blocks. If one is not placed solidly, the whole meaning can collapse. Melodically, the verses tend to be background in feel, leading on and up to the impending climax of the chorus. The verses can go straight into the chorus, or a pre-chorus/lift (a short, one- or two-line section that is different from the verse and serves to aid in the buildup to the chorus) could follow the verse.

In the verse/chorus structure, the title tends to be at the beginning of the chorus, in the first line. It may also be on every other line of the chorus, every line, or just the first and last lines, which is called *book-ending* or *bracketing* the chorus. The title is always in a prominent place and you should know what it is after one hearing of the song.

The title is almost always called the *hook*, because it grabs you and pulls you into the song. (Other kinds of hooks may be found in the lyrics, melody, or arrangement.) It is good to visualize the title as the hub of a wheel, with all the lines of the song pointing to and converging on the title like spokes. The title is what the song is about, the main message of the song.

The chorus lyrics explore the ramifications of the title, maybe saying the same thing in several different ways. The melody of the chorus lifts and stands out from the verse as a separate, and probably stronger, more dramatic section. It is usually best to make your verse and chorus sufficiently different from each other so that they are easily distinguished as separate sections. An easy way to guarantee the separation is to make sure your verse lines are much longer (more beats on the line) than those in your chorus (or vice versa). Varying the number of lines in each section helps, too. For example, a four-line verse could be followed by a six- or eight-line chorus.

After one verse and one chorus, a song in verse/chorus structure usually returns to a verse section, which gives more details to support the main point of the title. Ideally, the second verse should be identical to the first as far as beats on the line, placement of accented beats, and number of lines in the section. The lyrics should be different from those in the first verse, adding more information and, hopefully, introducing a new twist to the meaning of the chorus the second time around.

Choruses used to be repeated identically, almost without exception—both lyrics and melody. The narrowing of radio playlists and lengthening of the time a song is promoted as a single have moved the changing chorus from forbidden territory to desirable asset. More lyrical details make a song more interesting for longer staying power. In the changing chorus, the melody stays the same and some of the lyrics change, or all of the lyrics change except the title.

So far, we have had verse one, chorus, verse two, chorus repeat—and we might express that basic form as ABAB. Here is a diagram of verse/chorus structure dynamics:

One of our favorite examples of a verse/chorus song is "Live Like You Were Dying." The verses lead up to the chorus unerringly and the chorus takes off like it had wings. The only wandering from the pure verse/chorus form is the bridge before the last repeat of the chorus where the singer asks: "What would you do with it?"

Bridge is the term used loosely to refer to a small section of the song that is a departure from the rest, in lyrical point of view and/or melodic feel. In the verse/chorus structure, the bridge tends to be short, as in the example above. The basic form of a verse/chorus song with a small bridge (usually placed between the last two repeats of the chorus), would be ABABCB (A=Verse, B=Chorus, C=Bridge). In the verse/chorus structure, we don't write a bridge unless it really adds something wonderful. It is not always necessary between the last two repeats of the chorus, and extra excitement can be created by simply repeating the chorus a tone or a half tone higher (called modulation). The basic form would then be: A,B,A,B,B. On the positive side, a bridge may be just what your song needs to perk up interest at the end, to break up the monotony, or to add a new twist to the last go-round of the chorus.

Verse/Bridge Structure

In the verse/bridge structure, the bridge is a much more important element. Some ideas tend to write themselves into this form, and it's gaining more acceptance or, we should say, coming back into style. Many of the songs of the 1940s were verse/bridge forms, then called "pop" songs. In the verse/bridge structure, the title is in the verse. It may begin or end the verse but it always appears in the same place in every verse once the place is established in the first verse. Almost everyone has seen the classic motion picture *Casablanca*, starring Humphrey Bogart and Ingrid Bergman. If you haven't, check it out. It's considered by many as the best movie ever made. Featured in that film is the wonderful Herman Hupfeld song, "As Time Goes By". It's a straight verse/bridge structure, with the title at the end of each verse. The verse melody tends to have a completed feel, as opposed to the suspended feel of a verse that is leading up to a chorus. The thought contained in the verse is the main idea of the song and the melody seems to land in a resting place at the end of the verse, especially if the title is at the end. After verse one, there's usually another verse with exactly the same construction, but with different lyrics—except for the title.

Now we come to the bridge, which usually does not contain the title, but does build up to the emotional high point of the song. Usually the strongest emotional appeal in the lyrics comes at the end of the bridge in a verse/bridge song. It's "Woman needs man and man must have his mate, that no one can deny" in *As Time Goes By*. The melody builds to a high point there, and if you look at the bridge, you'll see it's no secondary or offhand construction. It's actually a major structural part of the song.

After the bridge, there is usually a third verse, which is again different lyrically except for the title. And that's the whole form: AABA (A=Verse, B=Bridge). The form is extended by repeating the bridge verbatim, and the verse of your choice (usually the first or the last). A diagram of the dynamics looks like this:

To further your understanding of song structure, simply turn on the radio and listen. Write down the lyrics and pick out the structures behind the songs.

Here's a list of titles of well-known songs. See if you know their structures:

1. *Just the Way You Are* by Billy Joel
2. *Live Like You Were Dying* by T. Nichols and C. Wiseman
3. *Killing Me Softly With His Song* by C. Fox & N. Gimble
4. *My Heart Will Go On* by J. Horner & W. Jennings
5. *The Way We Were* by A. & M. Bergman and M. Hamlisch
6. *Margaritaville* by Jimmy Buffett

1. Verse/bridge
2. Verse/chorus
3. Verse/chorus
4. Verse/chorus
5. Verse/bridge
6. Verse/chorus

12

WRITING YESTERDAY

*Don't try to write a song like today's hit;
don't write dated material*

Play a song from your past, any song, and you will remember who you were with when the song was a hit, what you were doing, and even which street you were walking or driving down when it came on the radio. Pat remembers the first time she heard Elvis Presley singing. She was nine years old and drifting off to sleep wondering what could be the meaning of a song playing on the radio called, "A Malt Shook Up."

You can mark the times of your life by songs because songs are so much a part of their time. Songs set, as well as express, the mood of the time. When a song is a huge hit, you can bet it has tapped into something going on in the world right at that time. Cole Porter's smooth sophistication, Dylan's anthems, the Beatles' psychedelic visions, the outraged and outrageous rappers, all express the values of the era from which they sprang. Should we conclude from this that it would be a good idea to consciously imitate the songs on the charts right now?

The answer to this is a definite *no*. The songs that are on the charts now were written a year ago, or more. We've

heard story after story of songwriters who pitched a song for more than a decade before someone cut it. Case in point: Keith Urban's hit "You'll Think of Me," by Darrell Brown, Ty Lacy, and Dennis Matofsky, which bounced around from rejection to rejection for thirteen years before its first cut became a number one hit.

When you are writing, you need to think about tomorrow, not yesterday. Certainly, there is a lot to be learned from the songs currently enjoying success. We can study and imitate their structures and production values—to a point. But if we really want to make an impact as songwriters, we have to go beyond today's songs and try to take the next step. It's our job as songwriters to express what's on everybody's mind before they are even aware of it.

Songwriters need to be students of society. You don't have to look too far for information about current events. It's coming at you from all directions: television, Internet, radio, newspapers, magazines, movies, advertising billboards, commercials, and jingles ad nauseam. It's a media jungle out there! It's hard to see the future through the media overload. Step back and make a point of thinking about where all the present madness is leading.

Some writers bring songs to our workshops that have gone beyond the today-is-too-late line and slipped right into the past. Musically, melodies can be updated in the arrangement. But lyrically, if the concept is old-fashioned, there's not much you can do about it except change the words. Here's a ditty we wrote back in the days when women's liberation was a new idea:

Hurtin' You Is Hurtin' Me

I told you you don't need no job
To satisfy your goals
A wife should keep the kitchen clean
And sew up socks with holes
But when I went and broke my leg
You stood up for us all
I'm sorry that I ever made you feel so small

> **Chorus:**
>
> *Every time I put you in your place*
> *Reality has hit me in the face*
> *It's finally penetrating into me*
> *Hurtin' you is hurtin' me*

I would come on big and strong
Superior to you
No way you could equal me
Physically it's true
So then I tried to prove my point
By pushing you around
You knocked me cold with a frying pan
This king got crowned

> **Chorus: repeat**

© Pea Pod Music

We still like this song, but it's obviously from another era. With the way the economy is today, men can no longer afford the luxury of being the sole breadwinners. Women are still being battered, and now that we look at this second verse, we realize that the image of the woman fighting back was ahead of its time.

The battle of the sexes rages on forever, but the style of fighting changes with the times. We need to consider how men and women relate to each other today and where that might lead tomorrow. Consider the changes that have taken place in the last few decades. People used to marry right out of high school or college and have babies right away. The wife stayed home and the husband worked.

Now people wait to get married and wait some more before having children. Many first-time mothers are between thirty and forty. That means today's young adults live as single dating persons for a longer time. Older singles get more set in their ways before marrying. Women develop careers before having children and stay in those careers as the children grow. Women and men choose to be single, parents, or they become single parents through divorce. The emergence of the gay population from the cultural closet adds a whole new category of music to the mainstream. The baby boomers, the big bulge in the population, are all becoming senior citizens at the same time. Your songs reflect this world. What do you think are the implications of these situations?

The fact that songwriting provides a constant stimulus to learn is one of its most attractive features as an occupation. Songwriters need to tune in to what's happening in the world on as many levels as possible. The information you gather reading sites on the Internet, in newspapers or books, talking with friends, and examining your own experiences and feelings is the stuff your songs are made of—the more input you have, the more intelligent your output can be.

You are the poets and the philosophers of tomorrow. Keep your eyes open and tell the world what you see coming down the road.

PART 2

WHAT IN THE WORD?

Watching What You Say in Your Lyrics

THE CASE OF THE MYSTERIOUS MESSAGE

Don't be intentionally obscure in your lyrics

Some songwriters think it's a good idea to leave their listeners guessing. They write songs that are like riddles. Try as the listener might to decipher it, the meaning of the song remains a mystery. For example, try to figure out this one, written by two songwriters we know pretty well (us!):

You're Not the One

Chorus:

You're not the one
You're the next best thing
You're not the one
My heart is taken
I need you
More than I want to
But you're not the one I love

The woman I love, she looks like you do
With auburn hair and smiling eyes
She sings to me just like you do but
She wouldn't leave and make me cry, saying

Chorus: repeat

The man you love, he's not like I am
He's just the opposite of me
He tells you lies and he's unfaithful
He throws away what I most need, saying

Chorus: repeat

© Pea Pod Music

It would take Sherlock Holmes to decipher that the singer loves the woman he is singing to, but she's *not* the one, because he loves the illusion of who he thought she was and not the reality of who she actually is. In the second verse, we can't even remember how to explain it, but the end result is that there are only two people referred to in the song, not four. It sounds like four because the lyrics refer to both the surface person and the secret or fantasy person within each character in the song. Have we tried your patience enough with this?

Patience is one thing a listener does not have, whether it's a publisher, producer, some other music business professional, or a kid listening to the radio. If you're asking your listeners to stop and think about what you're trying to say, you're asking too much. The beauty of a great song is that it says what it says so clearly. The listener doesn't have to think about it. The message hits home and all the listener has to do is say, "Yeah, that's exactly how it is."

We love a good mystery—book, that is. It's fun to read through the chapters and guess "who done it." But song is a craft with a different set of rules. The only mysteries allowed in songs are the multiple meanings evoked by very rich images. Even if phrases like "marshmallow skies," "moon river," or "the sound of silence" don't have an immediate concrete meaning, they do have an unmistakable emotional significance.

People don't want their newspapers to keep them guessing about what's happening. They want information clearly communicated. Can you imagine a newspaper writer trying to be more interesting by making the reader wonder what the story means? Perhaps because of the old troubadour connection, in which songs were a form of transmitting news, we want the message in a song to be clear and direct. Whatever the origin of their expectations, your listeners want to know right away who's doing it, what they're doing, and why they're doing it.

Truth, clearly delivered in words that communicate action and emotion through images, is fascinating. Don't try to be interesting by being obscure. It will frustrate and alienate your listeners.

14

NOWHERE PERSON

*Don't give the singer a negative
persona to identify with in your lyrics*

Some days you feel so low that worms could use your head for a doormat. This is a great time to write a song to express these feelings and relieve the pressure. Pain has its purpose; it forces you to grow. This fits right in with writing songs, so go on and do it. There's nothing wrong with that.

The problem comes in when you take that song too seriously just because it came from a serious place in yourself. Here's an example of a song we wrote on a particularly bad day:

Who Am I?

You're easy to talk to, you're easy to like
You make it seem easy to share
You're someone to look at and
someone to want
I love you, but then, who am I?

I'm no one to speak of and I've no
one who cares
I'm home and alone most of the time
I wait for the evenings when I find you here
I love you, but then, who am I?

Who am I to tell you I love you?
I can hardly say it to myself
Who am I to ask you to listen?
I love you, but then, who am I?

I'm so lonely, can't you see?
Everyone else is so special
Why not me?

© Pea Pod Music

There's even more to this sad tale, but we can't bear to subject you to it. Who will want to sing this song? Remember that when an artist sings a song, that artist takes on the image of the character expressed in the song. Who wants to be such a pathetic loser? Allen Reynolds, Garth Brooks' producer, put it well: "A person is known by the friends he keeps. Artists are known by the songs they sing." Among other duties, the A&R (Artist and Repertoire) staff at record labels helps artists find songs. An A&R person at George Strait's label told us, "George says, 'If I sing it they think I wrote it, and if they think I wrote it, they think I lived it.'" Don't underestimate the artist's need to look good to his audience!

Country music has room for losers, but they're losers on a grand scale. The loser in "Who Am I?" is too real, too ordinary. The country loser is bigger than life, as in "I'm Always on a Mountain When I Fall." When a lover is lost in a country song, he's really lost, as in "He Stopped Loving Her Today" (because he died). In those country songs, they lose so much, you have to admire them. Country is special that way. Then there are the blues, which by definition is the musical home for losers.

For the most part, however, a pop artist doesn't want to look like a loser, nor do we want our artists to look like losers. We want to see them as beautiful, successful, and glitteringly perfect, and imagine that such a thing exists in real life. They are the mythological creatures of our culture. We want to look up to them and identify with them. They take us with them to a place of beauty and power. We spend most of our time muddling about, trying to make sense of a crazy world. We want our artists to lift us up out of it, not drag us down into it.

That's why your real-life songs about your real-life down days need to be carefully considered before you invest time and money in pitching them to recording artists. Perhaps their usefulness stops with having helped you get through a rough day. Perhaps some parts are real gems that can be used as seeds to start a finely crafted song on a day when you're in top form.

There are some wonderful songs that carry painful messages. "Crazy" by Willie Nelson and "Love Hurts" by Boudleaux Bryant are two of our favorites. They are distinguished by a high level of craft and an air of wisdom in the point of view of the singer. But your ordinary "I'm bummed out and life stinks" song is best tucked away in the back of your file where you can find it years later and say, "Yuck, who wrote this?"

WHO IS "YOU"?

Don't mix up pronouns in a lyric

If you haven't seen the classic Abbott and Costello "Who's on First?" routine, check it out of your local video store and keep your tissue box nearby. You're going to laugh until you cry watching Lou Costello sputter and fume as he gets more and more confused.

Confusion in a song, however, is no laughing matter. One area to watch is your use of pronouns. Case in point: a beautiful song brought to the Santa Fe workshop by Candace Magner.

No Way Out

On a cold December afternoon
with a cold rain fallin' down
she packs the last box to leave in
*   her folks' storage room*
'cuz she plans to leave this town
She sets her suitcase on the seat of the bus
She tells him, "This town isn't big enough
for people like us,
but I'll be back, I'll be back, 'cuz there's

*   No way out*
*   No way out*
*   of a love that goes on and on*
*   on and on and on"*

On a warm May morning
with a warm wind blowin' through
she throws down her books and leaves
*   her last class at school*
as she wonders what she'll do
She writes, "I'm lookin' for a job in L.A.
I hope you're coming soon but if you
*   can't get away,*
then I'll be back, I'll be back, 'cuz there's

*   No way out*
*   No way out*
*   of a love that goes on and on*
*   on and on and on"*

He mails her a letter, sayin'
"This town feels too big
when you're far away, far away, but there's

*   no way out*
*   no way out"*

On a steamy August evening
with the storm clouds rollin' in
she dials him at home, and cries
*   "L.A.'s too big, and I feel I don't fit in*
too many people, there's too much to fear,
I haven't got friends, I don't know
*   anyone here,*
so I'll be back, I'll be back, 'cuz there's

No way out
No way out
of a love that goes on and on
on and on and on"

© Candace A. Magner

This song has a lovely melody. We wish we could have included a CD with this book so you could hear it. We love the unity Candace builds in this song with the similarity of the opening lines in each verse. The information about the season and the weather produces immediate emotional pictures.

For us, though, the song hit a major pronoun "bump" in the first verse: "She sets her suitcase on the seat of the bus/She tells him, 'This town isn't big enough for people like us.'" That bump sidetracked us. Was the heroine talking to the bus driver? Or might she have been talking to her father, since her folks were mentioned? Who is this "him," and where did he come from? Who is "us"?

Until that point, there's no mention of a love interest. All we know is that she's leaving home because she doesn't like small-town life. Even in our confusion, we can't believe she's really in love with the bus driver. But if she's talking to a lover and saying, "This town isn't big enough for people like *us*," why is he staying and she leaving? As we ponder these mysteries, half the song flies by unheard.

It's hard to take, but it's true. A little two- or three-letter word like "he" or "she," "him" or "her" can throw the whole sense of your song off track. This is especially true if you start out using "she" to refer to someone in the song and then switch to "you." We don't know the origin of the old saying "Don't switch horses in mid-stream," but we've seen enough songs go wrong to know why it's essential not to switch pronouns in mid-song.

16

NOT NAMING THE GAME
Make sure the title is not buried or nonexistent

David Ziems brought this moving lyric, written to a very pretty melody, to our workshop in Santa Fe:

I could never let you down
I will always be around
We will be the best of friends
'Til this life is through

I will always come to you
Any time you want me to
If you ever need my love
I will soon be there

There are times when the world is hard
Maybe times when your heart is tired
But you know you can always count on me

I'll forever trust in you
I'll forever love you too
'Til the rivers all run dry
You'll never be alone

© David Ziems

Now there's a friend all of us would like to have. Let's say we heard this song on the radio and wanted to run out and buy it. What would we ask for? Ah ha! Stumped you, haven't we? That's a big problem. How can we buy it? How can everyone who tracks income for it identify it? This is a song with no name. David told us when he presented it that he couldn't think of what to call it, so he just called it "Song for Kate."

There are a few exceptions to the rule that a title must be prominent, repeated, and obvious from just one hearing of the song. Billy Joel puts a fragment of the title of "Scenes from an Italian Restaurant" twice in that song; in the eighth line of the song and the last. Bruce Springsteen mentions "Born to Run" only twice in that song; at the end of the first verse and the end of the last verse. "Interstate Love Song" doesn't show up anywhere in the Stone Temple Pilots' song. Paul Simon only uses "Duncan" once on the fifth line of the first verse of that song: "Lincoln Duncan is my name and here's my song." Notice that all of these examples are writer/artists who do not have to pitch their songs to others to get them cut.

Conduct your own survey of the songs you hear on the radio or watch on MTV, VH1, CMT, GAC, BET, etc. How many times does the title get repeated in the song? Where is the title placed in the song? How does the placement of the title define the structure of the song? Just a bit of this should convince you that titles really are important. We feel so strongly about this that we wrote an entire course on the subject for www.SongU .com/luboff: "What's In A Name? The Central Importance of the Song Title."

The title is almost always our starting point for writing a song. The title is the hub of the wheel of the song. All the lyric lines should point to the title, enhance it, support it, and lead up to it. The title is your main idea, the essence of what you're communicating. Knowing this will help keep you focused on what your message is. Stick to your title and you won't wind up wandering all over the universe in your song. After you've finished writing your song, try this test: Put the song title after every line in the song. If every line makes sense next to the title, you know you've written a song that is focused on the title. That means it will be a unified, clear message.

The title needs to sit on the most exciting part of your melody. The emotional high point of the melody can be created very literally by having the highest notes in the melody at the title, but there are other ways of setting the title apart melodically. An interesting syncopated rhythm can do the trick. Notes of long duration in a very melodic phrase will stand out in the midst of narrow-range, quick notes that resemble speech. When you sing your song without lyrics, the place where the title should go should be obvious to your ears unless your melody has no single phrase that stands out from the rest of the song. In that case, you need to work on the melody until it does. (See chapter thirty-six, "Don't Play It Again, Please," for more on how to build some peaks and valleys into your songs.) The whole song vibrates when you sing your melody without words, but the part that jumps out and declares "Here's the title" should vibrate the most.

What makes a title great? Great titles are often drawn from everyday phrases in their usual form or in a slightly twisted form. A glance at the list of Song of the Year Grammy winners and Grammy-nominated best songs on www.Grammy .com in the R&B and country categories will give you plenty of examples: "That's What Friends Are For," "What's Love Got to Do With It," "Every Breath You Take," "We Belong Together," "If You Don't Know Me by Now," "Ordinary People," "Lean on Me," "I May Hate Myself In The Morning," "Politically Uncorrect," "9 to 5." All of these were commonly used phrases before they became song titles.

We like to look through a dictionary of American idioms for inspiration. For instance, the phrase "two heads are better than one" became our song title "Two Hearts Are Better Than One." Other song titles you can find as entries in this dictionary include "Behind Closed Doors," "Knock on Wood," "(I've Had) The Time of My Life," "That'll Be the Day," "I.O.U." and many more.

Our song on Patti LaBelle's *I'm in Love Again* album, "Body Language," was a book title and a common phrase in the jargon of popular psychology. While we were waiting for the album to be released, two other songs came out with the same title. Titles are not copyrightable, except in very rare circumstances, such as when the title word is a creation of the songwriters, such as "Supercalifragilisticexpialidocious." That is an example of a song title taking on what is known as "secondary meaning." The title becomes so identified with a particular song that the public would reasonably expect that song when they see that title. Another example is "Rudolph the Red-Nosed Reindeer." If you wrote a song using that title, the publishers who represent the original would have the right to sue you for copyright infringement. A search of ASCAP's repertoire on www.ascap.com will yield the one and only Rudolph, written by Johnny Marks. On the other hand, such common words as "Yesterday" cannot be copyrighted as titles. Searching the ASCAP, BMI, and SESAC repertoires (more about these performance rights organizations in chapter ninety, "What They Don't Know Will Hurt You") will yield more than two thousand songs with "Yesterday" as the title or part of the title.

There must be a million songs entitled "I Love You." If you are moved to write a song with that title, the song better be dynamite to make up for the ubiquitousness of the title. Better yet, add something special to those three little words to distinguish your song from 999,999 others. Four good examples are: "I Honestly Love You,"

"I Just Called to Say I Love You," "I Can't Help It If I'm Still in Love With You," and "(I Love You) For Sentimental Reasons."

Great titles have drama and conflict. They almost write the whole song by themselves because they call up so many images. A great title arouses your curiosity about the song. That's a great asset when you think about the professional listener who has a box of one hundred songs to go through. Add poetic devices to your conflict (see chapter twenty-four, "No Reason to Rhyme") and your title is stronger and more memorable. Country songs are often all that and humorous, too. "Size Matters," "Down In Mississippi (Up To No Good)," "Redneck Yacht Club," and "Something's Gotta Give" are a few examples of titles that do it all.

Let's get back to David's song with no name. Since the song has a verse/bridge structure and the melody calls for the title to be on the last line of the verse, we suggested that David pick one of his ending lines and settle on it as the title. For instance, he could choose "You'll never be alone" from the last verse and substitute it as the last line in verses one and two. The line carries the basic intent of the message of the song, and the repetition would establish it as the title.

Or he could choose to replace his current last line in each verse with a new line, such as "I'll be there for you." The problem with either of these choices is that they're not outstanding dramatic lines in themselves. With a dynamite title, this song could move up a dozen notches in impact. David will have to decide whether he's willing to spend some time coming up with about three hundred titles until he finds one that is strong and unique.

Then he'll have another problem to solve. The current rhyme scheme does not lead in well to the title. (For an extended definition of rhyme schemes, see chapter twenty-four.) It would be much more satisfying to the ear if the line just before the title set us up by rhyming with the title. The current rhyme scheme is *aabc*; that is, the first two lines rhyme and the second two don't. A better rhyme scheme would be *aabb*, or two sets of two lines that rhyme with each other. If David chooses to rewrite this song, it would be a good idea to show the devotion he's expressing through pictures of hands touching, shoulders to lean on, or lives intertwined like vines. His language is beautifully direct, but a few sharp images will makes this good song even stronger.

Remember the concept of the title as the hub of your song wheel. Your title shouldn't be an afterthought. A great title makes for a great song. Keep your ears out for the great titles that are constantly floating in the air around you and collect them. They make good starting points for writing sessions, either solo or with collaborators.

Once you have your great title, honor it. Stick with the message it wants to get across. Without a strong connection to your title throughout your song, the spokes collapse, and your song can't move on down the road.

17

I'M BIDING MY LINES

Get to the point in the first two lines of your song

In one workshop in Santa Fe, Denny Cicak presented the following song to the group:

Rhyming Lines

Where you been so long?
So good to see ya here;
C'mon and join our song.
Lend us all your ear.

The first time I saw you, you really
    turned me on;
I never thought I'd stand a chance,
You showed me I was wrong.

Life hands us people
We may never want to see again;
Reach out to someone,
Someone you could call a friend.

You know it's true,
Love is all around.
Feel it in your heart,
Remember where it's found.

It isn't always easy to be where you
    want to be.
To make your life do one thing right;
Imagine what comes naturally.

Make something happen;
Recognize the signs.

For the verses of destiny,
We write the Rhyming Lines.

© Denny Cicak

What's wrong with this song? Denny took the whole song to get around to his point, which is in the last two lines. The first two lines could have been an okay start to a song about meeting a long-lost lover again. The second two lines come from some other point of view, and it's not clear whose. The second three-line section goes back to the lover, but doesn't relate to the idea of how or why they've been apart. The next three sections are a philosophical discussion of love and friendship. The title idea, which is the foundation on which the entire song must rest, is not even hinted at until it shows up in the last two lines.

A song is a three-minute motion picture. In those three minutes, the songwriter has to give the who, what, where, when, and why of the situation. Most, if not all, of this information has to be stated or implied in the first two lines. If listeners can't relate to the people and the situation by then, they'll turn off their ears. Check out the first two lines in your favorite songs and see how much information they convey.

If a song is going to get through the gauntlet of publishers, producers, artists, record company executives, promoters, and radio programmers, and get out where it can be heard by the general public, it has to grab the listeners by the ears in the first line and never let them go. The message has to be emotionally intense, and we have to know who is singing and care about the person delivering the message right at the top of the song.

A song could be thought of as a commercial that sells the central idea you've chosen to express. Just like in the ad game, you have to tell them what you're going to say, say it, and then tell them what you said. In a song you start telling them what you're going to say in word number one.

We told Denny that the last two lines of the song were a good starting point for his rewrite. One way to go would be to make those the first two lines in his chorus. Because it's best to keep the language in a song conversational, it might be better to switch the order of the lines to say, "We write the rhyming lines for the verses of destiny." This is an interesting line, but a bit abstract and intellectual. Denny can counteract that by filling the rest of the lyric with some imagery that calls up distinct pictures to our minds. In Nashville, we call this imagery "furniture."

It's not unusual to come away from hundreds of lines of work with only one or two lines worth keeping. We have written as many as three hundred titles for one song before hitting the one that satisfied. Songwriting is like mining for diamonds: You have to move a lot of dirt to get to one little gem. Once you've sorted out the gem from the dirt, you're ready to begin writing the song.

We recommend starting with a strong title as the first step in writing a song. That's how we usually start the process. That means that we usually write the chorus first, then work "backwards" and write the first verse that leads up to the chorus. We talk about the who, what, where, why, and when of the story we're about to tell. Then we tackle the first two lines of the first verse.

Let's say that the song is about a fellow who comes home to find his wife/girlfriend has left him. Our first stab at the opening lines might be, "I came home and you were gone." That tells the facts, but doesn't have an ear-grabbing image. Also, it doesn't say that she's left him. She could have just gone out to the store. We call that a "what I'm trying to say" line. It says what we're trying to say, but we keep on trying to say it until something pops out that gets our juices flowing.

The next stab might be, "I saw the skid marks in the yard, you must have hit the road hard." That has an image that conveys some strong emotion on her part and it has some humor. But we'd press on for fifty or more tries at the line to find the one line that says the most. The lines would pack in imagery and emotion and stand up to the best objective scrutiny we could muster that they deliver all the necessary information. Maybe we'd wind up going back to that "yard/hard line," but we wouldn't stop there just because we liked the line. It does happen sometimes that the first or second thing you come up with is the best thing. But we've found, for the most part, that the deeper we dig, the better the payoff.

The opening lines of your song set the emotional tone and pull the listener into the story. It's worth the effort of working hard to make them as strong as they can be.

18

ONE SONG, MANY LANGUAGES

*Don't write lyrics with an inappropriate
mix of conversational tones*

We are fascinated by people who study language dialects and know them so well that they can tell where you come from after listening to you talk for a few minutes. With the egocentricity of youth, our son once said, "Everyone else has an accent, but I don't." We told him that, to other people, he does have an accent. Strangely enough—since he's a native Californian—it's a New York accent he picked up from Pat.

The language we use gives more information than just the literal meaning of the words. It identifies us in terms of education, social status, geographic origin, and level of relationship to the listener. This identification was the basis for the plot of George Bernard Shaw's *Pygmalion*, which in turn became the plot for Lerner and Lowe's *My Fair Lady*. The college professor says, "How do you do?" The teenager says, "Hi." The ghetto rapper says, "'Sup?" From the first word of greeting, we identify ourselves with a particular style of language.

This truth comes into play when we write lyrics. Every word we put into the singer's mouth must be authentic; it must come from the personality we created when we decided exactly who was singing this song.

Here's an example of tone gone wrong that we treasure because it is proof that top-of-the-line writers eliminate perfectly good writing from their songs. If the verse doesn't fit, don't keep it. Guess what song this verse never made it into:

You've got a long list
With so many choices
A ventriloquist with so many voices
And your friends in high places say
*   where the pieces fit*
You've got too many faces in your
*   make-up kit*

But I see your true colors ...

© Tom Kelly/Billy Steinberg

This was the original first verse to the wonderful hit song "True Colors," written by Billy Steinberg and Tom Kelly. Billy, the lyricist of the team, liked the writing in this verse very much. But he told us they decided that this verse limited the song because it spoke to a particular kind of woman. They saw that this song had universal potential, and they wanted to write

52

something that anyone might say to anyone else: father to son, daughter to mother, man to woman, friend to friend. So out went a perfectly good verse. It doesn't matter how good it is. If it doesn't serve the song, off with its lines!

We also feel that the language in this verse doesn't match the tone of the message. The song gives us something we all need, 100 percent unconditional support. This verse is slightly judgmental, a put-down. It's very clever, but clever is not what this message needs—sincerity is.

When choosing your words, consider both ends of the spectrum. Would this person use this word? Does this language suit the message? If the answer to both of these questions is yes, you've found the right word.

Do you remember why you loved, or hated, Winnie the Pooh? Maybe Sleeping Beauty or Tinker Bell was your favorite. Each of these fictional characters has a distinct personality, expressed in their physical appearance, their actions, their clothing, their dramatic situation, and their language. We are drawn to our favorites because we feel some kinship with the character. For us to feel that kinship the character must be, on some level, believable. We would never believe Tinker Bell if she talked like a truck driver. And you know what happens when you don't believe in Tinker Bell—her little light goes out!

Every recording artist also has a distinct personality, and it's no accident. They pay people lots of money to advise them about the image they present. Just like our fairy tale heroes and heroines, they have to project believable personalities. It has to do with the way they dress, their grooming, their performing style, and the songs they choose to sing. And what they choose to sing changes as their lives change. We were told at one pitch meeting that the artist recently got happily married and didn't want to sing any more cheating or drinking songs. The lyrics in the songs must fit perfectly into their jigsaw puzzle of personality or we won't believe enough to keep them alive as artists.

Thanks to the Internet, you can find out what's going on in artists' lives with ease. Do a search on the name and you'll be led to many sites. See if you can find the "official" site. There is often a way to sign up for a fan e-newsletter. Do that for artists you want to pitch songs to. We got a newsy e-mail from an artist saying that she was having a garage sale that day. We made a few phone calls to find out her address, and guess who showed up at her door with a CD?

Here's an exercise that will help you to identify the word choices of different genres of songs. Try listening to three distinctly different types of radio stations: country, rock, and urban. Jot down some of the words that jump out at you. After you've done this for at least a dozen songs, look at your lists of words. You will see the patterns of language and word choice for each genre that identifies it and distinguishes it from other genres. Here's our quick sample:

- **Country**—The straight and narrow, Jim Beam, angels everywhere, lonely miles, Mississippi, Carla Sue, two-dollar pistol, Momma, Daddy, Chevy, a baby to feed, butterflies, God
- **Rock**—Undercover, trigger, defending, pretending, misused, four-inch lens, persistent, generation, melancholy, gravitate, navigate
- **Urban**—Baby, baby, baby! Take off all your clothes, check you out, temptation, show me what you got, do it, tasty love, sexy, moan, players, and lots and lots of repetition of the title
- **Rap**—*%&@#?!

And those are just a few very broad divisions of songs. Satellite radio makes it possible for listeners to identify very specific genres. Our Sirius guide lists five different kinds of country and as many different types of rock. While that many categories may seem confusing at first, it is worth your while to explore them and find the one you like the most. That will be the one that's easiest for you to write because you will instinctively understand and speak the language. We can't stress enough the importance of immersing yourself in the genre closest to your heart. The more you listen thoughtfully, the more you will have the language and the culture of that genre in your bones.

Making sure your choice of words is precise and appropriate for the personality who is singing and the message you're expressing is the logical extension of the groundwork you laid in creating your original character, the singer and the singee (see chapter six, "Heard but Not Scene"). Putting the right lyrics into the singer's mouth creates a sense of unity and integrity that will make your listeners believe and will give real life to your song.

X-RATED

Be careful with sex in your songs

In workshops and collaborations, we've noticed that songwriters like to play with words, all kinds of words. When the word-play ball gets rolling, it often bounces back and forth from risky business to risqué business. This is good for some laughs, but should we put it in our songs?

The answer to that question is too complicated to boil down to a simple yes or no. Let's take the "no" side first. Sex is a big deal in everyone's life. Therefore, it's a natural subject for the songwriter to tackle. But if your intention is to pitch the song to a prominent recording artist, any references to sex have to be made in the porcupine style—very carefully. You can't get more direct than John Bettis, lyricist of "Slow Hand," with the lines:

I want a lover with a slow hand
I want a lover with an easy touch
I want somebody who will spend some time
Not come and go in a heated rush …

© Warner/Tamerlane & Sweet Harmony Music

Notice the high level of craft in these lines. There's nothing crude about the way John put them together. The phrase "slow hand" is fresh, unique, and creative; it conveys a precise and unmistakable image. That image is reinforced by the next line with the phrase "easy touch." John's talking about some really laid-back sex here, without sounding the slightest bit offensive. The third line says the same thing in another way and sets you up for the killer fourth line, where the censors are ready to hear "come and go" without so much as a twitch in the direction of their blue pencils.

On the contrary, the message conveyed by "Slow Hand" is one of sensitivity and thoughtfulness. This is a classy love scene. This is something we'd all like to experience, and the proof of its universal appeal is that it was a hit in both country and pop/R&B, by Conway Twitty and the Pointer Sisters, respectively.

By way of contrast, here's a song we wrote a million years ago:

Up Is In

Start out from the bottom
Take it from the top
I don't care where you begin
Long as you don't stop

Chorus:

Up is in … Get up, get up and do it
Up is in … Get up and get into it
Up is in … Use it or you'll lose it
Up is in … Down is out, up is in

Once you have it goin'
Give it all you got
Fill your cup up to the brim
Get it while it's hot

Chorus: repeat

Come on keep it coming
Come into your own
Get off on what's happening
Feel it in your bones

Chorus: repeat

© Pea Pod Music

No matter how much we tried to say that this was a song of encouragement and enthusiasm about life in general, those who listened heard it another way. All right, we meant it both ways. But the song never got anywhere, and we believe it was because of its crude undertones.

Our "no" answer to the question of sex in songs is a highly qualified one. It's interesting that we are constantly bombarded with sex and violence on television and in movies, but sex in songs causes such an uproar. What makes songs so much more powerful that people react so strongly to them?

When we say "yes" to sex in songs, we arouse the ire of well-meaning parents and vote-seeking politicians. Book burning and record burning are nothing new. You can check your history books to see who struck the matches, and we bet you won't like them. Yet the blatant sex and violence in rap, metal, and hard rock music might make you think that those historical bad guys didn't have such a bad idea. For your own sake, please think again.

Personally, we don't like songs with that lyrical content; we find them offensive, but we will defend the right of those creators to say what's on their minds. We don't buy it; we don't listen to it. That is the ultimate voting power, and everybody has it. Political resistance to this kind of music makes big headlines and boosts the sales of mediocre material that would otherwise have languished on the shelves.

Pardon our getting on a soapbox here, but we are in good company. The National Academy of Recording Arts and Sciences, (the Grammy organization, www.Grammy.com) is involved in the battle to curb the censorship of creators of music, songwriters, and artists. If we start to say that this or that songwriter/artist shouldn't be allowed to have his or her song heard, where will it stop? Where would we be now if the people who wanted to ban rock 'n' roll because it was "lewd" had prevailed? Before that, it was the Charleston that was too outrageous, and before that, the waltz!

Who's to say where the line is drawn between what is art and what is not? Art is in the eye of the beholder. Let's draw our own lines; we're the artists! If we are not free to choose what we express, how can we create?

So take your own position on sex in your songs. Crude sex in a song doesn't make it less of a creation, but it does narrow the song's appeal. Most people prefer candlelight and tenderness to elevate sex from a mere release of tension between battling genders to a romantic experience between caring lovers. For a good example of the latter, take a look at the lyrics of "Nothing On But the Radio." The words you choose will establish which of these two very different worlds of sex your song is expressing. Your listeners will respond negatively or positively according to their tastes and values. You won't be able to please them all, so make sure you please yourself by being true to your vision of the song and what it wants to say.

≡ 20 ≡

SING ME A ?

Don't depend on punctuation marks to give meaning to your song

Did you ever see Victor Borge do his punctuation marks act? He'd tell a story, indicating the punctuation marks by drawing them in the air and making hilarious noises with his mouth. A period was a finger pointing at the audience and a quick, rude blowing sound, like the opposite of a kiss. To make a question mark, he'd trace a curve in the air of the appropriate shape and make a ratchety sound in the back of his throat, like a New Year's Eve noisemaker, then finish it off with the period beneath.

As the story progressed, his speed accelerated and commas, periods, question marks, quotation marks came rapid-fire, until everyone in the audience had fallen out of their chairs in hysterics. This is the only known instance in the universe of punctuation marks being obvious in an aural presentation (we are not including dictation to a secretary in this unofficial survey of the aural universe).

We'd like to try an experiment with you. Don't read the lyric below with your own eyes. Ask someone to read it to you and listen without looking at it. Then you will have the real experience of the person who listens to the song, which is not the same experience as the person who reads the printed version. Have your helper start reading now:

Jane Aker brought this hard-hitting lyric to our Santa Fe workshop:

Gimme a Dime and I'll Call Somebody Who Cares

You been pokin' at some sore spots
I'd just as soon avoid—
Like, "Red on black
They're trading blood for oil."
Like, "When you gonna get a job?"
And, "Why so paranoid?"
Like, "Where you goin'?
Where you been?"

And "D'you believe in Sigmund Freud?"
The thing I'm trying to say is that
I ain't climbin' your front stairs
But gimme a dime
And I'll call somebody who cares.
It ain't much.

Can't afford to get involved
Been down this road before.
Like, "Ain't you Weasel Smith from Nam?"
And, "Ain't it a shame we didn't
*   win that war?"*

You say times have changed since then?
And life's not really fair?
Whoa! Flip me two bits
And I'll call somebody who cares.
It ain't much.

Lookin' to put some distance
'Tween my present and my past.
Today ain't much to brag about.
Yesterday's long gone—it flashed.
Paid my debts.
You got your share.
Ya' saying one check ain't been cashed?
Honey, lend me some coin
And I'll call somebody who cares.
It ain't much.
C'mon, gimme a dime
And I'll find somebody who cares.

© Jane Aker

Are you lost? Just listening to this lyric, it's easy to go down dead-end trails of what it might mean. That's because understanding it depends so heavily on knowing where the quotation marks are. Victor Borge is not here to guide you, so you hear, "You've been pokin' at some sore spots I'd just as soon avoid like red on black …" and you draw your own conclusion about the meaning.

Since there is no way to hear a quotation mark, you need to broadcast the fact that you're about to quote someone. You need to come right out and say it in words. We suggested to Jane that she substitute the words "You say" on the front of each of those lines that contain a quotation, instead of "like" or "and."

This will get her into a little trouble in the lines where she is already using the words "You say," because she has used those words to introduce indirect quotations and turn them into questions posed by the singer. Any solution she chooses will change the tone of those lines a bit.

Even with our eyes wide open and drinking in all those punctuation marks, there's confusion about what's going on here. We asked Jane, "Who is the singer in this song?" This is a question we should not have to ask; it is something we should be certain of from line number one. We thought we knew until we got to the Weasel Smith line and then we got lost. And who is the singee that the singer keeps quoting? How can we get our bearings if we don't know who's who and what's what?

Jane answered that the singer *is* Weasel Smith. The singee is someone who knew him vaguely in Vietnam. Knowing these two facts goes a long way toward helping us understand the song. So we suggested to Jane that she have Weasel introduce himself in the first line and singee in the second line. Once we know who the singer and singee are, the whole song makes a lot more sense.

If your song has a lot of punctuation marks in it, give it the aural test. Close your eyes and say the lyrics to yourself to see if understanding their message depends on those aurally invisible punctuations. Or try writing out the lyrics without any punctuation and see if any of the meaning is lost. Rewrite to remove the message's dependence on the punctuations. If that doesn't work, maybe it's time to revive Victor Borge's technique and sing those question marks.

21

LYRICAL HANGOVERS

Watch out for lyric phrases that hang over to the next melody line instead of ending with their own melodic phrase

There are many ways to envision how a song is built. We've already talked about the song as a wheel, with the title at its hub and each lyric line as a spoke. Another image we like to use is a tower of building blocks. We've all tried at some time in our childhood to see how high we could stack our wooden blocks before the tower tumbled.

Being the instinctive scientists we are, we soon figure out that the tower stands better if the biggest block is on the bottom and the blocks get smaller as the tower gets higher. We also see that the tower is more stable if the blocks are placed directly over the ones below. The block that hangs off to one side of the one beneath it is sure to fall, and soon.

In a song, each lyric line is like a building block. It holds up the ones that come after. Consider the tower that Ron Whitmore of Santa Fe built:

Love Is Holding You Tight

Ran around in circles, trying to find
looking for answers, locked in my mind
Didn't know if love was more than a score
Then you walked through my door, now

Chorus:

Love is holding you tight
Getting up at night
to see if baby is crying for you
and as you hold her to your breast,
I can't start to express
all the love I'm feeling for you
True love takes two

Did my share of looking, had my
*   share of fun*
every time I got too close, knew I had to run
When my eyes first looked in yours
Knew my race was through
now I spend my life loving you, cause

Chorus: repeat

© Ron Whitmore

Take a close look at Ron's first line. Do you notice how it doesn't complete a thought? This is what we call a lyrical hangover. The melody comes to the end of a phrase at this point, but the lyrics hang out waiting to—what? This question is partially answered in the next line. But the real subject matter, love, isn't introduced until the third line. If you look at the first two lines by themselves, Ron

60

could be talking about anything. He also painted the singer as a negative person. Where are his redeeming features?

Compare the first verse with the second. It's pretty clear that the first two lines of the second verse are talking about relationships. The singer has been around, had fun, and been afraid of commitment. He knows as soon as he meets his wife that she's the one for him and now they're happily married. That says a lot more and puts the singer in a much better light, all without lyrical hangovers.

We suggested to Ron that he scrap the first verse and use his current second verse to start out with. This is the equivalent of putting the biggest block on the bottom of your tower. To get people involved in listening to your song, open up with your strongest verse. Put your best lines forward. The professional listener at the publishing or production company doesn't have the time to wait for a song to get interesting. The song has to start knocking him or her out in the first line. By the second line, he or she should be totally hooked into the story and dying to hear what's going to happen. When you start with vague, incomplete thoughts, the listener *knows* what will happen next. Your demo is going to be thrown into the reject pile!

There was a unanimous feeling among the workshop participants that the line "True love takes two," which was such an afterthought that Ron had written it in at the bottom of his typed lyrics, was really the high point of the song, both melodically and lyrically. The alliteration, inner rhyme, and message of the line appealed to everyone. We all suggested that Ron rethink this song or start another one with that as the title.

Here is another example of a song with lyrical hangovers, written by Cindy Bellinger and brought to our Santa Fe workshop:

The Hardest Thing I've Done

Every night I go to bed
Wishing you'd call—instead +
The silence only pulls me down
to the quiet all around …

If you'd only trusted more
that I could be—your +
one reason to change your life
and take me as your wife …

© Cindy Bellinger

These are only the first four lines of the first two verses. These verses are excellent examples of the most common kind of lyrical hangover. At the points marked with a +, the thought is begun in one line and left hanging over to be completed in the next line. The musical phrase completes at the +, but the lyrics don't. This interrupts the natural flow of the language. It's like taking a long pause in mid-sentence. We cannot hear those dashes being sung, so it doesn't help to put them on the lyric sheet.

You may be able to point to some songs that have "made it" in spite of suffering from this flaw. Rules are made to be broken, but you must know the rules first. Some songwriters who are also artists break these rules because they can get away with it. A writer/artist doesn't have to work under the same rules as a songwriter who must pass through a gauntlet of ears between writing the song and getting an artist to record it.

Build your song carefully. Put the biggest, strongest lyric blocks down first and keep your thoughts complete within each melodic line. You may be able to build a song that reaches to the top of the charts.

TO SING THE UNSINGABLE WORD

Beware of tongue-twisting word combinations
and hard consonants on long notes

Singers sing because they love to sing. Like anyone who does anything well, a singer gets good at it by doing it over and over again until he gets it right. And like trapeze artists, singers seem to sing with the greatest of ease. But take a closer look. What's really happening is that the singer has turned his or her own body into a finely tuned musical instrument by studying and practicing for years. You will also notice that great singers are always singing great songs. They know what they like, and they choose a song because it feels great to sing it. Songwriters who do not take this into account will not endear themselves or their songs to singers.

You know what doesn't feel great to sing? Try singing a long, high note on the word "sing." Now try singing the same long, high note on the word "you." You can feel the difference easily. If you did extend the word "sing" by concentrating on the vowel sound in the middle and sticking the *ng* or the *g* on quickly at the end, you were trying to make the best of a bad word choice for a long note. The trouble is, the listener will wonder why you are singing about sin. The *g* will

probably get lost in the shuffle to the next word. Nasal tones and consonants are almost impossible to extend. They are more suited for shorter notes that flow into words starting with a vowel sound.

Why should a consonant flow into a vowel? Try singing or saying, "The best dog sits still." Notice how much your mouth has to work to get from the end of one word to another. Now sing or say, "I want to give you my heart." Your lips and tongue don't have to stumble over each other to make the transitions between these words, do they? The tongue-twisting variety of lyrics may have a place in a certain kind of song where they add to an expression of anger or agitation, but for the most part, for words to sing well, they must flow gently into each other.

The best sounds for those long, high notes are open vowel sounds. Check out all your favorite ballads and see if it isn't the case that the main sounds on the extended notes are *a, e, i, o,* or *u*. Singers just love to let loose on those sounds because it does feel good. Our vocal apparatus is physically suited to making those sounds with ease. Try opening your mouth and saying the vowels without moving your lips. It's easy.

You might think of the movements singers make with their mouths as a dance. You have to choreograph that dance so that it can be done smoothly. There are physical limitations. You can't ask a dancer to be in a totally curled-up position on one side of the stage and in a flying leap on the other side of the stage by the next beat. You can ask singers to sing the unsingable word, but chances are they will choose not to. Make your songs feel good to sing and you will increase your chances of attracting singers to it.

Do your own choreography check by paying attention to your lips as you sing the song. If they have to do too many twists and turns and flying leaps, you need to make adjustments in your choreography. Like our moms told us, "Watch your mouth!"

I CAN'T SEE IT

*Use picture words in your lyrics;
instead of talking about the subject, show it*

We are constantly bombarded with words. A steady stream of them washes over our ears from television and radio. Most of us have learned to tune out a great deal of it for the sake of what's left of our sanity. In this scenario, words are as meaningful as white noise. To illustrate the state of mind of the average listener, Pat sometimes wears a special pair of earrings to songwriting workshops. One earring says "IN"; the other says—you guessed it—"OUT."

Listening is an art that takes time and concentration to master. Wouldn't it be wonderful if the art of listening were recognized as a necessary component of everyone's education? It would be a very different world if we all really listened to each other. Unfortunately, this is not the case.

Songwriters listen to songs all the time, yet many new songwriters attending our workshops haven't noticed that the songs they're listening to have structure. There's listening, and then there's *really* listening to hear what's going on under the surface of the song that makes it great.

So, if even songwriters aren't hearing all there is to be heard in a song, what can you expect from the average listener, who doesn't have that extra interest? Not much. If you really want to get your message across to Mr. or Ms. Average Listener, you need to involve more than just their ears. You must grab the attention of their mind's eye with words that make them see what is happening in the song. This technique will quadruple the chances that your message will be received and remembered.

JoAnna O'Keefe, who writes beautiful inspirational poetry that is published on greeting cards and posters, came to our Santa Fe workshop to learn how to adapt her talents to lyric writing. She brought this lyric:

Remembering

*Many months have passed
since our time
of togetherness,
leaves of dark green
have turned to gold.*

Chorus:

*Autumn winds are blowing
embers are glowing
and I remember,
oh, I remember.
It was springtime
and I remember.*

It's been so long
since you've held me
in your arms
that I'm beginning
to lose the feel
of your touch,
and your face,
like an old photo,
fades in my memory.
Your gentle voice
grows softer:
still, I listen—

Chorus: repeat

Sometimes I wonder
if you are but a dream
if we met in the mist
of my imagination,
Then I ask my heart,
and I know.
You are real,
and you touched me.

Chorus: repeat

© JoAnna O'Keefe

What's wrong with this picture? There aren't enough pictures to make the message of the song stick in that space between our "IN" ear and our "OUT" ear. As it stands, all we know is that she once had a love, and now he's gone, but she remembers him. The words are lovely. They mean more every time you read them. But Average Listener is not going to be looking at the printed words. To get people to hear your song, you need to use picture words so they will see it. Especially since the title of the song is "Remember," we asked

JoAnna to fill in the blanks. What is it the singer remembers?

JoAnna wrote to us after the workshop, saying, "I would love to shape that poem into a song—guess I'll have to read your book to find out how." Well, JoAnna, here goes. You've got a good start here because you're capturing a special feeling that probably everyone experiences, looking back on a love that was good and is now gone.

Remembering that "Remembering" is your title, put it squarely in the center of your song wheel. "Remembering" needs to be the repeated word in the chorus, not "I remember," unless you want to change your title to "I Remember."

You are taking five lines at the top of the song to say what can be said in one picture phrase. You want to set the stage that they've been apart for a while. How about:

In the cool shade of this tree
We made the summer hotter
Now the branches are bare
in the cold winter air
But I still see us there

This establishes that they had a romance in the summer in the first two lines. The second two lines say that it's now winter. More than two seasons may have passed, but the images symbolize that the heat of the past has turned into coldness. The fifth line leads into the idea that you are remembering the love affair and, consequently, into your chorus.

Now, what is it that you remember? Close your eyes and picture it. Free-associate, using as many descriptive words as you can. What color were his eyes? What were you wearing? What color was his hair? What was so special about your relationship? Was it the long talks you had together, and the way he seemed to understand you? Was it his sensitivity to your needs? How did he show that? What kinds of things did you do together? You might want to keep the whole song in the one spot under the tree. You had a picnic there. You kissed. You talked about your future together. You fell asleep in each other's arms. You drank wine (symbolic of sharing an intoxicating experience of love). You laughed and played at tickling each other like children.

This kind of background material should be in your verses. Your chorus should give the overview. Are you glad to be remembering or is it painful? This might depend on why you're not together anymore. Remember the song Anna sings in *The King and I*? She's remembering her husband, who is dead. She has many good memories, but they're focused on one particular night. She sings about how the earth smelled, how the sky looked, and how the mists settled on the hills. Although she's sad that her husband is dead, she's grateful and glad for the love they shared because it makes her feel a part of all lovers. So she sings, "Hello, Young Lovers." You need to choose your emotional stance and then choose words that will deliver it in pictures.

When it comes to song lyrics, everyone is from Missouri (the "Show Me" state);

you have to show them. Don't talk about the situation in an indirect way. It's almost as if a song were a slide show. Each line of lyric needs to project a picture on the screen of the listener's mind. The picture the line projects is directly connected to the title and advances the central emotional message. Like a strand of DNA contains the code of your entire body, a lyric line contains the essence of the entire song. A listener could drop in and out of the song and still get the message from any line in the song.

Misty watercolors are nice in paintings and could set the mood for a particular kind of song. But, for the most part, the more distinctly colorful and emotional the picture, the more likely the listener will be moved by it. Think about the difference in impact between a phrase like "an old car" and this one: "a yellow '57 Chevy." The first is too vague. On hearing it, you might call up a picture in your mind, but not necessarily the one the writer has in mind. The second image is unmistakable.

Picture words are extremely important in a lyric, but don't stop with making your listeners *see* your song. Pull in as many senses as you can. If you can make them taste its strawberry sweetness, smell the smoke from a burnt-out desire, or feel the luxurious softness of velvet, you're going to have an involved, moved listener.

JoAnna, in the next chapter, we'll give you more about turning this poem into a song.

24

NO REASON TO RHYME

Avoid inconsistent or nonexistent rhyme schemes

Something else is missing from JoAnna's "Remembering" lyric in the last chapter. Did you notice there were no rhymes? It may not have struck you just reading the words on the paper, but if they had been sung to you, you would have missed the end rhymes you've come to expect in songs.

We call this a "bump"—the inner sense that something is "off" in the song. It reminds us of driving along a smooth road and then hitting a speed bump. Something inside you jumps. When a song is crafted to perfection, it doesn't have any of these bumps.

You may be able to find one or two examples of absolutely wonderful songs that don't have the usual complement of rhyming lines. "Gentle on My Mind," written by John Hartford, is an excellent example. Many of the lyric lines don't rhyme. Only one or two lines rhyme with the title line, but somehow you just don't miss the rhymes. Maybe it's because each line is so rich with images that the song flows gently by without any bumps. Those few exceptions aside, 99.44 percent of the time, song lyrics do rhyme.

Why? There's something in us that loves a rhyme. There's something immensely satisfying about the cadence of language that repeats word sounds and rhythms. As very young children, we love our Mother Goose. Pat will never forget our son's favorite book when he was two. It was a story told in rhyme, and he asked for it several times a day for months and months. After reading it five hundred or so times, Pat had it memorized. Ten years later, with a little prompting, she could probably still recite it.

That's another reason rhymes work in songs. Rhyming makes things easier to remember. No one likes to feel lost and confused. Rhymes are the signposts in a lyric. They say, "Here we are at the end of the line. Doesn't that make you feel just fine?"

How do we rhyme? Let us count the ways. There are *perfect*, *near*, and *inner* rhymes. In a *perfect rhyme*, the two words end in exactly the same sound: line-fine. Marilyn and Alan Bergman ("The Way We Were," "Windmills of Your Mind") are committed to perfect rhymes. They refuse to settle for less. But most songwriters feel a *near rhyme* is close enough for rock 'n' roll: line-mind. The slight difference in sound doesn't disqualify these two words from being a rhyming pair.

Inner rhymes (similar-sounding words scattered throughout one line of lyric) can be perfect or near rhymes. What makes them inner rhymes is their location. "The Rain in Spain" from *My Fair Lady* is an extreme example of inner rhymes. When you have too many in one line, it can get comical. But a few well-placed inner rhymes can pack a line with dynamite.

Rhyme schemes, or how the rhymes fall on the line, are usually referred to with lowercase letters. For example, an *abab* rhyme scheme is a four-line song section in which the first and third lines rhyme, and the second and fourth lines rhyme. Another common rhyme scheme is *abcb*; the first and third lines do not rhyme with each other, but the second and fourth lines do. A third possible rhyme scheme for four lines is *abcc*. Notice that in each of these rhyme schemes, it is the last word in the last line that rhymes with at least one other line in the section. That's what gives the feeling of completion to the section.

Whatever rhyme scheme you set up in the first verse, it is usual to stick with it for the rest of the verses. The repeating rhyme scheme gives listeners the satisfying feeling of knowing where they are and what to expect in the song. The same technological and corporate forces that have made a changing chorus acceptable have changed the rhyme scheme rules, too. Today, the scheme might change from verse to verse,

so your first verse may be *abab* and your second *aabb*. Just make sure it sounds good and flows smoothly. (Always run your songs by informed listeners to see if you've accomplished your goals. See chapter forty-nine, "No Up-Front Feedback.")

On the other ear, a problem of too much rhyming can occur when you fall into an *aaaa* rhyme scheme, a.k.a. the "moon, June, spoon, tune" syndrome. We call that writing yourself into a corner. All too quickly you find yourself grasping at ridiculous rhymes to meet the demands of the rhyme scheme. As a result, you wind up going for the rhyme and losing touch with the heart or emotional authenticity of the line. This is a sure-fire way to write a "bump" into your song.

If we find our lyrics falling into a rhyming rut like that, we steer in another direction. It's hard enough to carry off one such verse. The second verse is harder, the third impossible. If you do manage to come up with something that makes sense in the *aaaa* rhyme scheme, you run the risk of boring your listeners with too much repetition.

Every songwriter should have a rhyming dictionary to consult when stuck for a rhyme. There are rhyming dictionaries online and songwriting programs that contain rhyming lists you can modify to your tastes. These can be handy tools when you're searching for that perfect word.

Rhyming is the main poetic device to make your lyric memorable and impressive. There's nothing quite like a clever rhyme that really works. Another device that makes a lyric satisfying to the ear is *alliteration* (using several words with the same initial sound in a single lyric line). We've loved alliteration ever since Mary had a little lamb, little lamb, little lamb. There's no reason to stop now.

Take a minute to think of the titles of some of your favorite songs and you will see these poetic devices at work. Some of our favorites are: "Bigger Than My Body" (alliteration), "Let Me Love You" (alliteration), "Hardcore Troubadour" (inner rhyme), "The Late Great Golden State" (inner rhyme and alliteration).

Now do the same thing with some of the lyrics from your favorite songs. Take a close look at the rhyme scheme and the use of inner rhyme and alliteration. You'll be surprised at how much is going on in even the simplest song. It's a feat to pack all that in a song and make it sound so natural that you don't notice it. A quote from the classic movie *The Red Shoes* applies here: "A great impression of simplicity can only be achieved by a great agony of body and spirit."

Agony is not in your job description as a songwriter, but hard work is. Because the great songwriters make it look so easy, we are shocked when we get involved in the process and find out just how hard it is. Songwriter/singer Morgan Ames, one of the Inner Voices, said at a University of California at Los Angeles (UCLA) Extension seminar on women in songwriting:

> There's a difference between the romance of songwriting and the doing of it. The doing of it doesn't always smell good. You sit in a room and you sweat and it's not the dream. A lot of people get stuck between the dream of what they want and the unglamorous process of doing it.

So while you're sweating out the delicate balance between too little and too much rhyming, keep your cool. We dedicate the following poem to all of you brave and hard-working songwriters who stalk the wild word that not only rhymes but perfectly expresses your intended meaning, all the while sounding like it naturally fell off the tip of your tongue:

Ode to a Songwriter in Search of a Rhyme

When you're racking your brain for
 just the right rhyme
And you think you can take it no longer
Remember that writing a great
 song takes time
And what doesn't kill you is
 making you stronger!

25

EPIC PROPORTIONS
Write songs of reasonable length

Back in ancient Greece, the great-granddaddy of all rappers, Homer, had the *Iliad* and the *Odyssey* memorized. He would rhyme on for days about a giant hollow horse, lotus-eaters, Cyclops, Sirens, and battle after battle. But back then, they didn't have TV and radio. Homer didn't have to pause for a station break or a commercial.

Consider this song, brought to our workshop by Sharon Angell:

I Want You Back Just So I Can Dump You

When you left me, baby
You weren't much fun
It was cold Christmas Eve
At a quarter to one
I gave you ten presents
But you gave me none
Then you packed your things
And ignoring my gun, you said
Bye-Bye, Baby
I'm dumping you
You've been an angel
But I'm just passing through
Gotta hit the road
Gotta have my space
Gotta do my own thing

And all those other stupid things
That boys always say

> **Chorus:**
>
> *When you left me, baby*
> *You made me so blue*
> *Now I want you back*
> *Just so I can dump you!*

I'll be sweet for a while
Massaging your gums
You'll be so content
You won't know what's to come
Then you'll get 'pendicitis
Doubled over in pain
You'll beg me for help
That's when I'll explain

Bye-Bye, Baby
I'm dumping you
You've been a bad boy
And you know it, too
Gotta clean up your act
Gotta make it up to me
Gotta learn a lesson

And all those other stupid things
That girls always say

> **Chorus: (variation)**
>
> *When you left me, Baby*
> *You made me so blue*

Now I got you back
Just so I can dump you

I'll cut off the phones
There'll be no nine-one-one
I'll do you in
Without shooting my gun
My home fried chicken's
Germ warfare, it's true
You came back to me
And now I've poisoned you

Bye-Bye, Baby
I'm dumping you
And when I dump somebody
They're really through
Only a stomach pump
Can save you now
But the one I had
Got lost somehow

Chorus: repeat

You'll never make
Another girl cry
Lovers like you
Just have to die
Here's the red dress
I'll wear to your wake
Now kiss me goodbye
You coldhearted snake

Bye-bye, Baby
You've breathed your last
Let bygones be bygones
Let's forget the past
I won't hold a grudge
Cuz I got even with you
I got you back
Just so I could dump you

Chorus: repeat

Don't get mad ... get even ...
I saw Fatal Attraction twenty-seven times ...
No bad boy's gonna ruin my Christmas Eve ...
More fried chicken, honey? ...

© Sharon Angell

You have to hand it to Sharon, this song packs a wallop. The message comes across loud and clear. She's focused on the emotion of the moment, and she tells the story with definite images. The only problem is that a radio station would have to play the song in three parts to insert the required number of commercials in the time it takes to sing a song this long.

In order to fit the lyrics on one sheet, Sharon typed them in two side-by-side columns. The sight of that many words squeezed onto a lyric sheet might be enough to scare away a publisher who knows that the time limit for songs played on pop radio stations is about three minutes. This could be a fun album cut for Sharon if she wants to record it herself, but the length of it will probably limit its attraction for any other singer.

The current structure of the song is: verse A, verse B, bridge, chorus; verse A, verse B, bridge, chorus (variation); verse A, verse B, chorus; verse A, verse B, chorus, and tag. That's eight verses and four choruses. Usually a song has two or three verses. It's not just that we're a generation that insists on instant gratification. Songs have been that way for a long time.

The great ballads of the 1930s and 1940s were written into a strictly 32-bar form. Practically all of the Beatles' fantastic songs had three or fewer verses. You can't judge the length of the song you can write by the album cuts of artists who write their own material. They work under a different set of rules than the songwriter pitching songs from outside the artist's inner circle. Artists can get all the album cuts they need from within. The only songs they might consider from the outside are those that have hit written all over them. And hit is a very short word.

Let's look at the message of the song. If Sharon wanted to edit this song down a bit, we think the story wouldn't suffer if she eliminated the first two sets of verses A and B with their bridges, and the first chorus. Starting the song with the chorus (variation) and then picking up with "I'll cut off the phones" and going on from there will tell the story.

There is a problem with the literal sense of the second set of verses, anyway.

After hearing the threat of the first chorus— "I want you back just so I can dump you"— why would he come back? It makes more sense to pick up the story in the middle. She could emphasize that he has returned by repeating the line "Now I got you back" two or three times in the introductory chorus. That might also emphasize the humorous side of this otherwise dark song. If she decided to cut out the first four verses, she would have to rewrite the Christmas Eve line in the tag, too.

There are some wonderful epic-length songs in the folk field and special material such as soliloquies in musicals (for example, "My Boy Bill" in *Carousel*), but for the most part, your job as a songwriter is to write a three-minute miracle. That's one of the special things about a great song: so much meaning packed into such a nice, tight package. Great songs hit you quick and have a big impact. They strike you like lightning, brilliant and fast. After they hit you, you're never the same.

26

NOT ENOUGH IS NOT ENOUGH

Write enough to express your ideas completely

The flip side of the epic-length song is the mini-song. Some songwriters get the impression that a song has to be short. They take it to the extreme by cutting off the writing process before they get around to fully expressing the idea. Here's an example of a very short song by Joseph M. Tapia:

Love Shock

Every day is another
everything's a bother
I need to shake it
my soul just can't take it.

> **Chorus:**
>
> *You're gonna get me over this block*
> *Give me a love shock*
> *Give me a love shock*

I can't help the urge
being with you causes such a surge
night or day night or day
you lift me away

> **Chorus: repeat**

© Joseph M. Tapia

This is a great beginning for a song. The title is unique and calls to mind all kinds of wonderful images. The workshop participants had a ball free-associating on the electricity/love theme. The air virtually crackled with current, sparks, wires, plugs, positive and negative charges, magnetism, lightning, power, energy, and attraction. We encouraged the songwriters to go with the flow by exclaiming, "Socket to us!"

Although the structures of the verses do not match (the number of beats is 7, 6, 5, 6 in the first verse and 5, 9, 6, 5 in the second), the rhyme scheme shows careful thought. But the overall effect of the song in its present form is that it hasn't been taken to its limit.

Part of this might be due to many songwriters' mistaken idea that the song should flow out easily. Some think that the original thoughts should be accepted in the form in which they first arrive, especially if they pop out rhyming. The concept of writing a hundred lines to get one good line never occurs to them. They stop when the writing gets hard.

It gets hard rather early in the game, especially when the songwriter tries to make the first words they put on paper a "finished" line. The process of free-associating on the song's images and self-talking about the who, what, where, when, and why of the song before trying to write the finished product makes writing much easier by providing a wealth of raw material to work with. It beats trying to grab the perfect word out of thin air.

A temporary exhibit at the Country Music Hall of Fame and Museum in Nashville fascinated us. An entire room was dedicated to the preparation Thomas Hart Benton did for his wonderful painting "The Roots of Country Music," which is on permanent display in the Hall of Fame rotunda. There were pages and pages of sketches of body parts, larger sketches with grids on which various arrangements of the composition were tried, small sculptures of individuals, a miniature diorama of the figures in the painting—months and months of work. We can't help but wonder why some songwriters think a song needs to be instantaneous and perfect on arrival.

Without doing the groundwork of exploring all the possibilities of your idea, you run the risk, as Joseph did here, of not getting your message across. We suggested to Joseph that he play more with combining the ideas of electricity and love and use the associative phrases he comes up with in his verses. Also, as the song stands, the chorus is only the title. The chorus is where you need to make your point—hard to do if you haven't decided what your point is. Joseph needs to think that out and expand his chorus to make the song's point of view clear.

What's the difference between a song fragment and a complete song? A song fragment communicates *part* of the message and the complete song communicates the *entire* message. How can you tell if your song is doing the job you set out for it? That subject is worthy of a chapter all its own, so read chapter thirty-eight, "Stranger in a Strange Song," for hints on how to get an objective view of your songs.

In cooking, it's best to go easy on the salt because you can always add more later. If you put in too much salt at the outset, you've got a problem on your hands. But when you're cooking up a song, the opposite applies. Go ahead and write too much. Then you can cut it down to the strongest parts. If you write too little, you may never get to the good parts.

27

A POEM IS A POEM IS A POEM (NOT A LYRIC)

Don't mistake poetry for lyrics

When you're courting the muse, you take what she gives. You capture it on tape or paper with gratitude. Tuning in to what messages you have to give to the world is a worthy endeavor, no matter what comes of it. One of the most joyful aspects of being a songwriter is opening up to whatever is coming up from your subconscious, or down from on high, or wherever you envision the flow originating.

After you've taken down the first outpouring without hindering the flow by making judgments about it, it's time to consider what raw material you have to work with and what you want to do with it. Here's a song Dot Regelski brought to the Monday night workshop:

Haunted Dreams

When dreams disturb my slumbers
In the vastness of my bed
And I sink in solitude
In sunlight I do tread
Sol warms me with his fire
But my cheeks will never dry
For you are ever with me
Your spirit stays by my side

Chorus:

Haunted Dreams
Dreams of long lost love
Is it your face I see?
I reach but never touch

I turn to wine to lose
Your presence in my mind
But your face still appears
Even when I'm blind

Why give me endless pain?
Why won't you give me peace?
I pray through reddened eyes
That I will find surcease

Chorus: repeat

© Dot Regelski

After you have given the muse her day in court, it's time to sort. If what you've been given sounds like "Haunted Dreams," it's a poem, not a song lyric. How will you be able to tell the difference?

Conversational tone is a good basic measuring tool. The message in most contemporary pop songs is carried by words that are commonly used in conversations on the street. Word order in lyrics is generally best when the words flow in the order of normal conversation. For example, when talking about what you do in the morning, you say, "When I wake up." "When dreams disturb my slumbers" is a lovely poetic phrase that could have been written by Emily Dickinson, but it's not pop song lyrics. Some writers use conversational words, but put them in an order you'd never hear on the street. We call that Yoda talk: "Work on that, you must!"

Dot has a good image in her second line but again chose a less-than-conversational word: "vastness." The word "big" would be more accessible and even have the advantage of alliteration with "bed." The line could be rewritten into a more conversational phrase, such as "My bed's too big for me."

The conversational tone test is easy. Just picture yourself going up to someone on the street and saying the line. Then imagine the look on his face as he either lights up with your crystal-clear idea or fogs over in confusion. If someone came up to you and said, "And I sink in solitude," how would you react?

One response might be, "Take me to your poetry reading." It just doesn't sound like something said on the street; it's way too lofty in tone. Picture yourself as the singer in the song. You want the message to get across in all its urgency, with the most emotion you can muster. You could say, "I'm so lonely, lonely, lonely," thus getting the intensity across with repetition.

Or you might deal with a problem the lyric has in its current form, which is that the *you* or the *singee*, is not introduced until line seven. Up to that point, this could be a song about someone who is just constantly lonely because she can't form a decent relationship. Remember to get the who, where, when, what, and why in as early in the song as you can. With that in mind, line three could say something like, "Your cold pillow in my arms." It keeps the bed images going and tells in a picture that she's singing to someone she wants to hold but who isn't there.

Among the other words and phrases Dot uses that are more at home in a poem than a song lyric are: *tread, Sol, ever with me, presence, reddened eyes,* and *surcease.* These are all very good words, but they're not the way we talk to each other today.

Why she should jump out of bed and go treading outside is a good question. Especially when the title, "Haunted Dreams," calls up images of sleeping and, therefore, bed. You've heard the Latin proverb "carpe diem," which means "seize the day." As a rule, you don't have enough time in a song to seize a whole day. The idea in a song is to seize the instant, seize the moment, seize the emotion right now. Keep the lonely person in the bed right on the sword point of the pain and loneliness. These are the feelings that we've all had and can relate to on a gut level.

Also, remember that the title is the hub of your song wheel. The rest of your lyrics need to support the main image conveyed by the title. This title calls for lyrics that tell a story like this:

I woke up crying
My bed's too big for me
I hug your cold pillow
It's dark and I can't see

I heard you call my name
Just before I woke
I heard you say, "I love you"
Where did you go?

Chorus:

Haunted dreams
Tell me you're still here
But I can't find you
Through my tears

When choosing where to go from here, you have to keep in mind where "here" is. The singer just woke up from a dream; it's probably the middle of the night. She's in bed in a dark room. What does she do next? Does she turn on the light and look around the room and talk about all the evidence of his having been there? Does she stay in the dark and pretend he's there? Does she go over in her mind what led to the breakup or death? Or maybe he is really in the next room, but the relationship is in trouble and she's fantasizing about the inevitable end. We'll leave this story for you to finish.

What separates poetry from song lyrics is the method by which the message is delivered. Poetry can be read. You can hold it in your hand, look at it for a long time, and ponder its depths. Song lyrics, on the other hand, flow past you like a river. You can't put your toe in the same place twice. The information is received through your ears, not your eyes. Each line of lyrics has

to stand on its own and deliver a complete thought. Each line needs to lead to the next and relate to the central thought, expressed in the title. That way, your brain can put the picture together. Otherwise, you're lost, confused, bored, or even angry for being made to feel the fool because you can't understand what's going on.

If the muse hands you a poem, by all means do the poem the honor of pursuing it to its creative conclusion. Maybe you will be lucky enough to be given a poem so strong and beautiful that it can be set to music and be totally valid in both the worlds of poetry and song. "The Rose" by Amanda McBroom is such a poem song.

You may object to this division between poetry and song lyrics. You can provide many examples of extremely poetic song lyrics written by great songwriters such as Lennon and McCartney, Paul Simon, and Bob Dylan. Then there's rap music, which is a form of poetry spoken over rhythms. This is all true, and if you can write real poetry that sings, go for it. The problem is that so many songwriters get lost in the pursuit of poetic language and wind up obscuring the emotions of the song. That's why we recommend that you be direct and conversational with your lyrics if you're aiming at writing a mainstream pop, country, or R&B song.

All that rhymes is not poetry, and pure poetry does not a good song lyric make, necessarily.

Now, don't you wish we'd said that straight out?

PART 3

MAKING THE MUSIC

Melodic Mistakes

28

TO STUDY OR NOT TO STUDY MUSIC

*Don't think you have to study music theory extensively
or play a musical instrument expertly*

Some people who aspire to songwriting think they need to get an advanced degree in music theory to be a songwriter. Others think what is really needed is a highly refined skill on a musical instrument. They may even spend years studying theory and practicing their instrument. Then they try to write a song—and can't. This is one career in which a formal education can get in the way.

We're not saying "Don't bother to get educated." We're saying formal training in music theory is not the education you need to be songwriter. Some of the world's greatest songwriters cannot read or write musical notation. Many of them say that too much musical education hampers songwriting creativity. They find this out when they try to collaborate with someone who is highly trained. The trained musician often has trouble breaking from the rules that have become a habit from many years of practicing. Trained composers tend to lose sight of song structure, doing variations on a theme when they should be repeating the chorus.

Of course, there are excellent musicians who are also great songwriters. But

for those of you who don't have a gift for playing an instrument, the good news here is that you can be great songwriters, too. What you need to know to write great songs is what makes a song great. You can study this on your own and in your own way. You don't have to know the names of the chords being played or the theory behind their progression. If you can play by ear, that works, too.

Irving Berlin couldn't read music, and he played all his songs on the black keys of the piano. With today's keyboard technology, you don't have to be able to play up to speed. You can input the notes and indicate the times for the notes, and then the synthesizer will play them back.

You don't even need to know a black key from a white key to be a great songwriter. If you have a keen ear for how words sit on a melody, you are a valuable commodity. There are lots of people who can play instruments and write melodies; but very few can come up with just the right words.

We think playing a musical instrument is one of the finest occupations in the world. It's a beautiful and peaceful thing to do. Unfortunately, technology is taking over the livelihoods of musicians. Here's the situation: "There's a frog driving one way down the highway and a French horn player driving in the opposite direction. What's the difference?" The answer is: "The frog might be on his way to a gig."

Even so, some recording sessions still use real live musicians. If you are one of those musicians, you might be able to make connections for your songs. You can use musicianship in the aid of songwriting. Again, there are excellent musicians who are also great songwriters; one proficiency does not necessarily preclude the other. However, songwriting is a skill separate from musicianship. Songwriters are students of the world and of how it can be expressed through song. Being able to play a musical instrument or read and write music is not a prerequisite for adopting this lifetime course.

29

FREE SAMPLES

*Don't think you can sample from
previous recordings for free*

Songwriters who have their own at-home studio or access to studio time may feel free to sample the sounds from previously released records. *Sampling* is the process of taking the sounds from a record and using them in your song, either in their original form or electronically manipulated into another form. Samples can range from a one-time use of a small piece of an obscure song, to the looping of one bar of a song throughout a new song, to the use of a recognizable riff or hook from a hit song, to a rewrite of the lyric of an original song that is then treated as a parody.

Sampling is rampant today and very popular with newer songwriters who see it as a cheaper way to get great sounds in their songs. They may think they don't need anyone's permission to sample because the records they are sampling are thirty years old, or they're just using little pieces, or the original recordings weren't big hits in the first place.

You are on the wrong track if you think samples come for free. A writer/artist who uses samples without permission or payment up front for their use may find, if their sampled creation winds up on a record, that they pay more for those tracks than can be earned from the song.

Any sounds embodied in a commercially released recording have two layers of ownership. First, there is the owner of the copyright on the underlying work, usually the publisher. Second, there is the owner of the sounds on the record, usually the record company. You may think people won't know you used part of their record because you cut it up and switched it around and looped it, but you will be surprised what people can recognize. Samples need to be cleared on both levels of ownership, and each will want a fee or a percentage of the song depending on the nature of the use.

Publishers will want a piece of the new copyright with an advance based on 50,000 units or a specific dollar amount. Record companies/master owners want an average of $0.02 to $0.06 per unit, with an advance against 50,000 units. If the copyright owner discovers a use that was not agreed to, the same three seconds could cost hundreds of thousand of dollars in a lawsuit settlement, plus, possibly (but rarely) an order to pull all the stock off the shelf.

Since the use of samples can have such a drastic effect on the status of a song, it is very important to keep track of what you are doing when you use samples. If you are using samples, keep a written record of the origin of the samples' titles, writers, publishers, and record companies. This assumes you still have the original packaging where this information can be found. Also, take note of what parts you sample, the length of time sampled from the original, and how the sample is used in your song. The more information you can supply, the easier you'll make it for the person getting permission for the uses: called "clearing the samples." If you want to use a sample from an existing recording, you need to clear the underlying copyright for the song (from the publisher) *and* the copyright in the sound recording (from the record label).

One of the good guys in sample clearing is a lady named Madeleine Smith (Madeleine Smith Music Services, www .ms2.zoomshare.com). She says sampling is a booming business, not only in rap, but also in rock and pop. Smith states:

> Now every publishing company has a sampling division with its own VP of Sampling. Since artists rarely do covers anymore, publishers actively pursue sampling as a source of income. They send their catalogs to artists and ask for the songs to be sampled. Publishers and writers are happy because they get a better income at today's statutory rate than they did on the original recordings.

[Statutory rate is the number of pennies paid to the publisher and all the writers per song on the sales of recordings, which was 2 cents for many years, but is 9.1 cents now and slowly rising.]

While the demand for samples has increased, the number of record labels to get permission from has dwindled down to four. The four major labels have engulfed and devoured the rest. That means there are four VPs of Sampling in the U.S. handling all the requests. And that means they are generally too busy dealing with requests from other major labels to deal with independent artists and smaller labels with limited releases. But, if you have the time and the patience to wait, they will often get to your request.

The difficulty of dealing with this bottleneck has led to alternatives called *interpolations*. An interpolation means the song has been changed from its original state. There are two kinds—re-plays and re-sings. A re-play is when, instead of sampling a bass riff off a recording, the artist re-plays it exactly. A re-sing happens when, in the midst of their own song, artists re-sing a line of another song. Both of these are ways to avoid dealing with the record labels because only the publishing part has to be cleared.

Madeleine has seen samplers in action and knows they often work with stacks of vinyl records and CDs that haven't seen their packaging in years. She recommends www.allmusic.com as the site to visit for all the information you need to identify your sources. Enter the album name in the search box and it will yield the artist's name, album release date, record label, release number, and all the songs and their writers' names. You can use that information to search ASCAP, BMI, and SESAC's sites for the publishing company information.

Today's musical instrument technology is making it easier for samplers to kick the habit and create their own music, thereby avoiding sampling troubles. However, many writer/artists are still sampling. If you're among these samplers, remember, it's not a free ride.

30

MISMATCHMAKING

*Don't forget prosody: the marriage
between words and music*

Unfortunately, approximately 50 percent of American marriages end in divorce. Maybe it's due to the times and people's unwillingness to work through the tough challenges that face every relationship. Maybe when they "fell in love" they each fell in love with what they *wanted* to see in each other, and closer exposure eventually revealed what was really there, much to their mutual discomfort.

Songs are no different. The words and the melody/music get married after falling in love one day. Some of these marriages last and others don't. Alan Bergman uses the image of the words sitting on the melody like an old easy chair; they should be that comfortable with each other.

When it works, you have a great song/ marriage. For example, take Allan Rich and Jud Friedman's number one song "I Don't Have the Heart," recorded by James Ingram (see chart on page 87). The title line melody of the chorus descends and resonates emotionally with the sad meaning of the line as well as the cadence it would actually have in conversation. "To hurt you" starts a fifth higher than the note on "heart" and comes down on

"you" to give the feeling of an apology. The last line in the chorus, "Not the way you want me to," goes higher and ends higher than the title line melody, adding energy and torn emotions to the meaning of the lyric.

This is a songwriter's song, a timeless song, a perfect example of prosody. When a song has perfect prosody, the message of the lyrics, the feel of the music, and the emotional intensity and pitch of the melody are perfectly meshed. Have you ever noticed the shape of the melody in "The Sound of Music"? When the chime flies, it flies on the highest note in the melody. When the lyrics talk about a brook skipping and falling, the melody skips and falls. When the lark sings, it sings on a lovely long note. Prosody delivers the message on every possible level at once. How about the word "skydiving" in "Live Like You Were Dying"? Those three descending notes could be a person jumping from a plane.

In the heat of the moment when lyric and melody first meet, everything looks and sounds good, and the excitement of making contact makes the world seem right. As time goes on and things cool down a little, maybe the lyric could be stronger here, or the melody more interesting there, and you begin to see where each others' expectations aren't being met.

You can tell when the marriage isn't working. An obvious example would be a hot-blooded song with a lot of words about physical attraction on the dance floor set to a melody with long-held notes in 3/4 time. Such a lyric would be better set to a high-energy, fairly rapid-fire melody and feel. If you think this is obvious, it isn't. Would a heavy lyric about a break-up work set to a joyous melody like "Zip-A-Dee-Doo-Dah"? The attitude of the lyric and the melody have to work together, not against each other.

A lyric should be basically conversational; if there are too many inverted phrases such as "waiting, I stood in the rain," it may be difficult to write a melody with a natural flow that also meshes with the meaning of the lyric. We like melodies to flow rhythmically with the accents the words themselves would have in conversation; if they don't, it is because we are intentionally calling attention to that moment. Again, the point is to make the lyric and melody work together for the fullest impact rather than call attention to the craft, or lack of it.

We try to make the melody bring out the passion of the lyric like the music brings out the emotional intent of a scene in a film. In a song, the lyrics are like the pictures on the screen and the melody is the soundtrack; it tells us what to feel. Emotions are conveyed by employing a variety of techniques:

- melodic intervals from syllable to syllable that enhance the meaning
- melodic phrases that rise and fall to create pathos or passion
- rhythmic phrases that change from section to section to keep the interest up and to keep from boring us with repetition
- harmonic progressions that match the melody and lift us into an energetic chorus if necessar
- minor chords to sound sad or angry, or major chords to sound positive or happy

Ideally, the melody/arrangement expresses the intent of the lyric so well that you don't need to hear the words to know what the song is saying.

Just like a marriage in which two people have to learn to work together and help each other grow, so words and music help each other fully express themselves and be the best they can be, and they support each other through the hard times before getting a cut. When it's right, the combination of melody and lyric becomes synergistic, more than the sum of its parts. Together they create a new life that feels so natural it seems as if they were created simultaneously in one easy flow.

I DON'T HAVE THE HEART

by Allan Rich and
Jud Friedman

I don't have the heart _____ to hurt ___ you, ___ it's the

last thing I __ want to do _____ But I don't have the

heart _____ to love ___ you _____ not the

way you__ want me to. _____

31

LOST, LOST ON THE RANGE

Don't write a melody that has too wide a range for most singers

If you've ever tried to sing "The Star Spangled Banner" you know what a Herculean feat it is, even though Whitney Houston (whose performance at the 1991 Super Bowl is still cited as "the best") made it seem easy. It isn't. It's a very wide-ranging melody—you might sound good on the low notes in the beginning, but by the time you get to the chorus, the notes are beyond the top of your head voice. Perhaps one of the reasons this song survives, besides its political message, is that it gives singers a chance to show off their super vocal chops.

But for the most part, writing songs this difficult to sing is not a great idea. One reason is that you obviously limit the number of singers who would sound good performing it. If you're the artist, you know what your range is, and you can write a song with a very wide range if it suits your voice. But that song will have few outlets with artists not blessed with your range.

The range of a melody is a tool, like rhyming, song structure, modulations, and so forth. An orchestrator has to know the range of the instruments when writing an orchestration from a film composer's sketch or the instruments might literally not be able to play the written note. The human voice is the songwriter's ultimate instrument. Writing within a reasonable range is using the vocal instrument to its best advantage.

A general guesstimate of range limit is an octave plus five notes for most singers. Those who claim four-octave ranges are not talking about full voice alone. They are including falsetto and bass tones that are hard to sing words to while intoning. When we talk about range, we're talking about full voice. Even an octave plus five notes is pushing it for some singers with great voices.

Sometimes songs get too rangy because their melody is weak. The energy level is shored up by making the melody go high, and while this solves the problem of dynamic energy dropping off at an undesirable place, it creates the new range problem.

You want your singer to sound great throughout the song. At no time do you want the performance to sound strained because the singer had to reach for notes.

You want to avoid bringing the melody down too low when intensity, anger, or aggression is required. You might want the melody lower for intimacy, but upper-middle range when the dance partners are sweating. Rock choruses are often at the top of the singers' full voice so they can scream away. You basically want to keep a singer's voice at that point in his or her range that suits the emotional moment you're creating in the song.

The responsibility for making a singer sound great starts with the writing. Even if the message is great, the feel is terrific, and the melody has strong moments, if the singer doesn't love the way the song feels while singing it, the song will probably be rejected. You don't have to be a singer to know what works for the voice. An obvious corollary is that the song should also be in the right key for the singer so the energy or intimacy is there where it's needed.

If you are lucky enough to have made contact with a particular act looking for songs, find out not only the lead singer's range, but also at which note the singer is forced into falsetto. You could figure this out from previous recordings. Armed with this information and knowledge of quirks in the singer's voice—like where Kenny Rogers gets the growl in his range or Patti LaBelle does her high glissando holding the last note for four (not really!) minutes—you might build something into the melody to take advantage of it.

Of course you have to serve the song, and do whatever you must to make it work the best it can, which includes not being concerned about range unless you're over an octave plus five notes. But consider the average listener's ability to sing along and remember the music; watch people in their cars singing with the radio at the next stoplight, and hold fast to the image that they're singing your song.

32

THE LONG AND WINDING MELODY

Be sure your melodies lead to the hook;
don't let them wander

When a songwriter brings a song to the workshop with a melody that seems to wander aimlessly and not get home to a hook, we can guess how the song was written. More often than not, the lyrics came first and the melody was written after. When the lyrics are written without lines of a definite length and a rhythm structure grouped in clearly repetitive sections—that is, verses and choruses—the melody written to them will wander as well. The net result is a feeling of being lost in the musical desert and continuously crossing your own trail, thirsty for some clear, graspable melody.

This kind of writing is perfectly fine, but it's not really songwriting; it's tone-poem or song-poem writing, where the music is more accompaniment than an integral stand-alone melody wedded to a lyric.

Sometimes wandering melodies result from having been written first, developed along the lines of symphonic, film score, or New Age music that doesn't have the same requirements as popular song structure. This, too, can be very effective for atmosphere, especially if the lyric matches the emotional content of the mood of the music and has interesting imagery.

In some cases, the repeated musical theme may be eight or sixteen bars long and may not have a place to put a succinct title.

Sometimes the song fits a song structure melodically and lyrically, but the title line is buried in the middle of the verse or chorus and isn't placed strategically in the music. This situation also leads to an overall unresolved feeling in the song.

New variations on the basic verse/chorus and verse/bridge structures are being created daily. Country songs often have the title in the last line of the verse or in the prechorus, or "lift," leading into the chorus, as well as in the first line of the chorus. R&B/pop songs can open with a verse, go to a lift, into the chorus, to an extension of the chorus, back to the verse, lift, musical break, chorus, chorus extension, bridge, and so on. Some rap songs are written to be sung over a continuously repeated bass riff, with the only real distinction between sections being different rhythmic phrasing, harmonies, or extra production on the chorus. Even with all these variations on the theme of structure, the listener is never lost. The repetition of distinctive melodic segments helps us keep our bearings at all times.

Many lyricists hear melodies in their heads as they write lyrics; this is how they create the rhythmic patterns of each line, shape the overall flow of the verse, and match the pattern of syllables, accents, and rhymes in subsequent verses using the same melody. When the music person comes along to write a melody to these lyrics, his job will be much easier if the lyricist uses this method.

One exercise that can result in a commercially strong song is to write a new song based on the structure of a hit song you love. Here's how to do it: Write new lyrics to an existing hit melody, putting the title lyric in your tune in the same place as it is in the original. In fact, match it line for line, accent for accent, to the best of your ability. Then, bring your lyrics to your collaborator to have a new melody composed for them, without revealing the source of the structure. Or, if you are going to write the new melody yourself, do your best to forget the original melody. No one will ever know what you did, and you will have a guaranteed rock-solid interesting pattern and structure. Composers can use the same technique; they can write a new melody to already existing hit lyrics, then write new lyrics to their new melody.

You may not enjoy listening to Muzak when you get on the elevator or walk through your favorite department store, but, one day, we were in a Kmart and heard one of our songs being played sans lyric and we loved it. Melodies require the same focus the lyrics must have: both have to be great excuses for getting to the lyrical and musical title. Strong songs have strong melodies that can stand alone.

33

THE HOOK LINE IS SUNK

*Be certain you have a melodic hook
or that your title pays off melodically*

We didn't say this, and if you ask us to testify to it we won't: The first thing most listeners get into when they're hearing a new song is the music. Much of the time, even though songwriters slave over getting those lyrics just right, it is difficult or impossible to decipher the lyric on the first few hearings. The music has to attract you enough to listen again. Another way to say that is: The music invites the listener in; the lyrics bring them back.

If your listeners get into the music first, it's important to let someone leave your musical presence humming one of your babies. You have to give them something to remember. That something is a hook. It's the part of the melody that strikes your fancy the most. Usually, the title sits right on that part of the melody. You may not remember any other part of the song, but when that part comes around, you can sing it. You can't *stop* singing it sometimes. You're hooked.

A hook is the perfect image for this part of the song because it sticks out from the song and grabs you. The hook is to the melody what the title is to the lyric. It is the hub of the melody wheel. In the best

of all possible songs, all the melody lines lead up to and support the melody of the hook. Without this melodic focus to grab the listener, the song is so much mush, easily tuned out and forgotten.

The right location is important for a hook. Place the strongest melodic moment at a strategic place, such as the first line of the verse, last line of the verse, first and third line of the chorus, or first and last line of the chorus. If you can find a new place to put it and make it work, go for it. One of our latest songs has the hook/title on the second and fifth line of the chorus, but there's absolutely no melodic or lyrical doubt that it is the title.

Unfortunately, the failure to create a melodic moment around the title is glaring not by its visibility, but by its omission, so you don't "hear" it as wrong. There's just nothing about the song you can remember. Even if there is a lyric title hidden somewhere in the song, it's not set off musically so that anyone hearing it knows where it is. It sounds like just another line in the song—maybe one of the best lines in the song, but not the title.

In chapter thirty-two, we gave you a great technique to write stronger melodies and hooks. Imitation is one of the highest forms of compliment and a good learning technique.

If you've ever taught a child, you know you have to repeat something many times over before the child really learns it. We were not made to get everything the first time, despite what your inner critic might say. Treat your listeners like children, with respect and an understanding of their limitations: Repeat the hook as often as you can without driving them crazy or boring them, or at least enough to leave a good taste in their mouths. Then they will be able to hum the hook of your song after just one hearing on the radio.

34

JUST ONE HOOK

Include melodic, rhythmic, and instrumental subhooks

You might think, from reading the last chapter, that if you repeat your main hook line the optimum number of times, your listeners will be so irresistibly drawn into your song that their attention will not wander for an instant. That's a fine thought, but the reality is that listeners are super-fickle. If you give them a second without something interesting happening in the song, they'll start thinking about their shopping lists or carburetors.

After expending all the time and creative energy required to write and rewrite a great song, you don't want to lose your listeners' attention in the valleys between your main hooks. Your assignment, should you decide to accept it, is to dress your song up and take it out on the town.

Even when you're sitting 'round the campfire passing the guitar and singing songs, the ears have it when someone starts playing a short lead solo to get you into the song. Those first few notes can be a distinctive signature. You only need to hear the first five notes of "Imagine" to know exactly which song you're listening to. In fact, we can name it in two notes. How many notes of "I Can't Get No

Satisfaction" by The Rolling Stones do you need to hear before you're hooked? One? One and a half?

Notice in these songs and others how these distinctive note groups repeat in the spaces between the lyric lines, hooking the parts of the songs together. (There's that word "hook" again.) The best songs have more than one hook going for them. There is the main hook, which is the coming together of the high points in the lyric and the melody. And then there are all these little hooky bass or lead riffs, slides, or bent notes, between chorus and verse sections and between lyric lines that keep the listener's interest up and the excitement going through the song.

Without these minihooks, your song is stepping out in a plain old housecoat. Sprinkle minihooks throughout your song and you'll do for your song what the fairy godmother did for Cinderella: expose its beauty by dressing it up. The great thing is that you have to dress it up for the demo anyway, so your work won't be wasted down the line. Adding these minihooks helps you see if the song stands on its own as a piano or guitar vocal. We've found in listening to many original demos of hit songs that these catchy musical mini-hooks often turn up on the final record release. Today's producers basically copy your demo work verbatim when they produce the record because they don't want to mess with something that works.

This dressing up is even more necessary if the song is not particularly melodic. They add punch to a good song that's not particularly unique and needs all the help it can get to present it in a seductive light. The presence of these spicy subhooks also shows a professional mind at work.

You don't have to be an instrumentalist to create these addictive minihooks. You can communicate them to collaborators or hired musicians by singing them.

You can also catch your listeners' ears in other, more subtle, ways. Try to create rhythmic and melodic moments throughout the song that stimulate aural interest. Play with the rhythm, for instance, by singing a phrase in triplets rather than on the beat and making the accompaniment (drums, rhythm guitar, bass on a demo) track with it. Make the bass move in interesting rhythmic variations with or against the melody to strengthen the moment. Don't stick to root position chords even when just playing guitar.

These moments or "sound bites" are calculated and are peppered throughout hit songs in such a way that the listeners' attention is directed to the words and melody the entire time. They keep the interest up as the melody is sung and they also bridge the vocal silences. They can be as simple as rhythmic/thematic guitar licks or as technologically dependent as the latest drum samples. The better you dress your song, the more ears you'll turn.

35

IN SEARCH OF THE LOST CHORD

*Make sure your chords aren't
too complex or oversimplified*

You know the feeling: You're playing your instrument with some lines of inspired lyric in front of you. The melody you're creating sounds a little like the one you wrote three songs back and your hands are falling into familiar chord progressions. You're not stuck, but nothing you're coming up with is turning you on. You can't tell if anything you're playing is any good. It's time to break away from the all-too-familiar and do something different to make this song stand out. So you go out shopping at the Chord Store.

Did you know that rappers have been known to license a single chord sampled from a record label's copyrighted recording? One publisher tried to tell a rapper's representative, "We don't own the chord A." But the rapper's rep wasn't taking any chances and insisted on a license for the sampled chord. The publisher gave in and charged a five-hundred-dollar licensing fee, saying, "That's fine with me; we have plenty of chords where that one came from!" We're not talking about that kind of chord shopping, though. We mean when you go to your instrument of

choice and experiment with the possible chord combinations.

You buy an A flat when you're in the key of C, and go from the A flat to the C sharp 7 to the key of F sharp. This is fine, but unfortunately you're in the middle of the verse. It's different and draws a lot of attention, but is it working toward the intention of the lyric and melody? Maybe you're writing a country song and throw in several major seventh chords, ninth chords, or half-diminished chords. Are they in keeping with the tone of the song? Do they throw it into another genre, like jazz? Sometimes you make chord changes every half bar, which ultimately gives the song a restive feeling, as if it never settles into a groove and has no home key tonic feeling.

There is no question that you must keep yourself interested in your creations, trying new combinations of harmony, melody, and rhythm. But as both Tom Snow ("Let's Hear It for the Boys," "Somewhere Down the Road," "He's So Shy") and Tom Kelly ("True Colors," "Eternal Flame," "Like a Virgin," "I Touch Myself") have said, it wasn't until they simplified their work that they started to become successful.

From another angle, some chords and chord sequences are too simple. If you only play rudimentary piano or guitar, there might be a tendency to play all your chords in root position with the tonic in the bass. Granted, a moving melody and lyric will work *a cappella*, but by doing some simple chord manipulations you can make a song sound more interesting. Take a I-IV-V-I progression in the key of C and off the top of your head make up a simple melody. Sing the same melody over a C chord, going to an F with an A in the bass, a G with a B in the bass, and back to the C; or C going to an F with a G in the bass, to G7 and back to C; or C going to F with a D in the bass (which is a Dm7 or the II chord in the key of C), to Gsus, G7 and back to C; and so on. Suddenly a world of opportunity becomes available to give more feeling to your melodies. This is one area of study that many of the greatest songwriters today continue to pursue; it adds to their arsenal of skills and opens the doors to doing film scoring down the line.

Between making your arrangements so complicated that they distract the listener's attention from the song and making them so simple they lack harmonic interest, there is a middle ground you can only find by writing song after song. It takes time to find your own lyrical voice in the things you like to write about and the particular ways you like to express them. It takes time to find a way to keep your interest up as you search for new-to-you harmonic progressions while balancing the need to serve the emotional intent of the melody, lyric, and genre.

36

DON'T PLAY IT AGAIN, PLEASE

*Make sure your verses and chorus aren't
too alike in rhythm and melody*

Frequently in our workshops we see lyrics that could fit neatly into a rectangle drawn around them on the lyric sheet. The right margin of the words is almost as straight as the left margin throughout the verses and choruses. For example:

It's All the Same

When your song
Just goes along
And every rhyme
Is in a line

When your words
Can all be heard
To hit the beat
With the same feet

> **Chorus:**
>
> *It's all the same*
> *It's just too much*
> *We're losing touch*
> *Monotony's*
> *A deadly game*
> *It makes us sleep*
> *When it's all the same*

So syncopate
And variegate
It's not too late

To miss the gate
Escape the rut
And show us what
Can happen when
You take off in an exciting new direction!

© Pea Pod Music

In our workshops, we see the lyric sheet before we hear the song. If the verses and choruses are marching along in formation this way on the lyric sheet, a little flag goes up in our heads and written on the flag is "It's all the same." When the writer plays the song, our misgivings are usually confirmed. The verses, the chorus, and the bridge all have the same metric pattern, similar melodies, the same chord changes, and therefore, a uniform emotional intensity.

While repetition is an important device for driving home the hook or central idea in the song and for making the song memorable, it does have its limits. When repetition is carried too far, especially within the structure of the song, the song loses its power to grab and keep the listener's attention.

We didn't make these rules about varying the impact of the parts of a song. We learned about them many years ago from a cricket at the Exploratorium, a wonderful museum in San Francisco.

There was a cricket in a glass cage with an electrode implanted in its brain. The electrode was connected to a device that displayed the cricket's brain waves. If you knocked on the cricket's cage, the display screen would show the reaction in the cricket's brain, a big jump in the usually regular brain wave line. But if you stood there knocking in the same place, after a while the cricket's brain would not register any reaction. No new information is no information at all.

It's the same with a song. If a song drones on with the same metric pattern, the same melodic range, the same chord progressions, the same emotional intensity throughout, our ears will turn it off. The professional listener will hit the stop button on the tape machine. Should the song, by some miracle, get on the radio, the average listener will make a radio station's worst nightmare come true by switching stations.

In the three-minute movie of your song, you need to have a buildup and a climax. Try drawing your own "brain wave" graph of the ups and downs in your song and see how they compare to the diagrams shown in "Common Song Structures," on pages 32 and 34.

Notice that in a verse/chorus structure, the height of emotional intensity in the music and the lyrics should coincide with the most intense part of your message, the title or hook. The title is very often the first line of the chorus and is often repeated several times. In a verse/bridge structure the most intense point is usually the end of the bridge.

Is the graph of your song a flat line? If so, you need to play with it to build in some peaks and valleys. We want to be stimulated and excited by songs. One of the best ways to keep a song interesting from beginning to end is to keep new elements coming in with each part of the song's structure.

Here are some ways you can keep your songs from becoming flatliners:

- If the verse has notes of short duration and medium range, open up with some long, high notes in the chorus.
- Vary the length of the melody lines. significantly from one section to another—for example, make the verse lines long (twenty syllables) and the chorus lines shorter (ten syllables), or vice versa.
- Vary the length of the sections—if your verse is eight lines long, make the chorus a short four lines.
- Vary the rhythmic accents within the lines of a section.
- Vary the feel of the sections—make the verses rhythmic and less melodic, and become more melodic in the chorus.
- Keep the chord progression interesting by modulating out of the key of the verse into a new key for the chorus.

When experimenting with ways to vary the intensity of the parts of your song, make sure your title sits on the most outstanding point of the melody. Listen to your song as pure melody and chord progressions and be as objective as possible. Check to see if the part of the melody where you have the title stands out from the rest of the song and says, "This is it!" If not, you may need to move the title to the part of the melody that does.

PART 4

ONCE WRITTEN, LOOK TWICE

Rewriting Wrongs

37

DON'T SAY NOTHING
BAD ABOUT MY BABY

Learn to accept feedback on your songs

We are always amazed by the incredible amount of creativity and care songwriters put into their work. We know how much it takes to pull lyrics, melody, and chords out of the ether. As novelist Thomas Berger said, "Why do writers write? Because it isn't there." A tremendous amount of thought and effort is involved in the creation of a song. It's no wonder that many songwriters regard their songs as extensions of themselves. The song is not just scribbles on paper and notes in the air; it's your baby. You don't want anyone to tell you your baby's ugly. "Honest criticism is hard to take," said Franklin P. Jones, another author, "particularly from a relative, friend, an acquaintance, or a stranger."

For many writers, it's a case of "Love my song, love me." This kind of personal involvement with your songs really can't be helped in the early years of writing. Each new song is precious to you. You put your heart into every bit of the song, and you certainly don't want your heart trampled on. Fear of the pain that might come from exposing your song to criticism may keep you from showing your songs to anyone.

For some writers, this whole process is avoided by cloaking doubts and sensitivity in arrogance. These are the ones who show up at workshops expecting everyone who hears their song to fall down on the floor and worship the coming of the world's greatest songwriter, the one who can write no wrong note. After they show the song and the feedback begins, they become outraged that anyone would have the nerve to suggest an improvement to their obviously perfect song. Their defensiveness is a dead giveaway that they have a long way to go as songwriters.

The problem is that it's just during this stage, when you are so emotionally involved, that you need the most feedback on your songs. We spent years as songwriting students in various workshops and can recall vividly the awful feelings of annihilation we experienced as our songs were taken apart, rearranged, and rejected a thousand different ways. Our minds were screaming, "Our baby! How can you do this to our baby?" In such moments, it is important to write down or record what people are saying to you because your emotional distress makes it difficult to remember what went on during the time your song was in the hot seat.

As unpleasant as this may sound, it is a valuable experience and well worth living through. It does get easier. Through the process of seeking out and using feedback, you grow as a writer. You get used to looking at your songs as separate from yourself, and you don't take criticisms about your songs personally. We bring every song we write into our Sounding Board workshop. We crave the insights other songwriters can give us about whether we've communicated the message we intended when we wrote the song. At the Sounding Board, each writer distributes copies of his or her lyrics to all the attendees. As we all listen to the song and during the discussion afterward, everyone writes down ideas on the lyric sheets. Then, the presenting writer takes those written suggestions home and decides later which ideas ring true.

Where can you find feedback? Feedback can begin at home if you have a friend or relative whose opinion you value. The person must be able to express what's good about the song, what message she got from it, and where it was confusing. The person who loves you so much that he can only make glowing compliments is not the one you need for this process.

The wonderful songwriting team of Ray Evans and Jay Livingston that wrote "Que Sera, Sera," "Mona Lisa," "To Each His Own," "Secret Love," and the themes to *Bonanza* and *Mr. Ed*, wrote another song you probably know. Originally it was called "Tinkle Bells." Ray brought it home to get feedback from his wife. She said, "Don't you know what tinkle means?" It had never occurred to Ray and Jay! So Mrs. Evans was the midwife at the birth of the song we sing every December, now known as "Silver Bells." Without her, the song could have gone down the toilet.

Some relatives and friends may take the opportunity of being asked for feedback to put you down personally. Once you discover this is happening, don't ask for their opinions again. Being a songwriter is tough enough without asking for more trouble.

A more formalized source of feedback on your songs is the songwriting workshop. There are songwriting groups all over the country. Some are independent organizations, many with a Web sites that can be found by an Internet search on "songwriters in [Your Town]." If songwriters have not already formed a group in your area, you could take on the project yourself. Post notices, take out free ads, develop a mailing list, meet regularly to share songs, perhaps get a local club to sponsor a songwriters' night. This is exactly how the existing local songwriter organizations got started. Many towns and cities already have an NSAI regional workshop in place. Check their site at www.nashvillesongwriters.com to see if you're near one. NSAI will train and help you if you want to start a regional workshop in your area.

A great feeling of community develops in a songwriting workshop. We're all writers striving for similar goals. We share the same difficulties and desires. If the workshop is run with a respectful attitude toward everyone involved, the creative shot in the arm is phenomenal. When a workshop is done right, the participating songwriters grow to love each other. Each song becomes a group collaboration with the participating songwriters suggesting rewrites as if the "baby" in question were their own.

Unfortunately, some people seem to enjoy hurting others, and they occasionally show up in songwriting workshops as participants or even leaders. If you sense that such a destructive person is a participant in the workshop, talk to the leader about making some clear ground rules so negative behavior is not allowed to continue. If it's the leader of the workshop who is making nasty, cutting remarks, it's time to move on to a situation where you can get respectful, supportive feedback.

The Internet has opened up a whole new world of possibilities for getting feedback on your songs. We'll list a few. Just Plain Folks (www.jpfolks.com) has free peer feedback forums. NSAI members can send one song at a time to their song critique service. If you e-mail mp3 files of your songs, that allows for about a dozen songs a year. SongU students (www.SongU.com/luboff) can participate in live online feedback sessions with pro writers/songwriting teachers. TAXI (www.Taxi.com) members get feedback on songs they submit to listings. Songsalive!

(www.songsalive.org) offers critiques to its members for a fee. Songwriting consultants will give you individualized help with your songs. (See chapter one hundred one, "Dollars and Nonsense," for how to choose your personal songwriting consultant.) Searching for "songwriting feedback" and "songwriting consultation" on the Internet will yield you a couple million hits to explore. (See chapter ninety-eight, "Cyber Song Sharks," for how to tell the real thing from people who tell you your songs are great just to talk you out of your cash.)

It's part of your growth as a songwriter to develop a sense of where you can get intelligent and informed feedback on your songs. But, the song is your baby, and you may choose to ignore any and all suggestions to change it. That's your right as the creator of the song. (Q: How many songwriters does it take to change a light bulb? A: None. I think it's working!)

After collecting feedback from several sources, you may use some of the suggestions and toss the rest. That, too, is your prerogative. Eventually, the feedback process ceases to be a painful exposure of your innermost soul to insensitive criticism. As you mature as a writer, you'll understand that you have an endless supply of songs and that each one is not a matter of life and death. You'll come to value the process of getting feedback as a tool that you can use to fine-tune your songs.

≡ 38 ≡

STRANGER IN A STRANGE SONG

Check to see that your message is clear—
not hidden between the lines

When we write a song, there is a lifetime of meaning behind it. Everything we are at the moment when we write it comes into play. We know what we're talking about intimately. Naturally, we assume that everybody else should know what we mean.

Anyone who has tried to communicate complex emotions, even to those closest to us (or maybe especially to those closest to us), knows how hard it can be to be really understood. This is even more true when it comes to strangers. A stranger to your song doesn't know you well enough to guess at what you're trying to say. Your meaning has to be perfectly clear to the listener without the benefit of consulting your autobiography or your assumptions.

Don Curry impressed us with the skill he brought to a song he shared in our Santa Fe workshop:

Cowboy in the Western World

It's seven A.M. and the industrial world
Grinds out its dreams the American Way
The cloudy currents of the interstate
Stretch from Miami to the Golden Gate

Chorus:

I want to make it in the Western World
I want to rise to the top and
    spread the word
I want it all and I'm never gonna fall
I'm just a cowboy in the Western World

The winds are shifting in the face of time
Running to the deadline just around
    the bend
With morals drifting, slipping out of view
The future's in the hands of me and you

Chorus: repeat

Nobody told me that it couldn't be done
The moon was out of reach and
    belonged to no one
Don't even ask if you have any doubt
When you reach for the stars
That's what the game's all about

Chorus: repeat

© Don Curry

Don paints a remarkably strong picture in his first verse. You can almost see the smog drifting across the continent as the country wakes up and begins to grind its early morning gears. Let's start with lines one and two: great image, very unique,

105

sets the scene as early morning and the shot as a wide-angle aerial view of the United States. So far, so good. Lines three and four: another very interesting way to say that morning is arriving in industrialized America. We're ready for some new information. We were definitely hooked by this verse and ready to buy whatever Don was about to sell us in the chorus.

When we listened to the chorus, we figured the message was that the singer sees this industrial animal as the bronco he is going to bust by rising to the top in the business world. Okay, we'll buy that, too. The enthusiasm in the first line of the chorus leads us to believe that the singer approves of what's going on and wants to participate to the point of being on top of it and running the show. The phrase "spread the word" usually means someone is excited about something positive and wants others to know about it. So far, there is nothing in the words that would lead us to believe anything is wrong with this picture.

But with the second verse, we began to wonder. Now the picture is starting to change, and it sounds as though the singer doesn't approve of what's happening in the world. The second verse says, in effect: Times are changing, the pressure is on, morals are decaying, and we have to do something about it. How does the chorus, which we have assumed is positive and enthusiastic, fit into this turn in the lyrics?

Now we are strangers lost in a strange song, and the third verse, instead of putting us back on track, leads us even further down the path to confusion. It is in this confused state that we try to deal with deciphering the message of the first line, "Nobody told me that it couldn't be done." This line is a good example of how words can play tricks. It could either mean he feels he can do what he aims for because he has been told it is possible, or it could mean the thing actually can't be done, but no one informed him of that fact. Since we are currently lost, we have no context that will make us feel sure which way to take the line. The next line builds on this confusion, because it could mean either that we can't make claims on the moon or, as an extension of the previous line, that since no one told him the moon was out of reach and unclaimable, he could make a claim on it.

Since we are in doubt about what is going on, we won't ask about the next three lines. Our reaction to Don when the song was done was: "Great creative writing! But we don't know what you're trying to say. What's the message?"

He replied that he meant to say that the singer wants to become very successful in the business world so he can look down from the top of the pile and tell everyone how wrong it all is. Don felt he had expressed that in the phrase "spread the word" in the chorus. We never would have guessed he was trying to say that.

How can you tell if your listeners are going to get lost when your song makes perfectly good sense to you? We have a self-check technique that we call being a stranger to your song. Put your song in front of you and then put aside all your preconceptions about what it means. Pretend you never read these words before. Read the actual words printed on the paper without reading any meaning into them beyond what is actually contained in the words. Imagine yourself walking up to a stranger in the street and just saying those particular words from that particular lyric line. Would the stranger know exactly what you are talking about, or would she look at you as if you are talking a language she doesn't understand?

Take your song one line at a time and give it this test. Each lyric line is like an element in a mathematical equation. Each line must not only make sense on its own but must also be a logical part of the whole formed by all the lines added together.

Examining the song for the sense of each line, we can see that the trouble with Don's song is in the chorus, which set us up for something positive. Don's intended message is not there in black and white, and that is where it has to be. You cannot expect your listeners to fill in the blanks or to hear that you have your tongue in your cheek. We think the song would be better served by being definite about the intent of the song in the first line of the chorus. The chorus should also flesh out the reason for choosing the title. What does the cowboy concept have to do with all this? If the chorus truly stated the writer's concerns about where all this industrialization is leading us, the second verse would make a lot more sense.

We would still be a bit lost in the third verse, however. Don needs to put each of those lines to the "stranger" test. They can all be taken either positively or negatively, and that doesn't serve the purpose of the song, which is to communicate the writer's message.

Our thanks to Don, who did an outstanding job on this song, for allowing us to take it apart line by line. You need to do this to every song you write. Being able to remove your own prejudices and pre-knowledge of what you think the song is saying and see what it actually is saying is a very necessary skill in your bag of songwriting tricks. You must be a stranger to your song to see it for what it really is.

39

TWO DIFFERENT SONGS

*Be sure the verses and the chorus
aren't about two different things*

Sometimes, perhaps in an effort to distinguish the chorus from the verses, songwriters go overboard. The resulting song has separate sections, but with great gaps of meaning between them. Candace Magner's "Sing Your Song" is an example of a song that came to a fork in the road and went both ways.

Sing Your Song

*Take a trip out in the country
Take a spin around the town
Or take a walk and look around
And if you're lonely, fly away—
You'll meet a friend another day*

> **Chorus:**
>
> *Sing your song loud and lovely
> Sing it sweet, or sing it fine
> Sing it up or sing it down
> And if you're lonely, do it right,
> Sing it every day and night*

*You know me, I'm a country lady,
And I know you for a country man
And I'll come to you whenever I can,
And if you're lonely, you come to me*

*And I'll set your mind and your heart at
ease, 'cuz I*

> **Chorus: repeat**

© Candace A. Magner

The chorus in this song is very focused. It is about singing and singing only. But the verses have nothing to do with singing. Candace has the start of two or possibly three different songs here, as the verses don't have much in common with each other either. Starting with the chorus, she can write new verses that can easily be created out of a laundry list of reasons to sing: when you're happy, sad, scared, in or out of love. Since she has the word "lonely" in the chorus, she might build the verses around a good-bye situation. The leaver is going on a trip and will return, but it will be a long time, so the leaver advises the leavee to sing while she's gone to relieve the loneliness.

The structure of a verse/chorus is almost like a logical equation. We took logic in college and all we remember about it is: If *p*, then *q*. If you say, for example, that all broccoli is green, then if this is broccoli, it must be green. Such is the value of a higher education.

In the verse/chorus structure, the verses are the "if p" part. They give the underlying background information that supports the message of the chorus. The chorus is the "then q" part. The chorus gives the summation of the message, the main statement of the song. The verses support the chorus, and the chorus fulfills the verses. Together, they're undeniable. If they are divided in their impact, the song falls apart.

The best trick is to have each verse lead inexorably to the chorus, but each in its own fashion so that the chorus takes on a slightly different twist in meaning with each passing verse. This is called "recoloring" the chorus.

Remember, the chorus is the home of the title and the title is the hub of the song. All the lines of the song are like spokes in a wheel that point to that hub. A good test to see if you've focused on your title is to put the title after every line of lyric. Try doing that with Candace's lyric. "Take a trip out to the country—sing a song." "And I'll come to you whenever I can—sing a song." You can see the lines don't connect with the title. Now try it on a hit song; for example, "I Wish He Didn't Trust Me So Much," which Pete wrote with Harold Payne and James Eubanks. It's been cut many times, most notably by Bobby Womack and Snoop Dogg. "He's the best friend I've got—I wish he didn't trust me so much." "Each time he leaves me alone with his wife—I wish he didn't trust me so much." You can put the title behind every line of that song and see an obvious connection.

Remember that you are creating your own little world in each song. Sticking to the point of your chorus, which is at its highest expression in the title, is the gravity that will hold your song world together.

TOO MUCH IS MORE THAN ENOUGH

Don't include song parts or lyrics that don't add to the forward motion of the song

Abraham Lincoln couldn't have been talking about a songwriter when he said, "He can compress the most words into the smallest idea of any man I ever met." Songs are like diamonds, concentrated and crystal clear. You could say that writing a song is like wringing out a dishrag: You have to squeeze and twist until you get out every excess drop. Consider this song:

Summer Storms

Summer storms and memories
seem to get the best of me
and I'm hoping that this wine
will help get you off my mind

I'm drinking to forget the past
keep my world from spinning so fast
but when I get it spinning slow
your memory just won't go

I see your eyes shining bright
those warm summer nights
We loved all summer long
like storms without rainbows

As the storm starts blowing in
I think about what might have been
had it all gone a different way
where would we be today?

Not meaning what we say
our words seems to fly away
and before we can take them in
they're carried off by the wind
and turn to tears running down my face
those memories we can't erase
We loved all summer long
like storms without rainbows

Memories I just can't let go
I wish I could somehow know
that all the mistakes I've made
are worth the price I've paid

Afraid to ask for what we need
we think that others should plainly see
and not knowing what we want
our dreams turn to ghosts
that haunt when the nights are warm
carried by summer storms
We loved all summer long
like storms without rainbows

© DeEdda Freyer

This was one of DeEdda's first songs and the very first time she had shared a song with other people. There are a lot of great images in it that tell the story in an interesting way. She sticks to the central idea of the lost love, and all the lines clearly relate to that theme. This is a very good early songwriting effort, and it took a lot of courage to show it in the workshop. We congratulated DeEdda on a job well done.

Now using what you learned about song structure in chapter eleven, what would you say is the structure of this song? The opening four-line section does not repeat verbatim, so we can't call that section a chorus. The three longer sections, which have eight lines each and end with the same two lyric lines, feel like verses in a verse/bridge construction. There are two more four-line sections that follow the structure of the opening four lines. Looks like we have three bridges in this song. That's two bridges too many.

It's quite common for writers to come up with too many parts to a song. At a certain point, the song takes on a life of its own and requires that you make difficult choices in the interest of letting the song be the best it can be. This requires a certain amount of ruthlessness that you can only develop by writing so many songs that each one ceases to be precious.

It's fine to have too many parts; you can simply remove the parts that serve the song the least. In this case, we recommended that DeEdda start the song with the second and third four-line sections as her first verse. The lyrics in those sections use actions and pictures to express emotions, a great lyric writing device. We asked DeEdda to look at the song as a straight-ahead verse/bridge construction. Verse two would be the eight-line section beginning with "Not meaning what we say …" Then the current first four lines would make a fine strong bridge while keeping us drinking in the moment: "Summer storms and memories …" And "Afraid to ask for what we need …" would be the last verse, possibly followed by a repeat of the last two lines as a coda.

Speaking of the last two lines, they are the hook of the song. The title of this song is really "Storms Without Rainbows." Please don't cry because we cut those two extra bridges out. If they're strong enough, they can find a nice home in some other song.

Even in its cut-down version, this is a song of many words. They are well chosen, though, and we wouldn't recommend trying to edit this song down any further. But in general, when writing lyrics it's best to keep that dishrag in mind. Keep squeezing and twisting until every word is power-packed and no word is just along for a free ride. One of our favorite songs is Willie Nelson's "Crazy." You can count the number of words in that song on your fingers and toes but the emotional impact is like a locomotive with a full head of steam.

Fewer words with more meaning are the hallmark of a great lyric. Study the hit "I Don't Have the Heart," written by Allan Dennis Rich and Jud Friedman and recorded by James Ingram. The chorus is:

I don't have the heart to hurt you
That's the last thing I want to do
I don't have the heart to love you
Not the way you want me to

Look at how much is said in those few words. The first "I don't have the heart" carries the usual meaning of that idiom in our language: I don't have it in me to hurt you. This establishes the singer as a good guy, a sympathetic character who doesn't want to hurt the singee. The second "I don't have the heart," however, twists the meaning wonderfully. This time it means he doesn't have enough love in his heart to respond to the love coming from the singee. See how much emotional content and conflict they've packed into only seventeen words?

Songwriters are free to study all of the best examples of their craft. Take any song you love and purchase a copy of it. If you buy a CD, hopefully the lyrics will be on the CD insert. If they're not, or if you purchase a digital download of the song, you can transcribe the lyrics while you're listening. Examine closely the use of words and structures in the song. This is a different experience from just cranking up the radio and singing along. Look at the structure closely and name the parts.

Consider the question: How does one become a wine connoisseur? He drinks a lot of wine, thoughtfully! The same is true if you want to be a song expert. Thoughtful consideration of the way wonderful songs are put together will make you a better songwriter. Decide for yourself what makes a great song great. Chances are you'll find that the best songs are those that do the most with the least.

NEVER SAY REWRITE

Be willing to rewrite

Picture yourself in your special writing place. You open up, go within, listen to your muse, or whatever. Words, melodies, and chords come to you and you capture them. There is something holy about this picture.

The myth that songs come to songwriters in final, completed form is perpetuated by Hollywood. We've seen hundreds of movies that show childbirth, but never one that truly conveyed the experience. Movies depicting the birth of songs go to the opposite extreme. Hollywood makes having a baby look awfully hard and writing a song look way too easy.

The best songwriters in the world spend countless hours fine-tuning every note and word in their songs. We have a friend who collects Beatles recordings. Somehow, he obtained a work tape of John Lennon in the writing process of "Strawberry Fields." Listening to Lennon play the song over and over, making changes each time, talking to himself about what's right and what's not, is inspirational. It's guaranteed to make a "Never Say Rewrite" songwriter sing a different song.

As the saying goes, "Songs are not written, they're rewritten." The rewriting process starts concurrently with the writing process. It's not an insult to your muse to try for something better than what is first presented to you. It's a rare songwriter whose muse is so totally cooperative as to deliver perfect songs on demand. That's why they call it "courting the muse." We have to spend some time being nice to our muse, gratefully accepting what is offered but not necessarily keeping it all.

We have so many distractions and confusions in life; we can't expect to have a clear, open channel that only delivers perfection. We're going to get a lot of junk in the process of getting the good stuff. When junk comes, it's up to us to smile and say, "Thank you for sharing that with me," and then let it go. It's counterproductive to judge ourselves negatively for having less-than-wonderful ideas. These are just things we have to get out of the way so we can get down to the treasure beneath the junk.

Perhaps it is the fear of having to admit that not everything we think of is wonderful that makes some of us want to believe we mustn't tamper with the muse. Years ago, there was a series of margarine commercials in which Mother Nature tastes something and swears it's butter. When she's told otherwise, she disappears in a furious cloud of smoke, shouting, "It's not nice to fool Mother Nature!" Songwriters who don't want to fool with their muse are fooling themselves. Pretending to be perfect only rules out the trial-and-error process of true growth.

Some songwriters don't get to the "Never Say Rewrite" point until later in the game. They work and rework their songs to a certain level. At that point, they make the demo and bring it to a workshop or pitch it to publishers or producers. The listener who says, "I don't understand that line," or "I think you have too many verses," or anything of the kind might as well be talking to a brick wall. The songwriter in question believes the song is perfect, and anyone who has another opinion is just wrong. This attitude does not win friends in the music business. Being willing to consider constructive rewrite suggestions is the hallmark of a professional.

If you stand by your conscientious objections to rewriting at any stage of the game, you may eliminate your song from the running in a recording project. The rewriting sometimes goes on right up to the minute the lead vocals are being put to tape in the studio. This situation used to be expressed as, "It ain't final 'til it's vinyl." But that phrase and vinyl records have now gone the way of the dinosaurs.

We're absolutely not saying you should make rewrites against your will or rewrites you cannot live with creatively. Only you can know where to draw that line. It is a problem, though, if you draw the line so early in the game that you box your creativity into a corner. It's also a problem if you don't draw the line at all, as we shall see in our next songwriting wrong.

42

KILLING IT GRADUALLY WITH REWRITES

Don't rewrite a song to death

When a publisher or producer expresses interest in a song, it's music to a songwriter's ears. "A song I wrote could be heard by millions. It could change the world! What a concept!" As your mind rushes ahead to your Grammy acceptance speech, you can barely hear the "But …," from the other side of the desk over the roar of the crowd.

"But" can be a real kick in the … head. As a professional songwriter, however, you're going to sit tight as the "but" whizzes by your head and keep smiling, eager to hear what the person has to say. At least that is how you will act after you've tucked your tender ego away someplace safe.

Here's what could happen when the songwriter answers the existential question "to rewrite or not to rewrite" with endless rewrites. The publisher says, "I love your verse, but it doesn't have a strong chorus." So the writer takes this song and rewrites a new chorus. Then the writer takes it to someone else and that publisher says, "I love that song, but I don't like the lyrics to the second verse." The writer then rewrites the lyrics to the second verse and does another demo on the song. Then the writer

takes it to someone else who says, "That song needs a bridge." The writer takes that same song, writes a bridge, and re-demos the song. The song gets worked over and over and over, and somehow something—whatever was good about it to begin with—gets lost in the wash.

You may cut your song off from real opportunities by being unwilling to rewrite at all. But there's such a thing as being *too* willing to rewrite. You can rewrite a song to death. It's like killing the goose that laid the golden egg. If you take the song too far apart, you may lose the initial spark that inspired you to write it.

Only you and your collaborator, if there is one, can make the decision about where the rewriting stops. You are 100 percent responsible for the song, and you own 100 percent of the song. *You* have to live with the rewrites. A good rule of thumb is to make your best judgment about whether you really feel the rewrite has improved the song. If the answer is yes, go for it. Otherwise, forget it. If you decide not to rewrite, and the publisher is not interested in the song without the rewrite, all is not lost.

Remember, you are a songwriter. That means that you write songs. You don't just write one song and then stop writing until you've "made it" with that song. Believe it or not, we have met songwriters who have chosen this illogical course of action. If you're reasonably sane, you realize that this is just one song. You will write many more. Tell the publisher that you've made the effort but you're not happy with the rewrite. Perhaps this is not the right time or place for this song. Sometimes it's easier and more fruitful to try to learn something from the critique of the song and then write new songs. Let the publisher know you appreciate the interest and you'd like to come back with new songs, written with the feedback in mind. This way, even though this song didn't work out, you can keep the door open for the next song. If you do go back to the same publisher and your new song reflects what you learned, you will boost your credibility as a songwriter and begin to build a positive relationship with the publisher.

Pursue this relationship by bringing in your new, and always better, songs. Don't worry about angering the publisher.

If the publisher doesn't respect your prerogative as a songwriter to make the final decision on the song and can't recognize your sincere attempt to establish a positive relationship, you don't really want to deal with that person. Leave the scene gracefully. There are lots of really good people in the music business. If you're lucky enough to deal with one of the "good guys" (male or female), act accordingly. If possible, try to get an idea from the person of what projects are open to outside songs so that your next pitch can be geared to them.

Just because the song in question didn't feel right with the suggested rewrite, you don't need to abandon it. That was just one person's opinion. Try pitching the song to several other customers. If everyone says the same thing about it, you might reconsider the rewrite. But if you believe in the song just the way it is, stand by it. Many songs you hear as hits on the radio were rejected by over a hundred music business professionals before someone heard the potential of the song. Only you know what's best for your song, and only time and persistence will tell.

PART 5

TWO HEADS, OR MORE, ARE BETTER

Collaboration Misconceptions

43

DOING IT ALL

Don't think you can/must write it all yourself

Ever see a one-person band in the flesh? A friend of ours, Don Davis, was cited in the *Guinness Book of World Records* for playing the largest number of different instruments at once. Horns, whistles, drums, and cymbals, fretted and fantasy instruments loomed behind and over him on a giant backpack. In front, he wielded a huge accordion. More contraptions were strapped to his legs and suspended in front of his face. He couldn't be beat when it came to numbers of decibels produced by a human being. But, friends, don't try this at home. Don was a professional one-person band. You may put your growth as a songwriter in jeopardy if you attempt to write, play, and sing everything alone.

Creation in isolation has its good points. There's nothing like the courtship that goes on when it's just you and the muse. But if you only write alone, you miss out on a wealth of learning opportunities. We highly recommend collaboration as a songwriting learning tool. Billy Steinberg learned more about himself when he started to collaborate:

I didn't feel that I was stronger at writing lyrics than I was at writing music. I just thought I did both. I had really been sheltered as a songwriter. I had never co-written and I had never been around people with real musical gifts. I knew I wasn't a great guitar player but I wrote songs with my limited knowledge of chords. After a few years of working with Tom [Kelly], I started to realize that his musical talents far exceeded mine. Then I realized that I was also good at lyrics.

Note how long it took this realization to dawn on Billy. The slow business of show business requires infinite patience. Beware of wanting to do it all and make it all happen now. It will break your heart. Also, note that he had no way of knowing someone else could be so gifted or even what his own gift was until after the experience of working closely with another person.

We recently saw a nature program on public TV about hummingbirds. The show was overflowing with amazing facts about these flying jewels, but the image that floored us the most was the picture of a very special hummingbird.

Over millions of years of evolution, this bird had developed a bill with a certain length, curve, and twist to exactly fit the depth, curve, and twist of a particular nectar-holding flower. The feeding birds zip from flower to flower pollinating and thus ensuring the survival of the flowers. The flowers can't exist without the birds, and the birds can't exist without the flowers. They're a perfect match of gifts.

Believe it or not, you, too, are the result of millions of years of evolution, and your creative fit is just as perfect. It's our job as creative human beings to realize and identify what that means for each of us. We each need to dig into ourselves to identify the particular seed of creativity already planted and growing in there. A good place to start looking is your childhood. What did you really love to do as a kid? Chances are you loved doing it because it was the expression of your gift. Some are gifted with the variety of talents that it takes to "do it all"—or do most of it. Prince writes, produces, performs, and dances to his songs. He may not be your style, but his talent is undeniable. Most of us, however, have been given more specific gifts.

Billy's collaborator, Tom Kelly, told us:

The odds of somebody writing music and lyrics and hitting a home run on both ends are really pretty slim. There are some people that do it, but there are a lot more people that fall short because they try to do it. It's best to be able to recognize your strengths and really concentrate on them. Collaborate with somebody who can fill in the voids.

We'll talk about the pitfalls of collaborating in later chapters. For now, let's look at the bright side. Here are some of the advantages of collaborating:

- Making a date with someone else ensures that your writing session won't be put off while you engage in avoidance activities such as cleaning out the attic.
- Collaborators can provide instantaneous feedback, a new angle, a great lyric line, a beautiful melody, funds for making demos, music business connections, musical talents, recording equipment, enthusiasm, and commiseration.
- If you are lucky enough to find a steady collaborating partner, you can experience a rich, rewarding, and unique relationship. Since collaboration requires exposing your most vulnerable creative underbelly in the presence of another human being, trust and mutual respect are mandatory.
- The closeness of collaborating can be scary, but it can also be very educational. It provides an opportunity to learn from your co-writer and to learn about yourself as you relate to your co-writer.

Many writers are collaborating via the Internet. Those new to this express concerns about posting their material on collaboration boards or emailing it.

The Internet does not change the basic rules of copyright. Posting or emailing constitutes evidence of your date of creation. If you're worried about your ideas being stolen, give it up. Ideas are not copyrightable. Neither, for the most part, are titles. Only the presentation of the idea is protected by copyright. For more on this, see chapter sixty-nine, "Copyright It, Right?"

We teach a workshop called "Collaboration: The Key to Getting Cuts." The message of that workshop is: Develop your collaboration skills to the point where you can collaborate with anyone, anywhere. Then, when the chance to write with an artist comes up, you will be ready to seize the opportunity. Writing with the artist is your best bet for getting your song cut. You'll probably have to crawl, stumble, fall, and walk before you can run with that ball. The following chapters will alert you to some of the pitfalls along the collaboration way.

44

DIVING IN, CRAWLING OUT

Have an agreement with your collaborator
before you start working on a song

You're convinced that collaboration is the way to go. Now all you have to do is find your perfect match. How do you find collaborators? One ideal place is a songwriting workshop. It affords a unique setting that allows you to get to know the person and the songs she writes before you suggest a possible collaboration. Local clubs featuring original music are also good places to do your collaborator-hunting. Teaming up with an artist or a band that can provide a ready-made demo recording group and immediate live outlet for your songs is a wise move. Many songwriting-related Web sites have collaboration corners, places to meet people online. SongU (www.SongU.com/luboff) even has virtual writer's rooms, in which people on opposite sides of the globe can "meet" to collaborate.

Don't overlook schools as a resource. Many professional musicians and songwriters started out in high school bands. The creative writing studies and music departments of your local junior college or university probably have bulletin boards on which you can post an "I'm looking for a collaborator" announcement. If you are attending school, ask the teachers in those departments to recommend some outstanding students.

Find out if the songwriters in your community have organized to create some gathering point, such as an open mike night at a local club or monthly educational meetings. A simple Internet search for "songwriters in [Your Town]" often yields surprising results. If songwriters are not already gathering in your community and one of your gifts is a knack for making things happen, you can get help from NSAI (www.nashvillesongwriters.com). All you need is a dedicated core group of six songwriters to start an NSAI Regional Workshop. If this is something you want to do, contact NSAI to apply. You will be required to finance your trip to Nashville for a free training. Held in the spring and fall, these trainings are nicely scheduled with other educational and entertaining NSAI events: In the spring, it's Symposium classes and Tin Pan South concerts; in the fall, it's Songposium classes and concerts.

Cut to the scene of your first meeting with your potential collaborator. Now, do you sit right down at the keyboard and noodle until your new co-writer starts spontaneously singing the lyrics and melody over your riff? Isn't that the way it always happens in Hollywood movies about songwriting teams? Real life, as usual, is a different story.

It's a mistake to rush into writing right away. For the time you will be creating a song together, it will be like a mini-marriage. If you don't allow yourself time to get to know and trust each other, you may have the opportunity to experience the true meaning of "Marry in haste, repent at leisure." It's extremely important to have an understanding before you both invest your time and creativity into writing a song. Otherwise, you may find yourself crawling out of a confusing and painful experience with your confidence in tatters.

It's best to make a date to talk to your potential collaborator. We recommend you meet in a public place, such as a coffee shop, and talk about life, the universe, and everything. In this conversation, you can get a feel for whether you will be able to do the kind of wide-open communication that is a requirement for collaborating on a song.

Even if it is someone you know from a songwriting workshop, don't assume you understand what she or he has in mind. Now is the time to share enough information to let you feel safe to write with each other. Both of you should talk about the kinds of songs you love to listen to and write. Talk about your songwriting histories and goals. Talk about the kind of demo production equipment you have. Talk about your songwriting habits and your idea of how the potential collaboration will go.

A fruitful collaboration is based on mutual trust and respect. You can't expect your collaborator not to get on your nerves once in a while, but for the most part, you should be comfortable with each other. It is essential that you admire each other's writing. Use this talking time to develop a friendly rapport. If you are in the same philosophical ballpark, you will have more confidence in your ability to write together.

It's important to find out how well your collaborator knows the business aspects of music. Sharing information on this level can be a mutually educational experience. What contacts in the music business do each of you have? Does your potential collaborator have direct access to a recording artist? What are your preexisting contractual situations and opinions regarding the ownership of the publishing of the song? And last, but very far from least, there should be some sort of agreement as to how the ownership of the song will be split.

Will you be starting from scratch on an entirely new song? We think it's disrespectful and demoralizing to write a song and then try to pick it apart to see who wrote what percentage of it. If you're in the room together and you're both working on the song, the song's the thing. You're both giving your all. You have equal responsibility and deserve equal credit for the song. For us, it's important to make clear at the outset of writing the song that everyone who collaborates on it divides ownership of the song equally. We indicate this by writing in "50 percent [or 33⅓ percent, or 25 percent] words and music" under each writer's name on the copyright registration form. All expenses incurred in demoing and pitching the song are equally shared, and all income received is equally distributed among the writers. We believe this kind of business agreement is the basis of a trusting and respectful writing relationship with our collaborators. As we've said, trust and respect are absolutely necessary in the collaboration. Without them, we cannot drop our defenses enough to create spontaneously.

If you were presented with a complete melody and asked to write the lyric, you might expect to be identified strictly as the lyricist. That means you wouldn't get income from the song when it's recorded as an instrumental or in foreign translation. The standard procedure is to separate the lyricist's and composer's income streams. But we like to credit both writers with "50 percent words and music," even when the complete lyrics are written first by only one partner in the collaboration. Without those particular words, we wouldn't have found that particular melody.

Does the other writer have the melody and the chorus lyrics written and want you to write just the lyrics for the verses? In our collaborations, we still work on the premise that we're all equal writers. But your other writer may feel this situation calls for an adjustment in the percentage of the song, because he has already done more than half the work. It's best to have a frank discussion of the matter and agree up front about the value of your contribution to the song. It's far better to be in agreement *before* the writing is done than to fight about it *after* the fact. While you're busy arguing, another song will find its way to the producer you were going to approach. Arguments among collaborators after the song is written often result in songs that spend the rest of eternity in limbo because none of the writers want to deal with each other.

If you talk before you write, and you find out that you come from different universes and couldn't possibly get along, there is nothing lost and experience is gained. You must feel equal to your collaborator. If he or she is miles ahead of you in skills, knowledge, or contacts, you may be unable to function effectively because you feel inferior. Putting the shoe on the other foot, if you feel you are far superior, you won't have enough respect for your potential collaborator. Each of you needs to feel secure in your gifts and eager to pool your different but equally valuable talents.

Those hurdles overcome, you're ready to start writing together. You will be creating a piece of property, like a plot of land made out of the magic of your creativity. Anyone who wants to use your property will have to get your permission and pay you for the privilege. (Permission to record a song is only necessary for the first recording. After that, users will still have to pay you mechanical royalties as set by law, called the statutory rate, but will not have to ask permission to record the song. However, some users would rather negotiate with copyright owners for a lower mechanical royalty than statutory rate.) In other words, you're going into business together.

Some time during the writing of the song or, at the very latest, as soon as the song is completed, you need to enter into a collaboration agreement. This is a written contract between or among you that should contain the following information:

1. Title of song
2. Names of songwriters
3. Nationality of songwriters
4. Year of birth of songwriters
5. Percentages of words and music credited to each songwriter
6. Street, e-mail, and Web site addresses, and various phone numbers (landline/cell/fax) of songwriters
7. Social Security numbers of songwriters

This information is needed to fill in the blanks in the copyright registration form for your song. It will make life easier for whoever will fill out the form if all this information is already gathered. This is also a good time to talk about who will be filing the copyright registration, what the business address will be, and where the files related to the song will be kept.

In addition, a collaboration agreement might include language to the effect that:

- All writers share equally, or in proportion to their percentage of ownership, in the expenses of demoing the song.
- No money is to be spent without the consent of all writers.
- Writers are to notify the other writers in the agreement of any changes of address (this comes in handy when, ten years down the line, someone wants to record the song).
- No agreement is to be made regarding the song without the consent of all writers; however, you should make provision for the breaking of this rule (see chapter forty-eight, "Missing Persons"—the main reason for gathering of Social Security numbers at the time of the collaboration is to find long lost co-writers).
- Consent among the collaborators to agreements regarding the song may be given orally or in writing (you specify which).
- No changes are to be made in the song without the consent of all the writers (saves you from the nasty surprise of being written out of the song).
- If any writer becomes dissatisfied with the collaboration prior to its release or assignment to a publisher, the writer may withdraw his contribution to the collaboration freely, pro-

viding he makes no further claims on any subsequent collaboration on the song (separating out an individual's contribution may be difficult and troublesome).

- If a dispute arises over the collaboration agreement, the collaborators agree to submit to arbitration by a lawyer of unanimous choice or by the American Arbitration Association.

This is a document you can create yourself. We have a sample of the collaboration agreement we use posted on our Web site (www.writesongs.com), which you can use or modify to your needs. A lawyer would be able to write a more complicated agreement that covers many more subtle bases, but if money is an object, some kind of agreement is better than no agreement at all.

All writers sign and date the collaboration agreement, and everyone gets a copy. Then everyone lives happily every after, right?

Wrong again, collaboration breath! Read on and weep!

≡ 45 ≡

WHAT WE HAVE HERE IS A FAILURE TO COMMUNICATE

Talk openly with your co-writer
about every aspect of the song

Sometimes one member of a collaborating team will come to our songwriting workshop to get feedback on a co-written song. Let's say it's the lyricist. We'll play the song, and a participant in the workshop might say, "I think the melody was too upbeat for the subject matter. There's no prosody [emotional agreement] between the lyrics and the melody." Mr. or Ms. Lyricist often replies, "Oh, but that's the *melody*. I didn't write the melody."

What happened in the collaboration to make the lyricist disown the melody? Wasn't he allowed to give input on the writing of the melody? How can you create together if you can't relate honestly to each other? Now we come to the heart of the matter: communication. You want to communicate to the world through songs. But first you must overcome the communication barriers that come between you and your collaborator as you write the song together.

Avoid all the pitfalls from the outset by doing as we suggested in the first section of the book. Talk about the title, the intention, the mood, the setting, the situation, and the characters in the song.

Free-associate ideas of who the singer is and why she is singing. Consider which artists you think would relate to the message of your song. Listen to some of their current songs to get a feel for their musical style. Discuss the structure. Does the idea want to flow into a verse/chorus or verse/bridge form? As you have these discussions, you are building up to the trust it takes to show your creative underbelly.

What happens when you open up, become completely vulnerable, make a suggestion for a line in the song, and your collaborator says, "Yecch! That stinks!" in disgust? Your creativity slams shut like a clam; you're hurt and angry. You vow never to collaborate again. We thought we had discovered one of the secrets of life when we learned through repeated experience that extremely painful situations always turn out to be opportunities for growth. Then we found that it's no secret. In research conducted at California State University, more than 87 percent of people studied said that a painful event (for example, death, illness, breakup, or divorce) caused them to find a more positive meaning in life.

So when your collaborator makes a stabbing remark, look upon it as a golden opportunity for you to practice your assertiveness skills. You will be doing yourself, your collaborator, and the song a favor if you simply say you feel it's not productive to cut each other down. If the line isn't to your collaborator's liking, there are ways to say it without attacking. For instance, "That's not quite there yet; I think we can get a stronger line. Let's keep trying."

We've taught a workshop called "12 Steps to Building Better Songs" all over the United States. In that workshop, we lead a group collaboration on a song, starting with choosing the title from among dozens offered by the audience of writers. We've done this with groups of one hundred adults and with groups of six-year-olds. (They're the best. No creative blocks there!) To avoid the creative shutdown negativity brings, we lay down a simple rule that the six-year-olds helped us to refine. Pointing to our noses and shaking our heads, we say "No nos!" This rule can be set and easily followed. We learned that truth while being trained in creating in groups, conducted by a corporate think tank. The first one who said, "That won't work," or "That would be too expensive" got to wear a baseball cap with a fake turd on the front! Guess how many people made the mistake of being negative? One! That was all it took for the rest of us to take the positive high road.

Arthur Hamilton, who wrote the fabulous song "Cry Me a River," a hit for Julie London and recorded by over one hundred artists in the fifty years between its debut and its appearance in the 2006 motion picture, *V for Vendetta*, related a story about his collaboration with Barry Mann. Barry is co-writer of "You've Lost That Loving Feeling," "Somewhere Out There," and "Sometimes When We Touch," to name a few of the monumental songs he has co-written over the last forty years. You may have heard him singing, too. Barry is the writer/artist who brought us the immortal "Who Put the Bomp."

Arthur talked about a lyric he had given to Barry. After working separately on the melody, Barry invited Arthur to hear what he had done. Barry played the melody and sang the lyrics, then turned to Arthur and said, "I'm having a problem with this spot right here. It's probably my fault, but I just don't think the words and melody go together." Arthur saw immediately that the melody did call for a change in the lyrics. In the end, Arthur wound up rewriting two entire lines of lyric because of the changes in the word or two where the lyric and melody weren't meshing. Arthur was thrilled by the sweet and gentle way Barry suggested the change. The point is that it's not what you say, but how you say it. Truly great songwriters know better than to be arrogant.

It's really a matter of respect. If you respect the ability of your collaborator, you will not criticize the occasional awful suggestion. We all have trash that we have to get out of the way before we get down to the good stuff. (In fact, that "stupid" idea that comes into your head may be just the thing your collaborator needs to hear to trigger the brilliant solution to your song problem. We feel an obligation to say every dumb thing we think of.) If you react negatively, you start to function as the too-early editor for your collaborator, and the result is the shutdown of the creative flow. If you make the mistake of putting your collaborator down, you can make amends by apologizing and cleaning up your act. That kind of an attack is often, if not always, caused by the attacker's insecurities and defensiveness. Examine yourself honestly. Stop blaming your collaborator for your frustrations with the song. Give yourself the reassurances you need to carry on with confidence.

If you keep clear and direct communication lines open throughout the writing process, every iota of the song will be agreed to by all the writers. By agreeing to each word, note, chord, rhythm, and feel, each writer is responsible for that part of the song, even if it clearly came from another writer in the team. You cannot simultaneously keep score on who wrote what note or which word and be creatively spontaneous. You are all responsible for the total song. If there's a part of the song you really can't own, it's up to you to make your feelings known. Then what?

We'll talk about collaboration impasses in the next chapter.

46

LET'S DO IT MY WAY

Don't insist on your way when a collaborator disagrees

You're collaborating with a new partner. The song is coming along pretty well. You have the title, the first verse, and part of the chorus written. You're both working on finishing off the chorus lyric, and you've both tried a lot of possible lyric lines on each other. None have made either of you jump up and down and shout. Suddenly, your co-writer exclaims, "Eureka!" You eagerly listen, wanting it to be the answer to your search.

Despite an enthusiastic presentation of the line, you're not thrilled with it. You do your best to respectfully express that you think a better lyric could be just a line away. You suggest some more work on the line. Your co-writer gets all bent out of shape, claims it's the perfect line, and insists there's no way you're going to find a better one; you've already spent enough time on it, and you should just go with this line.

Now is the moment of truth. You discover that, in all your prewriting talk, you forgot to lay a very important ground rule: Not one jot of lyric or melody goes into the song without all the writers' agreement. And giving in to pressure does not qualify as agreement. Pressure has no place in a creative collaboration.

Likewise, if you're the writer offering a line that is not greeted with great joy by your collaborator, you need to learn to accept that gracefully. You might state a few calm reasons why you think it fits perfectly. If, after giving it a second look, your collaborator isn't turned on to the line, you need to let it go.

We attended a workshop given by Marilyn and Alan Bergman, world-class lyricists whose collaborations have won them Oscars and Grammys galore. "The Windmills of Your Mind," "The Way We Were," the theme from the movie *Tootsie*, and "What Are You Doing the Rest of Your Life?" are among the standards they have written. During the workshop, they spoke at length about their policy of mutual respect. If the lyric line doesn't make them both absolutely happy, it's tossed without a second glance. There are a hundred, a thousand more where that came from, and one of those yet-unconceived lyric lines *will* make them both happy. We heard these words of wisdom over twenty years ago, and we've never forgotten them.

With this philosophy, the Bergmans are expressing their complete confidence and trust in each other. They know they have what it takes to keep at it until they are both totally satisfied. The thought of running out of ideas never occurs to them. Of course, they've been writing lyrics eight hours a day for umpteen years, and their skills are razor-sharp. They find the lines they're looking for faster than we do. That only means that we have to be more patient with ourselves as we stumble around learning to walk the songwriter way.

It's fantastic when a song comes fast and easy. Some songwriters are known for creating lyrics at lightning speed. Sammy Cahn, lyricist of "All the Way," "High Hopes," "Let It Snow, Let It Snow, Let It Snow" and "Come Fly With Me," to name just a few, used to write lyrics as fast as his collaborators could play the melodies for him. Most of us, however, take a bit longer. Some songs take weeks, months, even years to come together.

We had a strange experience while writing a song with Harold Payne. Contrary to our usual procedure, we had written the melody first without a title. We knew where the title fit on the melody, so the three of us worked separately on finding the perfect title. It may have been two or three days of writing and some four hundred rejected titles later when Pat came up with an idea she liked and typed it on her computer. She looked down and noticed that Pete, who was working at a desk beside her, had just written the same title on his piece of paper. She turned to him and said, "Oh, you like that one?" thinking that he had seen it on the monitor and copied it. He replied, "Yes, I just wrote it." As we sat staring at each other, wondering at this coincidence, Harold burst in from the backyard, saying, "I've got the title." It was the same title. Working independently, we had all written the same title at the same time. This had to be the title we had been looking for all those hours. There's a saying that applies to this situation: Don't give up before the miracle happens.

Suppose you realize your error of omission and take an intermission from writing to discuss the basic ground rules of the collaboration. You could say something like, "I understand you feel strongly about the line, but I think we should have a basic rule in the collaboration that we both agree fully to every line in the song, or the line is not in the song. Let's try a few more lines, and if we really can't find anything better, we may still use it." What happens if you work and work and work and still you don't find anything? You can choose to:

- accept the lyric that your co-writer loves and you're not so crazy about, with the condition that it can be changed later if a better line is found
- take a break from the song and come back to it another day
- take two aspirins—songwriting is a dirty job, but somebody has to do it

When your collaborator develops a hard head after you've written a dozen great songs together, it can be an even bigger headache. We had that experience, and it was devastating. The writing went so well at first. We were all excited by the process and the product of our collaboration. Then, all of a sudden, something went wrong. Our collaborator started to insist that there was one right way for things to go, and of course, it was the way she had in mind. We tried to reinstate the "everybody must be happy" rule, but it fell on deaf ears.

The songs that followed also fell far below the quality of the previous songs we had written. It meant the ending of a relationship for which we had high hopes. It's pointless to try to create when the relationship between collaborators has deteriorated from a democracy to a tyranny.

Life goes on and you will find more and better collaborators. We did.

47

I TAKE THAT BACK

*Don't try to change your collaboration
agreement after the song is written*

Once upon a time we had a collaborator. And the collaborator was a very nice person who wrote songs about brotherly love, so we expected this person to be familiar with the Golden Rule. We had a long acquaintance with this person through our mutual involvement in several music business organizations. We all thought it was a very good idea to collaborate.

We talked about our business understanding before beginning to write; we all agreed this would be a three-way collaboration and an even three-way split of ownership. So we sat down to write, and the writing went very well. We were enthusiastic about the song, ideas flowed freely, and we completed a song with no problems.

We went on to write song number two together. Again, the writing went smoothly, with everyone contributing continually in the process. After song number two, the collaborator called for a meeting. We don't want to give away this person's identity, so we'll use the name Chris, which could belong to either a man or woman.

Chris said, "Look, I think I'm contributing more to this collaboration than you are. I think I deserve half of it, and you two should split the other half." You could have knocked us over with a guitar pick. We had trouble believing what Chris was doing: Chris was trying to "take back" the deal we had all agreed to. When we understood that Chris was serious, we felt betrayed and angry. That ain't no way to treat a collaborator! The collaboration was over immediately. The two good songs we wrote together have gathered dust on our shelf ever since.

What if you do feel that, on one song or another in a collaboration relationship, your actual contribution was more than your percentage? If the writing relationship is a good one, you need to think about the long run. Perhaps two or three songs from now your contribution will be less than your percentage. We feel strongly that petty quibbling over who wrote what is anathema to a collaborative relationship. Write a few more songs together, and if you still believe you're doing most of the work, talk to your collaborator. You won't be able to go on with the relationship with this feeling of inequality.

Honesty is the best policy, but a little bit of tact goes a long way. First, make it clear you are not talking about changing the deal on the songs you have already written together. Even if you did not put your agreement in writing, you are honor-bound to live up to it. You need to let your collaborator know you value the relationship.

Tell your collaborator that you feel you are consistently contributing the greater part of all or most of the songs you have written together. Ask if she thinks this is happening, too. If the answer is yes, you can breathe a sigh of relief and talk about what kind of deal would more fairly reflect the way songs are being created in your collaboration. If the answer is no, you've got trouble in collaboration city, but it can be overcome if both of you are committed to the relationship.

You could always choose to continue the relationship on an even-split basis. But if you resent this arrangement, your writing will suffer. You could both agree to write the next song, observe who contributes what, and decide accordingly how it should be split. We hate this idea, but maybe you can make it work. We don't think you can do math and songwriting simultaneously. You could agree to modify your writing process so that it becomes more clear who is doing what, or so that the work is shared more evenly.

Collaborators bring much more than their writing skills to the songwriting process. They bring recording equipment, music business connections, business skills, office facilities, vocal talent, musicianship, inspiration, and enthusiasm. Be sure you add in all the factors when you start crunching numbers—you wouldn't want a good collaboration that could last a lifetime to get lost in the crunch.

═48═

MISSING PERSONS

*Know how to deal with a song when there's interest
but you can't find your collaborator*

On a day like any other day, you get a call unlike any other. The caller wants to record your song. You sent a record company a CD two years ago, and unbeknownst to you, they have been holding it for consideration. Since this is the first time this song will be recorded, the record company needs you to issue a mechanical license. A mechanical license is a piece of paper that says they are permitted to mechanically reproduce your song on a CD, and they have to pay you *x* amount for each copy sold.

Your problem is that you wrote that song with Sam Songwriter four years ago. You never knew him well, and you have no idea where he is now. If you have no collaboration agreement with Sam, you're out of luck. Sam owns the song just as much as you do. You can't issue the license without his agreement.

To avoid this awful situation, you must include some provision in your collaboration agreement for each of you to act on opportunities for the song, in case you cannot get in touch with each other. Even if you're best buddies and never lose touch, it's useful to have such a provision

for those times when one of you is traveling around the world and hard to reach.

The collaboration agreement should state that all collaborators on the song will notify each other of changes of address. Put your old collaborators on your holiday card list; they will at least know where you are at the end of each year. The planet seems to be spinning much faster these days, and we guess a few people fly off the face of the earth each year, because cards bounce back undelivered from a couple of our old friends each December. Despite the best intentions to stay in touch, this provision in your collaboration agreement doesn't guarantee that you'll always be able to find old Sam Songwriter.

The Internet can be helpful in finding lost co-writers, especially if they have a Web site. Someone with an unusual name and whose general location is known can be found in seconds. But if your missing writer isn't technologically inclined and has a common name like Bruce Williams (Bruce, where are you?), you're out of luck.

The provision to deal with your missing collaborator should state that, if unable to contact or locate the other collaborator(s), any of the writers on the song has full power of attorney to make an agreement regarding the song. (For the power of attorney to be binding, it must be notarized.)

When you are dealing directly with a record company like this, you are acting as your own publisher. Another way to deal with the situation of missing collaborators is to form a publishing company owned by all the writers. Then all of you sign a publishing contract to that company for that song. As co-owners of the company, each of you will have the power to do business with the song. For more about being your own publisher, see chapter seventy-five, "One Hundred Percent of Nothing."

If you thought ahead and were prepared when that call came, you are now able to issue the license on the song you and Sam wrote. The song is recorded and released and winds up on an album that does fairly well. In a year or so, money starts to come in for you and Sam. Now what do you do?

Even if you didn't go through the formality of forming a publishing company with Sam, you are one in fact. Money from the record company will come to you as Your Name Music Publishing and Sam Songwriter Music Publishing. Half (or whatever percentage you agreed on) of that money belongs to Sam. You need to keep an accounting of the money received and the money that belongs to Sam. There is no law that says how you have to keep this money for Sam, but you need to be

ready to show him the accounts and give him his money should he hear about the recording and find you.

There is no answer to the question of what to do if Sam never shows up. It seems reasonable that some of Sam's money could be spent on locating him. Since you should have Sam's Social Security number on the collaboration agreement, you might be able to use that information to find him. If you know Sam loves to read *Rolling Stone* magazine, try a personal ad in their classified section.

Another missing persons problem that songwriters run into is the case of the disappearing publisher. What happens when you sign a single song contract with Pat Publisher and then Pat vanishes? If you signed a contract without a reversion clause, you have a problem, because that means you gave Pat complete ownership of the copyright and all power to do any business with the song until thirty-five years later when copyright termination will allow you to recapture your copyright.

This is only one of the reasons—but it seems sufficient—that we advise you to insist on a reversion clause in any publishing contract. The reversion clause states that the ownership of the song reverts to you after a stated period of time if there is no commercially recorded release. The time can range from six months to two or three years.

If the problem is that you can't find the publisher, it stands to reason that the reversion of the ownership of the song should not depend on your being able to find the publisher to give notice that the time is up. Make sure your reversion clause has language that provides for the situation of the disappearance of the publisher. It can say something to the effect that ownership of the song reverts to the songwriter upon written notice sent to the publisher by registered mail. The reversion clause should also state that if the publisher refuses to accept your certified mail or if the publisher moves without providing a forwarding address, the attempt to give notice by certified mail will be considered the legal equivalent of giving notice.

Providing for the possibility of losing track of your collaborators or your publisher in your agreements with them may make the difference between a hit song and a dead issue. Don't forget to take care of this important little bit of business that can mean a lot.

PART 6

GETTING IT RECORDED

Demo No-Nos

49

NO UP-FRONT FEEDBACK

Don't spend money on demos before getting informed feedback on the song

After your song is written, the next step is to make a demo (short for demonstration recording). The demo will be the only embodiment of your song that the publisher, producer, or artist will hear. In most cases, you will not be there in person to present the song. The demo will have to present itself. It will have to be strong enough to stand on its own without your being there to say, "This part needs horns," or "The record would have backup vocals here."

There are a million ways to go wrong in the demo-making process. In the chapters that follow, we'll cover a variety of preparation mistakes and ways to avoid or undo them. Some of the most important steps you need to take to get your demos produced are the things you do *before* you go anywhere near a recording studio.

Taking first things first, the song is the thing. No amount of horns, backup singers, or money poured into a demo is going to make a weak song strong. Too often in workshops we are presented with incredibly elaborate demos of songs that are shining examples of all the errors we've covered so far in this book. The lyrics are confusing, the melody is monotonous,

the character the singer is representing is an unsympathetic lout, and so on.

We literally wince when such an empty demo is played because we hate to tell a writer that she just wasted five hundred dollars (in a recent case, two thousand dollars!) or whatever she spent making the demo. It hurts us to have to point out this painful truth. The writer could have spent half of that money on taking a songwriting workshop and then made a much better demo with the other half of the money. The only thing we can recommend to the songwriter is to create a file like the one we did when we bought a lemon of a car from "a little old lady from Pasadena." The label on the file read "Four-Hundred-Dollar Lessons We Have Learned."

To save yourself the pain of creating your own "very expensive lessons learned" file, do not spend penny number one on a demo until you have some informed feedback on the strength of the song. Review chapter thirty-seven to refresh your memory about where you can find this feedback. Don't just ask your mom—you know she loves you too much to see your flaws or those in your song. Get feedback from several people whose opinions you value.

A good demo can cost a lot of money, and it can be money well spent. But before you start spending, stop to listen to your song. A very good thing to do before you make a demo is to make a pre-demo. A pre-demo is the demo you make at home with whatever equipment you have on hand. If all you have is a little cassette deck, just sing and play into it and make the best recording you can.

If you have synthesizers, MIDI, drum machines, DAWs (digital audio workstations), and so forth, your investment in that equipment is a testimonial to your seriousness. You can make your own elaborate demo at home with a minimum of further cash expenditure. However, do not discount your most irreplaceable and therefore valuable asset: your time. No one gets more than twenty-four hours each day. You can spend a long time making a terrific in-home studio demo of a song that could have been terrific, too, if you'd sought some feedback and done that necessary rewrite.

Make every effort to have the pre-demo at least suggest the sound you will be going for in the ultimate demo. Use your guitar or piano to play the hooky rhythmic riffs that you imagine will be played by horns later. You can use your voice to indicate musical ideas you "hear" for instrumental solos or fills. Try to capture the feel that you want to express in the demo. The amount of thought and creativity you put into your pre-demo

will have a big effect on the quality of the final demo. The demo-making process is really a decision-making process. The more decisions you make before the meter starts ticking in the studio, the less money you'll spend and the less stress you'll experience.

A pre-demo is a handy tool. You can play it to your esteemed feedback providers. You can give your ears a rest from the song for a day or two, then play the pre-demo again. Does the song grab your interest and hold it all the way through? Do the emotions in the song build and pay off? Is the melody memorable? Is this a message the world needs now? This is the moment of truth. You have to distance yourself from the song and look at it with a critical eye. Ask your song, "If I spend five hundred dollars making a demo of you, will you pay back on my investment?"

If you honestly think the answer to that question is no, it's time to get your hand out of your wallet and get back to work on the learning process of songwriting. Maybe this song is as strong as it's ever going to be. Maybe the idea wasn't that strong in the first place. It wasn't a wasted effort, because you learned so much while you were writing. Maybe it's time to write another, better song and put this one in a file marked "Lessons I Learned for Free."

This is not an easy thing to do. Songwriters want to be heard. We want the world to sing our songs. We want that so badly that sometimes we think we can make it happen if we only spend enough money. The only thing we really gain by spending money without a lot of thought first is more space in our wallets.

If, when you play your pre-demo, the feedback is totally positive and your most critical listening of it still leaves you knocked out, you're ready to start thinking about your demo. Your pre-demo comes in handy again. Give a copy to the vocalist with a lyric sheet so he can become familiar with the song before the recording date. Give copies to the musicians who are going to play on the demo session. Give a copy to the producer or engineer you will be working with on the demo. Or send a copy to the mail-order demo service to help them know what you're trying to get at with the song.

Notice we said "a copy." Never let your original out of your hands. It will find a way to get lost. Label your pre-demo as you will your demo. Mark all items with a copyright notice (© and your name or your publishing company's name) and your phone number.

Remember, you create a song, it's like creating a piece of real estate. The song is the land itself; it is the basis of the value of the property. The demo is the house you build on the land. If you build on sand, the house will fall. You have to make sure your song is as solid as a rock before you start construction on top of it.

50

POISONING THE PRODUCTION WELL

*Don't have an overbearing or put-down
attitude in the studio*

D-day has arrived—Demo day, that is. You've booked the studio. It's your song, your money, and you're in charge. You're drunk with the power of the moment. You tell the musicians what to do. You tell the engineer what to do. If anyone makes a mistake, you let him know you don't like it a bit. Your money is being spent and mistakes take time.

You put your coffee cup on the top of the mixing console, your feet up on some outboard gear, and say to yourself, *Today, I am a producer, and I say what goes.*

This doesn't really happen, you think. Well, the picture we've painted is mild compared to what has actually happened in recording studios: fistfights, food fights, even gunfights. Coffee in the console, smoke and sparks in the air, engineers being held hostage—that's what happens when people forget to check their egos at the door of the recording studio.

When you are the producer, your attitude sets the tone for the session. If you are encouraging everyone to do their best instead of insisting they toe your line, you will get a much better performance. If your attitude is overbearing, if you

criticize and put down the people you are working with, expect the worst. You'll get it, because you're poisoning the production well. No one can be creative while being put down.

Remember when you wrote the song? You had to open up to a sensitive place in yourself to reach the emotions you needed to put into the song. The people you hire to record your demo are having the same experience. In the same way that you didn't need your inner critic or a criticizing collaborator then, they don't need your criticism now. You need to make the recording session a safe place where everyone feels free to open up and give her creative best.

Old-fashioned manners can go a long way. "Please" and "thank you" should be mainstays in your vocabulary. Be sure to emphasize what's going great. A suggestion for improvement does not have to be couched as a criticism of what's been done.

But what if someone really is making a lot of mistakes and giving a bad performance? You cannot afford to pay for someone else's bad day. Try calling a ten-minute break and speaking to the person privately. Ask if there's something wrong or something you can help with. You probably can't help, but just the offer may be enough to lift the person's mood.

If there's no improvement after the break, you may have to accept that you cannot work with the person in question. If you hired the person on the recommendation of the studio, they may accept some financial responsibility if it's clear the person is not performing. They want your business, so they want you to be happy. Consult with the engineer. You can be sure the engineer is hearing what's really going on. That's the first item in their job description.

Engineers are a special breed. If you are going off the deep end, they will suggest the saner route once or twice in a mild way. If you are insistent, they will clam up and do as you say. Their job is to serve the producer, even if they think the producer is wildly incompetent. They won't fight you if you're determined to do it your way.

If it's the engineer you're having trouble with, speak to the studio owner. If the engineer *is* the studio owner, you've just learned not to make demos there. You will have to decide whether to make the best of a bad situation or get out while you're ahead.

You may be paying the bill, but don't forget that what you're paying for includes the expertise of the people you have hired. Megalomania and defensiveness will get you nowhere fast. Open communication and respect for everyone involved will get you everything you need.

51

TOO MANY DEMOS SPOIL THE WALLET

Don't make too many demos at once

The only thing worse than a songwriter blowing a lot of money on a demo of a song that isn't ready is a songwriter blowing lots and *lots* of money on *many* demos of *many* unready songs. We've had songwriters in workshops tell us they've sent off twenty songs at once to a mail-order demo service. At two hundred dollars per song, that's way too much money to spend at once, for several reasons.

First, demo production is an educational process. How can you learn from your mistakes when you make them all at once? If you make one or two demos at a time, you can learn from the mistakes you make on those. That way, demos number three and four can be better than one and two. You have to give yourself time to process the information.

Second, sending a huge quantity of songs to a mail-order demo service cuts you out of the process. This is your education you're paying for; don't miss out on the field trips. Even if you feel totally incompetent to make your own demo, it is preferable to get your body into the studio and watch the process if you can. Musicians and engineers do have to take

breaks, and you will have the opportunity to strike up relationships that may be mutually beneficial. You never know what connections you might make in a studio. Perhaps you'll find a collaborator. Maybe one of the musicians is a member of a band that needs material. A good friend of ours wound up marrying the owner of the studio! Whatever happens, it wouldn't have happened to you sitting at home staring at your depleted checking account balance.

Third, it's highly unlikely, no matter how good a songwriter you are, that you have twenty hits on your hands at once that need to be demoed right now. You are far better off concentrating on the one or two most powerful songs you have. Take your time and do a bang-up pre-demo. Study the songs currently on the charts. Who do you want to pitch these two hits to? Record their latest songs off the radio or pay for a download from the Internet to study their vocal range and "image." Record or legally download songs that have the feel you want on your final demo. They will serve as the audio equivalent of "a picture is worth a thousand words" in communicating your musical ideas to the demo producer. Audition vocalists and choose the one you think will best serve the song. Research your recording options; for instance, some studios offer discounts if you buy blocks of time, and some give better rates when business is slow.

If there is no studio close enough for you to be physically present at the recording, use mail order as a last resort. If you're unhappy with the results, at least you'll only be unhappy with two songs, not twenty. We'll cover the subject of how to get the best demo possible from mail-order demo studios in chapter sixty-one, "Sending Money Down the Demo Hole."

Emptying your wallet is not going to make you a better songwriter. Filling your mind with experience will. The great thing about songwriting is that it's a never-ending learning process. There is so much to learn; don't let any opportunities pass you by. You can get a lot more learning out of doing fewer demos at one time. It's the difference between wolfing down a meal and savoring every bite. The latter is a more exquisite experience, and it's better for your digestion.

≡ 52 ≡

TOO MANY PRODUCERS
SPOIL THE DEMO
Don't let everyone else make your demo decisions

On your obstacle course to songwriting success, you've managed to avoid sinking in the mud puddle of confusion. You've finely focused your ideas and expressed them clearly and with passion. You've asked for input and rewritten as you felt necessary. You've chosen two or three of your best songs to demo. You've asked around and booked a studio that several other writers have highly recommended. The engineer and the musicians are warmed up and ready to roll. What could go wrong now? Plenty.

As the songwriter hiring the studio and the musicians to demo your song, you are officially the producer of that recording session. What does a producer do? We asked Quincy Jones that question. His reply:

> There are thousands of decisions to make about the right musicians, the engineer, the studio, the perfect tempo, the right key, the arrangement, the instrumentation, the mood, the feel. Basically, you're trying to bottle lightning all the time.

These thousands of choices can be overwhelming. It's highly likely that the situation will cause decision overload—this is when your eyes roll up in your head and little "tilt" signs appear where your irises used to be. You feel the lights going out in your brain, like a scene from a movie on the New York City blackout. On the outside, you try to look cool. The band plays on to the end of the song, and when everyone looks to you for your opinion, you turn to the engineer and say, "What do you think?"

There's a variation on the old light-bulb riddle going around the music business:

Joker: "How many record producers does it take to screw in a light bulb?"

Jokee: "How many?"

Joker: "I don't know. What do you think?"

You start collecting opinions. Before you know it, the drummer is producing the drum part, the guitarist is producing the guitar part, the bass player is producing the bass part, the vocalists are producing the vocals, the engineer is producing everyone else's production, and you're not producing anything but a cold sweat. The confusion compounds if there are several collaborators stirring up the works as well.

The only antidote for this affliction is to know that the purpose of the demo-making process is to realize *your* dream for the song. If you have collaborators, part of preparing to make the demo is to come to a consensus about the direction you all want the song to take. You must agree before you get into the studio that either the same respect and "everyone must be happy" ground rules apply in the demo recording as in your collaboration process, or that one of you should take the lead in the production of the demo. Since every tick of the clock in the studio is usually echoed by chimes of the cash register drawer opening and swallowing more of your hard-earned money, the pressure is on. Even so, this is not the time to pass the buck. Someone has to be in charge of the vision for the song. As the songwriter who is paying for the demo session, that honor is yours.

It is one thing to ask for the engineer's opinion or the musician's opinion or the vocalist's opinion. It is another to let them start running the show. As lost as you may feel, it's your responsibility to let the people you are paying know that you value their input but that, ultimately, the decisions are yours to make.

It's a fact of songwriting that the only thing you have to "sell" is your opinion. It's your unique point of view that makes you irreplaceable. Making all the difficult decisions in the writing and demo-making processes is the method by which you educate and refine your opinion.

Exercising your decision-making muscles is the only way to build them up. At first, expect your demos to miss the bull's-eye of your hopes for how they should sound. Most producers at the top of the music business charts can think of changes they'd like to make long after their songs have become hits.

Ask successful producers how they know when the recording is right; their answer will probably feature the phrase "gut feeling." They know in their guts when it's right. They were not born with these informed intestines; they developed them through trial and error and by learning from the great talents that went before them. You, too, can have smart guts, and the way to get them is this: When the music stops, you might ask your engineer, "What do you think?" But the answer is just one of the variables you will consider when you ask yourself the most important question of all: What do *I* think? Then tune into your own gut reaction.

If you are very new at demo production, and making so many decisions in rapid succession seems an impossible task, you could defer to the engineer while you listen and learn. Or it may be time to hire someone to act as producer. It will still be up to you to communicate to the best of your ability your idea of how the demo should sound. If you do hire someone, you have to let that person do the job. Of course, you will need to express your opinions about how things are sounding as you go along, but don't drive yourself and everyone else crazy by engaging in a power struggle with the producer during the demo session.

Remember, you're not only paying for this person's experience as a producer, you're paying for your own education. The recording studio is the graduate school of songwriting. Make like a sponge and soak up every bit of information you can. Before long, you will know enough about demo production to take on the exhilarating and challenging job of bottling lightning.

53

BIG-BUDGET BLUES
Don't spend too much money on one demo

The demo is an extremely important part of the songwriting process. It's the only way to have your song heard by people in the music business. Someone might come to a club and hear you sing your song and say, "I love it." But the next sentence will invariably be, "Give me a CD." You cannot overestimate the importance of a good demo. Although there are still a few people in the music business who claim they can "hear" a song through a poorly produced demo, they are rare birds. There's no getting around the necessity of making the best possible demo of your song.

You know this to be true, so you hire the philharmonic and a star vocalist who charges several thousand dollars. Don't laugh! Just such a multi-thousand dollar demo found its way into our workshop. One of the writers was a brewery heir for whom money was no object.

Many writers cannot afford these extremes. All things are relative, though; we've heard a bunch of way-too-expensive demos over the years. There's nothing like going broke to get a person discouraged about being a songwriter, however. The big-budget blues can get you down so low, you don't feel like singing anymore.

When is a demo too expensive, and how does it get that way? A demo gets too expensive when it's not a demo. Remember, the purpose of the demo is to display the song. It is not meant for commercial release. The more elaborately produced recording that becomes the record is called a "master." The master is a finished product, ready to be mechanically reproduced onto CDs or downloaded from the Internet. If you are trying to record a master when you should be making a demo, you will definitely spend too much money.

You will also spend too much money if you spend too much time in the studio. Make as many decisions as you can before you get into the studio and the clock starts ticking your money away. If possible, get a rough demo of the song to the musicians and vocalists before the session and an example of a recording you want your song to sound like.

You will spend too much money if you hire a studio that has a closet full of vintage mikes and charges two thousand dollars a day. Do you really need all the "A" players who get double- or triple-scale Musicians Union wages? That could cost around four hundred dollars for a three-hour session. In Nashville, there are up-and-coming musicians who will make your demo shine for thirty dollars per song.

Demos can get too expensive without your spending a dime in someone else's recording studio. Many songwriters build demo studios in their own homes. This is a great idea if you know when to stop buying equipment. However, some songwriters get hooked on accumulating every new gadget that comes out, and their home studios become black holes that suck in every available dollar. Songwriters who fall into this hole often wind up producing demos for other people in order to justify and recoup the money they spend on recording gizmos. Then they don't have any time to write and record their own songs. If you intend to use your home studio strictly for demo making, you can do what you need without going nuts in the recording equipment store.

It's a different story if your intention is to produce the finished product in your home. Composer Ray Lynch recorded his *Deep Breakfast* album at home and sold twenty-five thousand copies from his dining room table before being picked up by Music West Records. Songwriting can be a cottage industry. If that's your intention, your investment in sophisticated equipment is warranted. Lucky for you, this equipment is getting more compact and less expensive every day.

What are the essential elements of a good demo? By far the most important element of a good demo is a great vocal. If you can get a special singer to deliver an emotionally convincing performance of the song, you've got 80 percent of what you need in the demo.

The basic tracks usually call for a drummer/drum machine, keyboard/synthesizer or rhythm/lead guitars, and bass. "Sweetening" the basic tracks with horns, dobro, mandolin, and/or strings (acoustic or synthesized) is optional. With today's technology, you can make a demo that sounds like it has a full complement of musicians with just one talented person, a sequencer, and synthesizers/samplers.

How much money should a writer spend on a demo? You can get a good demo made for $300–$800 per song. This depends on whether the studio owner functions as a multi-instrumentalist or you hire a studio and record five songs with live musicians in a three-hour session. Good lead vocalists cost $75–$250, which is included in the price range mentioned above. Top-of-the-line singers, often up-and-coming artists themselves, are well worth it. Their gift of making every note and word sound heartfelt will add tremendously to the impact of your demo. We're not talking about mail-order demos here. You'll find them in a later chapter.

What are some ways to cut demo-making costs? Collaborating cuts costs by spreading the cost of hiring outside studios among the collaborators.

Collaborating with someone who has a home studio is a good way to cut costs. Make sure you bring something to the collaboration as well, so friction doesn't develop because of unequal contributions. Ask your studio-owner/collaborator how he would like to split the expenses of the demo. He may want to tally up his usual costs and figure your split from that. Or he may just ask you to pay for the singer.

Shop around before you hire a studio, as rates and services offered vary. Ask about lower prices for down time; some studios are eager to sell certain undesirable time slots. Some studios are also willing to make deals for lower prices if you hire them for several blocks of time. Make sure you find out what equipment and services are included. Ask if there's a separate charge for the engineer.

If you are hiring a studio, the best way to economize is to do as much preparation as possible before you enter the studio. Have your chord sheets or number charts clearly written and copied for everyone who needs one. Know what "feel" you're going for and be ready to communicate that to the musicians and vocalists by playing a hit record with the desired "feel." Make sure your lead vocalist has a copy of your rough demo well in advance of the session so she can be familiar with the song. When the session starts, get down to business and keep focused and positive. This is some of the best fun you will ever have. Enjoy it.

54

JUST JAM IT

*Have a clear idea of the feel and
sound you're going for in the demo*

Once upon a time, there were four musicians: a drummer, a bass player, a piano player, and a guitarist. These musicians were being paid a substantial fee by a songwriter. The songwriter figured that if the musicians could charge so much money, they should be able to perform magic. The songwriter called the musicians together in a recording studio and said, "Play and make beautiful music together." And they lived unhappily ever after.

Believing in the fairy tale that musicians make music by magic is a good way to enlarge your demo-recording studio bill. It can seem like magic among the top-of-the-line musicians working in music industry centers who make their living as studio musicians. These musicians can read charts and are ready to start laying down tracks within ten minutes of encountering a song. Musicians are subject to the laws of supply and demand. In Nashville, where great musicians abound, you can expect to pay each player around $30–$50 per song. In Los Angeles and New York, where the demand and the costs of living are high, good musicians can run you $100–$150. (In fact, that cost differential might make it feasible for you to travel to Nashville to record your demos.)

Even if you are dealing with high-caliber musicians, you can't expect them to know how you want your demo to sound. You must let them know what you want. This presumes that you have first decided what you` want. Here are some questions to answer that will help you decide:

- Which artists would I like to record this song?
- Is this a pop, rock, R&B, country, New Age, jazz, or inspirational song?
- What records have the feel I would like in this song?
- What tempo do I want for this song?
- What instruments do I want on this demo?

Once you have answered these questions for yourself, you can tell your musicians the answers. You must provide them with chord sheets. A chord sheet is not the same as a lead sheet or sheet music. You need not write down every single note. Just indicate rhythms and chord changes. An example of a chord sheet is shown on page 153.

In Nashville, musicians favor what is called the Nashville Number System. The number charts use Arabic numbers instead of chord symbols. Musicians can then play the song in any key. An example of a number chart for the same song follows the lead sheet. If you want to learn this system, read *The Nashville Number System* by Chas Williams (www.nashvillenumber system.com).

It helps to play pieces of several records that have the feel you want for your demo. As our friend Harold Payne wrote in a song, "Music speaks louder than words." This is true when it comes to communicating your song, too. Playing the song on the spot is one way to show it to the musicians. It's even better if you have a rough demo to play. The rough demo process gives you time to work out the little touches that add to your song, such as hooky riffs between the vocal lines.

After communicating as much as you can, sit back and let the musicians add those things that never occurred to you. They didn't get to be top studio musicians for no reason. They will have special gifts to offer, and you would be foolish to get so stuck in your own ideas that you aren't open to their suggestions. However, don't lose sight of the fact that you have the final word.

Not everyone in every town is lucky enough to have access to musicians this talented. Unless you are sure that the musicians you hire are very fast and very good, it will probably be worth your while, and save you money on studio time, if you arrange a rehearsal a day or two before the actual recording date. This will give you time to work out the arrangements of the songs before the recording studio clock starts ticking. Rehearsing is necessary if you are dealing with a group of musicians not used to playing with each other; that is, musicians who are not members of the same band. Bands already have their musical communication lines in place. Individual musicians have to spend a little extra time setting up those lines of communication.

Unless you are an excellent musician yourself or your intention is to be a writer/artist/musician on your own recording, don't play on your own demo. You will have enough decisions to make without having to worry about your performance as well. It's fine to go into the studio with the musicians and play the song with them a couple of times to show them some of your ideas, but once they have the ball rolling, let them run with it.

If you take time to decide what you want in your demo and you communicate that clearly to the musicians you hire, you have a much greater chance of being happy with the results. You are asking for trouble if you expect it to magically come together, but do leave some room for the spontaneous magic that can happen in the studio.

WHO DO YOU WANT FOR CHRISTMAS?

by Pat & Pete Luboff and Bruce Williams

VERSE I

Who do you want for Christmas   to help you string the lights

to dance with at the parties   to keep you warm at night

VERSE II

Who do you want for Christmas   to share the giving   with

To watch the children's faces   as   they unwrap our   gifts

BRIDGE

Tinsel in the windows carols in the air   still it won't be Christmas

VERSE III

if you don't want me there   Who do you want for Christmas

when there's love beneath the tree   Who do you want for Chirstmas

I hope   I hope   It's   me

55

SELF-SUNG DEMO HERO
Avoid singing the demo yourself; hire a dynamite singer

Clothes may or may not make the person, but lead vocals definitely *do* make the demo. We know you love to sing your songs. Living in Nashville, we have the luxury of being able to go out any night and hear the writers of amazing songs singing their own creations. We revere these people as national treasures for the contributions they have made to our culture.

Once in a while, a great songwriter performs who can barely sing. You love them all the more for getting up in front of so many people to display their vulnerability and love for what they do. But when these writers make demos of their songs, you can bet they don't sing on them. Barry Mann can sing (who can forget him on "Who Put the Bomp"), but when he and Cynthia Weil made the demo for "Just Once," they hired a hot demo singer. The demo singer was James Ingram, and that demo was his ticket to a record deal. Our friend Ben Weisman, who wrote fifty-two platinum-record songs for Elvis Presley, once played a demo of a song he wrote for us and Elvis recorded. The demo singer was a session guitarist named Glen Campbell. Take a tip from the writers on top: Don't sing on your own demos.

This practice has the side benefit of forging a personal connection between you and a potential hit artist.

Of course, it's a different story if your goal is to be a writer/artist, and you intend to be the one who ultimately records your songs. If you can honestly listen to your own vocal performance on the song and judge it to be outstanding, by all means sing on your own demos. But if you have to admit that you're just an okay singer, go out and hire a dynamite singer. It will be well worth the investment. An outstanding lead vocal is the single most important part of your demo.

If you write songs for other artists to record, you need to do your homework. Every song has a personality. The song itself calls out for a certain type of voice to sing its message. Who should record the song you have written? Male or female? Big, raspy growl or light, young tone? Are there long, high notes that require an advanced mastery of breath control? Have a clear picture of the vocal sound your song requires.

Now you need to find the perfect singer. Ask around among your songwriting friends. Listen to singers in clubs and choirs. Ask for recorded samples of their singing skills. Singers who want to make money doing demos should be ready with a demo CD. Get to know as many singers as you can for future reference, as each of your songs will call for a different voice. If you're going to do your demo in a small studio, the studio owner will know a number of singers and be able to make recommendations.

When you've chosen the singer, give that person a rough demo and lyrics of the song you're about to record. Allow sufficient time for the singer to get to know the song.

At last you are in the studio, ready to record the all-important lead vocal. Before the singer sings one note, you need to focus on the emotional content of the song. As the producer of the recording session, you are very much like the director on a movie set. Talk about the situation of the song, about the feeling you want the singer to go for, about the dynamics (loudness and softness) of the various parts of the song. You might mention the artist you ultimately intend to pitch the song to. That will help the singer to know what tonality to go for. Talk the entire song out before you try to record it for the first time. Don't expect to catch the song on the first take. The singer will be warming up to the song and getting comfortable in the recording situation.

After the initial take, talk about what you loved in the performance *first*. The singer needs encouragement and support in order to take the risks involved in an outstanding performance. After you praise the performance, point out areas where you'd like changes. Try a second recording. Again, praise first, then ask specifically for certain changes. Once you get a basically good take, you can "punch in" the particular lines that you feel need improvement.

Just remember the Golden Rule when you're dealing with your singer, and you will get the best results. When someone is putting their creativity on the line, the last thing they need is a disparaging remark. Don't say, "You're flat," when you could just as easily say, "Let's try that line again," and demonstrate, either by singing or playing on an instrument, the notes in question. Only an atmosphere of trust and respect will allow an outstanding performance to come through your singer. It's up to you to provide that atmosphere.

When you have that excellent lead vocal on your demo and compare it to your own rough demo, you'll be glad you hired someone else to sing it. Having a "set of pipes" is a wonderful gift; so is the gift of being able to write great songs. They don't necessarily come in the same package. Part of the pleasure of being a songwriter is giving others an opportunity to express their gifts through your songs. Everyone benefits. You have a great demo. The singer has a great work sample. And if the singer happens to be an artist who is shopping for a record deal, this demo may be a ticket to the top of the charts for both of you.

56

LITTLE VOICE LOST

Put the vocal up front in the mix

Musicians love to hear themselves play. You can't blame them. If they didn't love it, they wouldn't be doing it. If you're a songwriter who is also a musician, you know what we mean. You put a lot of creativity and work into the chords and melody of your songs. Then, when it's time to make a demo, you're the one who plays the keyboard, the guitar, or bass. Your performance of the music is extremely important to you. You have every right to be proud of what you create and to want everyone to hear it.

But sometimes this desire to be heard can cloud your judgment when it comes to mixing down the demo. You want so much for everyone to notice that terrific chord change—or that great lead guitar lick or fantastic drum track—that you can't find it in your heart to pull back the faders on those tracks. It just sounds so great to you.

You know the vocal is important. You may have gone to the trouble and expense of hiring a great singer to do the lead vocal. Still, that doesn't make you want to put your music in the background. It can all be up front, can't it?

The answer is *no*. In a demo, something has to be up front and something has to be in back. And the something that has to be up front is, without a doubt, the lead vocal. If the lead vocal is overpowered by the musical instruments, the melody and the lyrics are lost to the listener. In a demo, that's the same as saying the song is lost.

Many people are familiar with the famous Japanese film *Rashomon*. Three characters in the film tell the story of the same event, which they all experienced together. However, each one tells an entirely different story. The point is that we see things the way we want to see them. We also hear things the way we want to hear them.

A musician/songwriter may hear more than enough vocal interfering with the music in the demo. That songwriter is surprised when others respond to the demo with, "I couldn't hear the vocal," or, "I think the vocal should be more up front." If you have had this experience, you have some psychological factors working against you. You can remedy the situation by putting the vocal much further up front than you think it should go, thereby getting it where it needs to be. Or you can ask for feedback from other people in the mixing process and rely on their less prejudiced perceptions.

Musicians/songwriters aren't the only ones who need to be aware of the placement of the vocal in the mix. Many non-musician songwriters get so entranced with all the new toys in the studio that they lose sight of the song's essence. Unless a song *is* an instrumental—a song with no lyrics—the essence of the song is its message. The message is conveyed by the music. The emotional feel of the arrangement communicates the message as well. But the bulk of the message is contained in the lyrics and the melody. It is the vocal delivery of that message with all its emotional content that sells the song. If you bury that vocal, you're selling your song short.

Picture the song as it is being performed by Celine Dion, for example. The curtain rises and the orchestra begins to play. Now where is Celine? Is she sitting down among the violin players? Is she back there with the kettle drums? Oh no, she's right up front and center, glittering in a skintight gown. All eyes are on her and all ears hear her voice towering above the musical instruments. That's the right place for the singer to be, both on the stage and in your demo.

≡ 57 ≡

I CAN'T FIND YOUR KEY

Be sure to lay the tracks in the singer's key

It used to be that all demos were made by live musicians. A person banging away on an actual drum set, another person playing bass, and a guitarist and/or piano player were needed to lay down the basic rhythm tracks. Back in the bad old days, we learned one lesson the hard way. We had a song and a friend who is an excellent singer (she went on to tour with Ray Charles for years). She agreed to sing the demo for us. We laid the basic rhythm tracks in the studio, then invited her in.

We discovered, to our great chagrin, that we had recorded the tracks in a key that didn't suit her voice. She tried singing it high; it was too high. An octave lower was too low. Finally, she went for the higher octave, but the demo was never right. She couldn't hit some of the notes with the conviction we needed. You only need to waste hundreds of dollars like this once. It's not a lesson you forget.

A few demos are still made the old-fashioned way: They play the tracks, sing the vocal, and record live. This is fast, provided they've rehearsed, and captures the spontaneity of an ensemble performance. Some piano/vocal demos or guitar/vocal

demos might be recorded live. For the most part, though, the tracks are recorded before the vocalist is brought into the picture. It is crucial to choose the correct key for your vocalist before you start recording and it's a more subtle choice than just, "Can the singer hit all these notes?"

If you're going to make a great demo, you want a great vocal performance. You have to tell the vocalist what kind of emotional atmosphere you want to create in the song. Knowing the singer's high note, range, or the note where falsetto voice kicks in is not enough. If you want a certain lyric line to be expressed forcefully, you have to know if the singer can go beyond just hitting the note to pushing it, punching it, growling it, screaming it, or whatever it takes to deliver the emotion you choose. This requires knowing the singer's voice and where the sweet spots are in her voice. Think of Kenny Rogers' gravelly growl, Josh Turner's bassy rumble, and Mariah Carey's strong head voice. If your singer has a special quality, put the song in a key that lets her show it off.

The only way to know these things is to test the song with the singer *before* you record. Quincy Jones is not the only producer to tell us that choice of key is a make-it-or-break-it proposition for a song, but his word alone would be good enough for us. If you are using live musicians, get the musicians and the vocalist in the studio together to pick the key. If this isn't possible, get a recording of the song to the singer and try to communicate verbally the kind of performance you want. Describe the vocal quality you want in the song. Point out the areas where you want the most intensity and ask the singer to tell you what key he thinks is best.

Garth Brooks' producer, Allen Reynolds, divulged one of the secrets of his success at a meeting of the Nashville Publishers Network. After the artist and Allen have agreed that a song will be cut from the thousands Allen screened for the project, they go into the studio and record a simple guitar or piano vocal version of the song. That recording tells him if the song, the key, and the artist are meant for each other. Allen brings that simple demo into the master recording session. He doesn't want the original demo he was pitched to influence the creativity of the musicians who will be recording the final version. He wants to build on the magic that happened with just the artist and one instrument.

Some of the worry about choosing the key can be eliminated by using MIDI sequencer technology. You can create basic rhythm tracks (bass, drums, keyboards) and, when your singer comes in, try several keys until you find the right one. But for the most part, the key is chosen before the basic tracks are recorded. The tracks are recorded with a dummy vocal. Then, the final vocal and back-ups vocals are recorded. Finally, lead instruments, fills, and any "sweetening" (lead guitars, string pads, etc.) are added.

Remember, your musical setting needs to highlight and accent (maybe even praise) the vocal performance, not bury it.

58

INSERT INSTRUMENTAL INTERMISSION
Don't put long instrumental breaks in a song demo

Songwriters love songs. We all have our favorites, and we can't help but emulate the songs we think are the best. We go to concerts and see the bands in action: They begin with a long instrumental lead-in as the audience roars in recognition and the lead singer bows in response; the lead guitarist wails away on a long solo; the drummer takes a minute to show off in mid-song; the song ends with many repetitions of the chorus as the lead singer improvises variations. We buy CDs or downloads and listen to and thoughtfully study what's going on in these five- to seven-minute songs. And we get some very wrong ideas about how to present a song.

Then we engage our local demo studio and call together the musicians. We ask for a long instrumental lead-in, a couple of solos mid-song by the lead guitarist and drummer we've hired, and choruses ad infinitum until the demo is seven minutes long. All this, of course, takes extra time and money, but it's worth it, isn't it? Now our song sounds like our favorite band.

The trouble is, we've probably just bought a one-way ticket to the eject button on the publisher's CD player. Time

is at a premium for everyone in our mad, mad world. Ask people about their time and they'll tell you how busy they are, how much they have to do, how they can't get around to doing a zillion things they think they should.

A publisher's or producer's time is like that to the tenth power. The good ones want to give songwriters a chance, and they really make an effort to listen to the mountain of CDs on their desks, around their desks, and under their desks. Every minute is golden. When they pop in a CD, eager to hear a hit song, and you make them wait through a minute or even thirty seconds of wheel spinning, you are not winning your way into their hearts. After a quick intro, you have thirty seconds to get through the first verse and into the hook. They want to be knocked out of their chairs and *fast*.

The same is true of long, mid-song instrumental breaks and long end-of-song productions. If you are a songwriter showing a song with the intent of getting an artist to record it, give them the song, the whole song, and nothing but the song. Get in fast, get to the hook fast, and get it over with as soon as you have demonstrated the song's key elements. Catchy, quick instrumental riffs should be included; long instrumental solos should not.

Many of the greatest rock 'n' roll classics of the fifties were under two minutes long. Those songs are packed with so much fun that two minutes feel like forever. Check out the Leiber and Stoller classics "Charlie Brown," "Alley Oop," "Love Potion Number 9," and "Hound Dog" for sterling examples of how to get to the point quickly, stick to it, and make it in a big way. Use them as models for making your song demos and leave the extended productions to the producer of the ultimate commercial recording.

You enhance your chances of having your song recorded if you use your demo to show the song in its most concentrated form. The professional listener will appreciate the subliminal message you send when your demo is short and sweet: "I appreciate and value your time."

Try using a stopwatch to time the songs you hear on the radio. This is not the same world as the concert hall or the album you listen to at your leisure in your home. For a radio station, songs are vehicles to get the audience from one commercial to the next. Some stations like to brag about how many songs they play in a row. These are short songs, usually around three minutes in length. The radio stations don't mention that between these blocks of songs they play just as many or more commercials back to back.

Radio makes songs into commercial successes because the bulk of the money you earn when a song becomes a success is from performances (ASCAP, BMI, or SESAC). If you sell a million copies of your song, the money you earn from selling the CDs or downloads is just a fraction of the money you earn from performance royalties for radio airplay. A close study of the types and lengths of songs used on the radio station you want your songs to play on would be an excellent investment of your time.

The entire picture changes if you intend to sell yourself as a performing artist, especially as a self-contained band. In that case, you *do* need to show off your potential as a live performing group. You're selling more than the song: You're selling yourselves as an image, a lifestyle. You're selling *your* ability to carry off an extended performance of the song. But remember that time is money at record companies, and use good judgment when deciding how long you draw out your songs in your presentation.

When you're in the demo studio, keep time on your side.

≡ 59 ≡

A BIG OVERPRODUCTION
Keep your demo uncluttered

Letting a songwriter loose in a demo studio is like letting a toddler loose in a toy store. There's no end to the toys that can be gathered and played with. Samplers and synthesizers enable us to create full orchestras right in our own bedrooms or garages. It's so much fun, that we add this, and that, and that!

When a songwriter gets carried away in the studio, the result is something like what an artist gets when she mixes all the colors of paint together: mud. When everything sounds the same because all the parts of the song have every possible instrument going at once, the ear takes a little nap. It says, "Wake me up when something new and different happens."

In time, the song demo can be viewed as a work of art. For convenience, let's break the song down into three-second pieces. If the average song is three minutes long, we should have sixty of these three-second pieces. You could draw a line graph of what's going on in each of these time intervals with the height of the line determined by the number of instruments playing. If everything is going on at once all the time, your graph will be a straight line.

Variety is the spice of life and of demos. A straight line doesn't offer variety; a graph with peaks and valleys does. To make your demo interesting, you need to add a pinch of guitar lick here, a bit of drum pattern there, a background vocal in this spot, a hooky lick on a saxophone right there, so if the vocal is not the center of attention for a moment, some catchy instrumental part is. These little touches can be repeated as appropriate.

But don't let these light touches get in the way of your lead vocal. The lead vocal is the gem in the center of your setting; the licks, riffs, rolls, and solos are the little stones surrounding it that are meant to show off the centerpiece in the best way.

You are less likely to get carried away in a studio that you have hired by the hour. That situation has the built-in restraint of the ticking clock and access to feedback from the engineer and musicians you hire. But left alone in your home studio, it is easy to let yourself go. You paid good money for all these toys, and you want to use them.

You need to separate playing for pleasure and playing to serve your demo.

This requires a level of objectivity that is sometimes difficult to achieve. Asking for feedback from someone you trust and whose opinion you value is a way to get around the problem of subjectivity. Play your demo and ask if there is any place in the demo where your listener's interest lags. It helps to hear your song through another's ears.

It also helps to listen to the radio and take note of the way other songs are arranged. The songwriters who come to our workshops are always amazed when we play tapes from our collection of original demos of hit songs. You can literally hear the record in the demo. The riffs, the arrangements, the vocals—they're all there. They're in a less finished form, but definitely there. So what you hear on the radio is usually what was on the demo.

When you're making a demo, use a light and tasty touch. The important thing is quality, not quantity, of sound.

≡ 60 ≡

CAN'T STOP NOW

Don't continue to work when the session is going badly

Let's say you've done your homework. You've planned and prepared your demo recording session. You've hired the musicians and the vocalist. You've supplied them all with rough demos of the songs, and you've given them an idea of the kind of feel you want. You plan to record three songs, so you've booked the studio for three hours to record the instrumental tracks. The musicians arrive in the studio on time, and you go right to work.

The session starts off fine, and you're happy with the way things are going. After two hours, you realize you only have one song down and two to go with less than half the time left. You start to panic and get impatient with the inevitable delays. You pressure the whole situation and call an end to all coffee breaks. You find out that the studio is available for a couple of hours after your session is supposed to end, so you push on past your time.

Now you're dealing with tired, harassed, and even angry musicians. The engineer is starting to mutter unpleasantries. The situation has gotten out of hand, and it's your responsibility. This is what happens when you get so fixated on how you

think things should be that you can't see how they really are.

The same thing can happen when you book the session to record the lead vocals. Expect to spend about forty-five to ninety minutes on each song on the lead vocal alone. Remember, the lead vocal is the most important ingredient of your demo. If you don't push the singer to take some risks, you won't get an exciting performance. But if you push the singer too long or too hard, you will destroy your chances of getting a salvageable performance.

From start to finish, recording sessions are 100 percent emotion. As the producer of the session, whether in a hired studio or your home studio, it's your job to be sensitive to the emotional tone of what's going on. If it doesn't feel good while you're doing it, chances are it won't sound good.

Even after you have the tracks down and the musicians and singers are gone, you still run the risk of doing your songs a disservice if you rush the mixing process or push past the emotional and physical limits of the engineer and yourself. Many songwriters who are new to the recording process are shocked to find that the mixing process takes as long as laying the tracks. That is, if it takes two or three hours for the instruments and three hours for the vocal, expect to take six hours to do the mixing. These time estimates presume you are working with competent professional musicians and vocalists.

In fact, some songwriters are shocked to the point of disbelief. Whenever we do a workshop in another city, we interview local people who work in the music business. We want to show the participating songwriters that people in their own hometown are actively involved in making music. In Santa Fe, we invited James Townsend, a singer/songwriter who had produced his own album and who was selling it locally and getting airplay on local radio stations. We asked him, "What was the biggest lesson you learned in this process?" His immediate response was, "The mixing took much longer than I expected."

The day before, we had interviewed Max Highstein, the owner of the recording studio where the album was cut. Max explained his approach to such projects. He talked about how he sits down with the songwriter and discusses the kind of music the songwriter has in mind. Then he gives the songwriter an estimate of how long it will take and how much it will cost.

So we asked James, "Didn't Max tell you the mixing would take a long time?" James said, "Yes, but I didn't believe him." If you haven't been through it, it *is* hard to believe. But believe us, we're not exaggerating. Laying down the tracks is only the beginning. The recording is really made in the mix.

Mixing entails sitting down and listening to the same song over and over and over again as you get the sound of each and every instrument exactly the way you want it; build a frequency balance among all the instruments; compress, limit, EQ (equalize), and tune the vocal and place it prominently in the mix; pan tracks left, right, or center; adjust relative volume levels; and generally whip the song into a cohesive sound image that is constantly interesting. It is exhausting work and requires a tremendous amount of concentration.

There is also the physical reality of fatigue. Your ears do get tired of listening; the nerves don't fire as well. To minimize loss of hearing sensitivity, we recommend you do your mixing at low sound levels. If it sounds good when the volume is down low, it will sound good when it's loud.

Any creative process is really a series of decisions. Recording a demo involves nonstop decision-making. Each of us has his own level of tolerance for this kind of intense mental work. It's up to us to stay in tune with ourselves and those we hire so we know when to take a break. A quick walk out in the fresh air may be all you need. Or you may need to come back another day. When the session is not going well, it is far better to call it a day than to antagonize everyone involved.

There comes a moment in the demo-making process when the most important thing to know is when to stop.

61

SENDING MONEY DOWN THE DEMO HOLE
Make the best of mail-order demos

We've heard from songwriters who have sent off ten or twenty songs to a mail-order demo service, along with a great big check, only to receive a great big disappointment in the mail a couple of weeks later.

Making demos of your songs is an important part of learning the songwriting process. We recommend that you participate personally in the process. If you think that's impossible because you live far away from any recording facilities or because you feel you are not technically inclined enough to do your own recording at home, think again.

There is probably a recording studio near you no matter where you live. An Internet search for "recording studios in [Your Town]" will yield a number of possibilities.

Wherever there is a radio station, there is recording equipment. Some local cable TV stations make their facilities available for free to the public. You can also approach your local radio station about using their audio recording facilities.

Networking and collaborating with other songwriters can put you in touch with people who do not operate official recording studio businesses, but are willing to help you record your project. The proliferation of easy-to-use, in-home recording studio equipment has made the process possible even for just about anyone. With a little money and a little more experimentation, you can record your own demos—at least your own rough demos.

If, after researching your possibilities, you still feel you want to go the mail-order demo route, you're going to need that rough demo. When you order a demo by mail, you are not there to give any input during the process. Therefore, you need to make your up-front input as clear as possible. Making a rough demo with at least an indication of the feel and the parts you want included will go a long way toward ensuring the final product is something you can live with.

How do you find a mail-order demo studio? Call your nearest songwriters' organization for recommendations. You can search online, but don't confuse a legitimate mail-order demo service with a song shark (see chapter sixty-eight). A legitimate mail-order demo service will *not* charge you an exorbitant fee or promise to make you a star or release a record of your song.

Legitimate mail-order demo services will have sites with contact information for a specific person, usually the studio owner. You'll be able to call her up, talk with her about your ideas for the demo, and discuss your choice of instrumentation. The more instruments you want, the more the demo will cost. Many times, legitimate mail-order demo sites will have samples of previous productions you can listen to online.

When you've found a couple of likely studios, e-mail or call them. If they are legit, they will gladly furnish you with information about their recording equipment, instruments, services available, and what they cost. Some demo studios specialize in certain styles, such as country. Ask the demo producers what styles of music they do best. Check with them about what information they need from you.

When you have made your studio choice, send as much information as possible about your song and how you want it demoed. The more you communicate, the better your chances are of getting what you want. Your package should include:

- a rough demo of the song
- a neatly typed lyric sheet
- a chord sheet or a number chart—a lead sheet is not necessary
- instructions about the feel you want in the demo, including references to recognizable songs, and possibly a recording of a song that you want your demo to sound like
- your choice of male or female lead vocal
- your choice of instrumentation
- a money order or credit card number for the cost of recording the demo (Projects paid for by personal checks are not recorded until after the checks clear the bank.)

If you're sending a cassette or CD through snail mail, use delivery confirmation or certified mail (no return receipt) so you can track it. Never send your only copy of a song. Alternately, the whole process can be transacted online. Using mp3 files, you can e-mail the studio your rough demo and get the finished product back to burn to a CD.

We recommend that you try a mail-order demo service on only one song at first. If you don't like the product, you can change to another service for the next song. If you send a bunch of songs at once, you may be stuck with a bunch of demos you don't like.

When you're deciding which song to try first, keep this is mind: It's a rare song that will impress the professional listener with just a piano or guitar vocal demo. That's because most professional listeners have no imagination. They want the finished product, or as close as you can get to it, handed to them on a silver platter. If you do have to go with a simple guitar or piano demo, you absolutely have to have a dynamite singer to do the lead vocal. A big, soulful ballad is your best choice when a guitar- or piano-vocal demo is all you can do. Save up for a bigger production on your grooving up-tempo rocker.

PART 7

ALLOW ME TO PRESENT MY SONG

Pitching Package Pratfalls

62

NO WAY IN

*Don't seal your demo package with a
roll of tape and a thousand staples*

We've opened countless song packages while judging various song competitions. You wouldn't believe the lengths some writers go to in packaging their tapes and CDs for mailing.

One package started out with an 11x14-inch padded envelope fastened by twenty or thirty staples. Having fought past that, we were greeted with a similar envelope, only smaller. Frazzled and covered with mangled staples, we found the CD inside the smaller envelope. It was wrapped tightly in seven layers of plastic bubble wrap, secured by full-mummy wrap of fiber-reinforced packaging tape.

By now we had cultivated a distinct dislike for the song inside, whatever it was, and an even deeper dislike for the songwriter, whoever he was. Dedicated listeners that we are, we hunted up a pair of scissors and cut our way through this last barrier. Finally, panting from our efforts, we got the CD in the player and got what we expected, a song that contained most of the mistakes in this book. If only the writer had taken as much care in writing the song as in wrapping it up.

This is just one of many stories we could tell you about impregnable song packages: stories about Styrofoam, rubber bands, boxes within boxes, duct tape, and more. Professional listeners at publishing companies and record labels deal with hundreds and hundreds of CDs, as well as thousands of other details in their jobs. They simply don't have time to struggle through bizarre packaging barriers.

Building a fortress around your song is an expression of tremendous insecurity. It shows that you are terribly worried about this song. A nervous voice in your head tells you, "It must be protected by many layers of non-biodegradable materials. As much money as possible must be spent to ship it." But the message the person on the receiving end gets is that you do not care one bit about making her job a little easier by allowing hassle-free access to your precious song. In short, it plainly states that you do not have a professional attitude.

If you've been building the unbreakable song package, now's the time to stop. You need to relax your grip on your songs if you want other people to hear them. Show some consideration for the listener by making your package easy to open. The best presentation package is the simplest: a brief cover letter, a lyric sheet, a CD in an envelope with a little piece of tape across the flap of the envelope in case the glue doesn't hold. If you are in the position to drop off a CD at a publisher's office, omit the cover letter and the envelope. Put your contact information inside the CD case and make it effortless for the listener to access the CD.

The inclusion of a self-addressed, stamped envelope (SASE) for the return of your CD is optional. We found that most publishers didn't return the CD anyway, so we were out the cost of the envelope and the stamp. We decided that including the SASE sent a message that we assumed the listener would want to return our CD. We prefer the message that the listener will want to keep our CD. So we stopped including the SASE.

Hounding the listener for the return of your CD is a sure way to earn his or her eternal animosity. We think of demos as our calling cards—bread on the waters of the music business. Let them go (keeping a record of where you sent them for your information and for tax deduction); you never know what will come back to you. Here's a story to illustrate the value of letting go:

A songwriter we know had decided to quit trying. She packed her recording equipment in boxes and put it in storage. While she was putting things away, she came across some demo copies and sent them off to a couple of people just to get rid of them. The owner of an independent record label in Nashville liked her songs and called her. The last we heard, she had a record on the country charts and had married the record company owner.

It's not the wrapping around your CD that establishes it as precious; it's what's on the CD. Put your utmost effort into the writing of the song and the production of the demo, but when it comes to packaging the CD for mailing, make it easy on yourself and the potential listener.

63

LYRICS IN LONGHAND

Don't send handwritten lyric sheets

One of the essential parts of a CD presentation package is the lyric sheet. Every lyric sheet tells a story about the songwriter who sent it. There's the frantic tale told by the lyric sheet that's been scribbled in pencil on a page from a spiral notebook, then ripped out and thrown in with the CD. Doubtless the songwriter was in a big hurry to get somewhere else and just threw the package together on the way to more important things.

There's the lyric sheet that's ever-so-neatly printed in teeny-tiny letters, with a teeny-tiny pen, presumably by a teeny-tiny songwriter.

Have you heard the one about the lyric sheet that's hand-printed, semi-legibly, on hotel stationery? It's even more interesting when some of the words are crossed out and rewrites are added for that extra plot twist.

For those whose tastes run to horror, there's the frightening tale of the invisible lyric sheet. This is a tale of two possibilities: There is no lyric sheet at all in the package; or there is one, but it is the twenty-fifth-generation copy of a light original that has slipped into a dimension somewhere between visibility and a blank sheet of paper.

The more sophisticated lyric sheet stories always involve dramatic devices called computers and printers. Even with these, songwriters will find a way to make their lyric sheets difficult to read. Some of these are the lyric sheet war stories, where the words are typed in one long run-on sentence. This margin-to-margin smokescreen of words camouflages the song structure.

Others go to the opposite extreme. They want so much for the reader to know each and every component of the structure and how it relates to the whole. They label every few lines—Verse I, Verse II, Pre-Chorus, Chorus, Bridge, Verse III, Pre-Chorus, Repeat Chorus, Repeat Bridge, Repeat, Repeat, and so on—until there are more part names on the sheet than lyrics.

Some songwriters like to create an air of mystery: They'll leave clues, but don't want to give away "who done it." Their lyric sheets are cleanly typed and beautifully copied. However, the only identifying feature on the lyric sheet is their publishing company's name, which may or may not be registered with a performance rights organization. An interested publisher may not be interested in trying to find out who the writer is and how she can be contacted.

Some songwriters like to spell *everything* out. They insert handwritten letters over their typed lyrics indicating chord changes: F, C, G, F, C, G, and so forth. Sometimes the insertion of chord names partially obscures the printed lyrics, calling for an extra deciphering effort. Imagine how a publisher welcomes this. Even when confined to the space between the lyric lines, the chord names create a cluttered, confused look on the lyric sheet.

We're not making up these stories, faithful readers. We have examples of every one right before us as we write.

Make sure that everything your lyric sheet has to say about you is good. It should say, "Here is a person who cares enough about songwriting to type and print the lyrics out so that the structure of the song is clear. This songwriter wants to be contacted if there's interest in the song; here is a name, e-mail address, and telephone number. This songwriter knows something about the music business, because here is a copyright notice."

For all those songwriters with sad lyric sheet tales to tell, we wrote a little song. It's called "Example of a Lyric Sheet" and it goes something like this (actually, it goes exactly like this):

EXAMPLE OF A LYRIC SHEET

by Fred Music and Sylvia Lyricist

All lyric sheets should be typed
On standard-sized paper (8½ x 11-inch)
With the title and the authors at the top

THE CHORUS SHOULD BE
IN CAPITAL LETTERS
OR INDENTED, OR BOTH;
IN VERSE/BRIDGE STRUCTURE
THE TITLE SHOULD BE IN CAPS

Include your name, e-mail address,
and telephone number
At the bottom of the page
Under the copyright notice

CHORUS: repeat

The bridge reminds you to
completely circle the ©
In the copyright notice;
(parentheses) won't do

CHORUS: repeat

© Fred Music and Sylvia Lyricist
(or you may use your company name)
Fred Music and Sylvia Lyricist
info@fredandsylvia.com
(111) 111-1111

Okay, so it doesn't rhyme, but it does show how a lyric sheet should look. Your lyric sheet tells the publisher or producer who you are. If it's less than professional-looking, the listener may not take the time to look at it.

64

READ THIS LEAD SHEET

Don't send the lyrics on a four-page lead sheet

We are often presented with songs in our workshops that have been written out on six or seven sheets of paper full of hand-drawn musical staffs. The song is fully written out in musical notation, every note in every chord is there for all to see, as are vocal harmonies, chord names, dynamics, and, buried in the midst of all of this, the lyrics. Of course, to fit below the proper notes, the lyrics must be hy-phen-a-ted.

Henry Mancini told us he used to hand-draw all his staffs in the very beginning of his career, but only because he didn't know he could buy paper with staffs already printed on it. So you are in great company with your hand-drawn staffs. With today's technology, even hand-written notes on printed staffs are obsolete. There are computers that will produce laser printouts of ready-to-print sheet music at the touch of a button. The problem is, no one in the music business wants to see your staffs, hand-drawn or printed.

You want your song to be taken seriously. You might think that creating a complicated lead sheet will impress the professional listener with your musical training and seriousness. The listener will be impressed, all right, impressed with how much time and energy you wasted and how out of touch you are with how songs are pitched in today's market. Pitching fully written lead sheets went out with the days when songwriters actually went into music publishers' offices and played their songs on pianos. Practically none of the professional listeners you pitch to today can read music.

Putting your song in lead sheet form does more than waste your time; it makes your demo presentation package harder to handle. Instead of a nice, neatly typed one-page lyric sheet, the listener is now fumbling with three or four pieces of paper that either fall apart and fly to every corner of the office or are taped together in a way that is reminiscent of a road map and impossible to refold.

Publishers and producers don't want to sift through sheets and sheets of paper and endless hyphens to follow the lyric. They don't care one bit about your skills in writing down a musical arrangement. They just want to listen to your tape and be totally knocked out by your song. They want a nice, clean, uncluttered lyric sheet to glance at while they listen. Save the trees by limiting your demo tape presentation to one pithy cover letter, one lyric sheet, and one outer envelope.

In the past, you needed a lead sheet to register your song with the Copyright Office in Washington, DC, but that has changed. Now all you need is a copy of the song on tape or CD. We like to include a lyric sheet with the CD on our copyright registrations, but it isn't required.

In the summer of 2007, the Copyright Office began to offer online registration. With this new method, if your song is not published, you don't even need a CD. See chapter sixty-nine, "Copyright It, Right?" for more about registering your songs.

Don't let your urge to impress lead to unnecessary work. Concentrate on putting all of your energy into important tasks: writing the best possible song and making the best possible demo.

≡ 65 ≡

SAVING THE BEST FOR LAST

*Don't put your best song at the
end of a twelve-song demo CD*

There's something we want to say in this chapter, but we don't want to say it just yet. We're going to beat around the bush for a while. It doesn't really matter what we say here because we're going to say something very important later, much later, in fact. We just want you to wade through a lot of words first. Maybe it will be boring. You might even get a little mad at us for putting you through this. We really don't care about that. You have plenty of time, haven't you?

We could keep up this much ado about nothing for a great number of paragraphs, maybe even pages. You'll have to be patient with us. We'll get around to the point sometime. After all, we are taking the time and trouble to write all of this stuff, and you owe it to us to read it, whether you think it's good or not.

Here we are in paragraph number three. This isn't our best writing, but we expect you to keep slogging away at it. There's going to be something great at the end, so just keep reading. We'll get to it eventually. How would you appreciate it if you didn't have to go through some trouble to get to it?

Have you ever noticed that your mind begins to wander when you're getting bored? Bet you have the urge to shut this book right now and go do something else more fun. Do you think life is about having fun? Where would this world be if everyone thought that?

Okay, joke's over. Wasn't very funny, was it? What we've been doing here is trying to give you the emotional experience of the publisher or producer who is sent a CD with a half-dozen or a dozen songs on it. The songwriter who puts this CD together feels the need to give the listener an overview of the collected works of Me, Myself, and I. By some unfathomable leap of calculation, the songwriter figures the ideal order of these songs is to put the worst first and the best last.

As a result of this scheme, the listener incurs the expense of purchasing a wig, having pulled out every hair on his head long before the best song comes around. And those are the listeners who care enough to try to wade through the entire CD. Most professional listeners can't afford to care that much about someone who obviously doesn't care enough about their time to be selective. They will listen to snippets of the first few songs, make a judgment, and toss the CD into the circular file for recycling. The masterpiece at the end will never be heard.

First of all, there should never be that many songs on a demo CD. You are far, far better off sending only your single best song. Impress the listener with your selectivity, not your fecundity. At the very most, put three songs on your demo CD. If your package is easy to get into and your songs are about three minutes long, you're still asking for ten minutes of the listener's time. Considering the pressures people in the music business have to deal with, that's asking a lot. When you send only your very best two or three songs, you also send a message that you know the value of the listener's time. If the listener likes something on the CD, she can always ask for more.

Even if you only send your best three songs, don't save the very best for last. Remember how we talked about grabbing the listener by the ears in the first few lines of the song? The same is true for the lineup on the CD. If you have your absolutely hottest song first on the CD, you increase the chances of having the second and third song heard. If the first and second songs aren't knockouts, the listener probably won't have the patience for the third.

You may think this is heartless, cruel, and irresponsible behavior on the listeners' part. Try to remember that they're only human. They have indigestion, fights with their spouses, car accidents on the way to work, and plenty of job-related stress. Your CD can make their day if you knock them out with a song. They want that more than anything.

Unfortunately, they rarely get what they want. Usually, listeners have to go through at least a hundred CDs to find one that interests them. Their patience wears thin. Remember how you felt when you read the first part of this chapter? Admit it: You were beginning to resent us for wasting your time and attention. Now you know how the listener feels when a songwriter doesn't care enough to put the best song forward.

66

FEAR OF FIRST CLASS

Don't send songs by certified or registered mail

After all the time, effort, creativity, blood, sweat, and tears, not to mention money, you've put into your demo, there's no way you're going to trust your CD to the perils of the regular U.S. Postal Service, right? You're going to walk that baby right up to the counter and fork out whatever sum it takes to send it certified, registered, return receipt requested, insured, special delivery, Priority Mail. Little do you realize that you have just turned your demo package into a super bouncing ball. It will end up back on your doorstep, unopened. It may even beat you home from the post office.

Mailing your CD by anything but regular first-class mail spells *p-a-r-a-n-o-i-a* to the person on the receiving end. It indicates that you want proof for the infringement lawsuit you are planning to institute against their company and their songwriters. Successful songwriters constantly have to deal with what they call "nuisance" lawsuits by not-so-successful songwriters who claim that they wrote the latest hit and the song on the air was stolen from them.

This has become so prevalent that doors have slammed shut all over the music business. The professionals are driven, in self-defense, to protect themselves from the amateurs. Many people who used to listen to "unsolicited material" have stopped doing so. These litigious songwriters have made it harder for the rest of us who are trying to get our toes in any door that's even slightly ajar. (We'll talk about how to transform your demo from "unsolicited material" to an inside pitch in part eight, "Making Disconnections.")

If you can't bear the idea of releasing your CD into the wind, rain, snow, and dark night of first-class mail, you might draw inspiration from stories we've heard of unusual demo deliveries. One songwriter landed in a helicopter on the front lawn of an artist's home to deliver a demo. Another songwriter cornered Donna Summer in the ladies' room at a disco club; even more interesting, this songwriter was of the male persuasion. We've heard of a demo arriving at a publisher's office with a Walkman encased in a beautiful antique box. Someone who knew the passion of Arista Records' president Clive Davis for a certain ball club packed the demo with a baseball signed by all the members of the team.

Creativity counts in demo delivery. Even if you can't afford a helicopter, you can do something to make your CD stand out from the others that are piled on a desk somewhere. Most of those envelopes are of the plain white or mild-mannered manila varieties. Spice up your demo presentation with color-coordinated envelopes, stationery, and CD labels to make them stand out from the crowd. Anything you can do to make your outer envelope and its contents more attractive and appealing to the eye will count in your favor. Publishers are people, too. They get bored looking at all that white and beige.

But be sure not to get too cutesy. You want to look professional. If you need it, get help in choosing your image. The typeface you use on your personalized stationery can make a statement about you and your music. Do you write New Age music? Consider having your name, company name, and so on, done in calligraphy.

Aiming for the top of the pop charts? Look into having your stationery typeset in a hot, modern typeface. If you have a publishing company name (see chapter seventy-five, "One Hundred Percent of Nothing," for more information on this), a coordinated logo printed on your envelopes and stationery will make your package stand out. Get help from an artist friend; you can pay her a handsome fee after your first big hit.

After you have done all of this careful creation of an outstanding and unique presentation package, you still will have to stick on a regular first-class stamp to cover the latest postage price hike and drop your dreams in your local mailbox. Talk about an act of faith. Seriously, we find this the perfect moment to say a little prayer, releasing the results of our efforts into the universe and congratulating ourselves on having done our best.

67

GUESS WHO WROTE THIS

*Put your name and phone number on
all parts of your presentation package*

More than once (and even once is one time too many) we've heard a request like this one at the California Copyright Conference: "We have a CD here; the song title is_____, but there's no name or phone number on the CD. We want to record the song. If you know who the writer is, please contact us." The producer of film music making the announcement is hoping someone among the music business attorneys and publishers assembled there will recognize the song title. The producer will not be able to record the song unless its writer is located.

We know writing the song was no big deal, right? As Gene Fowler said, "Writing is easy. All you do is stare at a blank sheet of paper until drops of blood form on your forehead." Making the demo was a breeze, wasn't it? You couldn't wait to separate yourself from all that cash. So, it doesn't matter to you that someone is actually interested in recording the song, and they can't tell who the writer is? What a catastrophe! We can hardly think of anything worse.

Don't ever let this happen to you. It's so easily avoided. Every piece of your demo presentation package—your CD, your lyric sheet, and your cover letter—must have your name, phone number (including area code), and e-mail address on it. That's all.

Disaster averted.

PART 8

MAKING DISCONNECTIONS

How Not to Get Your Songs Heard

68

PITCHING PARANOIA

*Avoid coming across with a defensive attitude,
afraid of being ripped off*

Recently, a young, self-contained band asked us to advise them on how to proceed with their careers. They've been working around town and have started to generate a "buzz."

The group feels that any day now someone is going to approach them with a contract, and they're afraid they will be taken advantage of because they are young and naïve in the ways of the music business. We suggested that they attend our workshop to get feedback on their songs. But they were afraid to show the songs because they hadn't registered them with the Copyright Office.

We wonder where the buzz is coming from if they're afraid to show their songs, but we're getting used to holding two contradictory thoughts in our heads at the same time, so let's bypass that mystery. Let's try to solve the conundrum of how a songwriter gets songs out in the world when he thinks they will be stolen as soon as they are shown.

First of all, the copyright law protects your songs as soon as you put them in a fixed form. That means as soon as you scribble them in pencil on a scrap of paper or sing them *a cappella* into your recording device, you have created a piece of property that belongs to you and you alone. If someone steals that property, you can take that person to court and sue him.

For a more detailed explanation of copyright registration, see the next chapter, "Copyright It, Right?" If you are a songwriter with songs signed to publishers, chances are your single song publishing contracts will provide that the publisher do the paperwork and pay the fee for the copyright registrations.

It's easy to say you have protection under U.S. copyright law. The reality is that your protection is only as good as your lawyers and the amount of money you are willing to spend on a lawsuit. Look at George Harrison's "My Sweet Lord." We'll never forget the first time we heard that: We said to each other, "Hey, George Harrison wrote new words for 'He's So Fine!' " Somehow, he had no idea that was what he was doing. The copyright owners of "He's So Fine" had to bring him to court, where the judge decided it didn't matter that George

Harrison didn't know what he was doing. He must have heard the original song and unconsciously remembered and repeated it. The court ruled that he had to share his royalties for "My Sweet Lord" with the copyright owners of "He's So Fine."

As we mentioned, Steve Allen admitted to us that melodies ran through his head in such rapid succession that he couldn't tell whether they were his or playbacks of other people's songs. He, too, had a song published that he later found, to his embarrassment, was entirely someone else's melody. Once he realized this, he gave the other writer half the royalties.

Are there people in the music business lying in wait to pounce upon your songs and steal them? We don't think so. There are, however, *song sharks*. These are the creeps who advertise that they will get your song recorded, then hit you up for money. They may even produce a recording with your song on it. A stack of these will only add to the clutter in your closet. Never pay anyone to publish or "make a record" of your song. This is different from paying for time in a recording studio to record a demo or master of your song. For more on the new, improved Internet version of song sharks, see chapter ninety-eight, "Cyber Song Sharks."

In the legitimate music business, people are too busy to bother with stealing from songwriters. If you write a hit song, they want to be your friend because you are going to make them lots of money. It doesn't make sense to kill the relationship with a songwriter who writes a gold record.

If you're still afraid of being ripped off, take a tip from the great country songwriter, Tom T. Hall. He said that early in his career he considered it a compliment to be stolen from, because it meant someone thought enough of his writing to steal it. A similar idea is expressed in the movie *The Red Shoes*: "It's much more disheartening to have to steal than to be stolen from."

You must go forth boldly with your songs in full display. Shout them from the highest hills. Sing them in your church or synagogue and community meeting room. Give your CDs to friends, family, co-workers. Get them out in the world where they can be heard. Don't hold back one iota. You never know where the connection is going to come from. If you keep your songs hidden, you are guaranteed not to make that connection. No one is going to go into your closet and dig around, looking for a hit.

No one can steal your ability to write songs. That talent is uniquely yours in the universe. It is perfectly safe. And besides that, you are an unending source of creativity.

Are there people in the music business who will hand you contracts that contain clauses in fine print that can be very detrimental to your career and your income? You bet your bippy! Still, you have nothing to fear. No one will force you to sign anything. Never, never, never sign anything unless you have been advised by an attorney specializing in the music business and you understand the basic meaning of what you are signing. Ask your nearest songwriter organization for a referral to a reputable music business attorney.

Contracts are not written and signed on the spot; they are negotiated. They go back and forth while attorneys on either side adjust the deal according to the clout of the parties involved. You don't have to worry about being taken advantage of if you follow the simple rule of always being represented by someone who has only your interests in mind.

There's a definition for fear that we like: *False Evidence Appearing Real*. There is nothing to fear but fear itself. If fear is keeping you from getting your songs out, we hope we've helped. If you can't shake your fear, we recommend you read the article, "Fear and Songwriting" on our site (www.writesongs.com) and try the A.R.T.S. program to heal the cause (see chapter three, "The Too-Early Editor").

≡ 69 ≡

COPYRIGHT IT, RIGHT?

Don't register every song individually with the Copyright Office

If you're a prolific songwriter, like our friend Lisa Aschmann who writes a song a day, you could spend more than fifteen thousand dollars a year on registering each song individually. Even registering a song a month would cost over five hundred dollars a year. Is it worth it? One of the most common questions songwriters ask us is, "Should I copyright my songs before I show them?" Our short answer is, "No." This chapter will give you the long background on that short answer.

Back when sheet music was the main way songs were sold, you could lose your copyright ownership of the song if you forgot to include the copyright notice at the bottom of the first page. Fortunately, the copyright law changes in 1976 eliminated that danger. Still, it's best if you do put a copyright notice on your lyric sheets and CDs to tell the world that you own them *and* to make it possible for someone who wants to use your song to find you. Don't write a long, drawn-out warning about all rights being reserved for the known universe. A simple copyright notice at the bottom of your lyric sheet and on the label of your CD will do. That consists of the symbol © or

the word "Copyright" or the abbreviation "Copr," the year, and your name (or your publishing company name). On our songs, it looks like this: © 2010 Pea Pod Music. (We don't include the year when we're pitching our songs because we don't want to have the listener prejudiced against them for being "old.")

But if we haven't registered the song with the Copyright Office, aren't we cheating by putting the notice on it? No. The law says you have a copyright the minute your song is fixed in tangible form. That is, as soon as you write it down on a piece of paper or record it on tape or CD, your song is "protected" by the copyright law. It's a limited protection because you will not be able to institute an infringement lawsuit until you file the official registration. And if you don't have your song registered when the infringement takes place, and you sue and win, you will not be entitled to some of the money you could have recieved if the song had been registered prior to the suit. These include statutory damages, compulsory license royalties, and attorneys' fees. Also, having a copyright registration gives you legal presumption, which means everything in the copyright certificate is presumed to be true and the other party has the burden of proving at trial that it's not.

Many songwriters cherish the illusion that registering their songs with the Copyright Office somehow protects them. You could send in a copy of the Lennon and McCartney song "Yesterday," however, and eventually you'd get a nice official document in the mail. There's no one at the Copyright Office checking to see what's in the packages. There are crooks in every walk of life, but generally speaking, no one in the legitimate music business is going to "steal" your songs. But let's say you think someone actually heard your song and thought enough of it to use all or part of it and claim it as their own. If you registered the song with the Copyright Office, you can hire yourself some expensive lawyers and musicologists and spend thousands of dollars in court proving your song was created first, that the infringer had access to your song and that the infringing song is substantially the same as yours. This is not an easy thing to do, as their attorney will come up with "common source" examples of previously existing songs that pre-date the two in contention. All of your effort and expense would only be worth it if the infringing song were a huge success. The horrible truth is that the likelihood of any of this being an issue is so slim that it's hardly worth thinking about.

Getting back to the moment when you automatically achieved copyright, the date of creation: How do you prove that date? Although some people say it won't hold up in court, Donald S. Passman, author of the excellent book *All You Need to Know About the Music Business* (New York: Free Press, 2006), maintains that mailing yourself a copy does establish a date of creation. Sometimes called "the poor man's copyright," this practice of sealing up a song in a tape-surrounded envelope and sending it to yourself via registered or certified mail may help you sleep better at night. Another way to economize on copyrights is to put a bunch of songs together and register them as an unpublished collection. You can only do that if the copyright owner or owners are the same for all the songs in the collection. You have to give the collection a title, though you may list the individual song titles on a continuation sheet. If something happens with an individual song in the collection, it's best to file a new, separate registration for that song. Our favorite way of establishing a date of creation is to bring all our songs into our workshop. We distribute lyric sheets to all present. They write their creative ideas about the song on the lyric sheets and sign and date them. And we receive a bunch of great ideas and fifteen witnesses that we had created the song as of that date.

But, you've got money to burn and nothing but the real thing will do for you. Or a miracle occurs and someone wants to record a song of yours that is not already signed to a publisher. Since the Copyright Office says that "the distribution of copies or phonorecords of a work to the public by sale" constitutes publication, that makes you the publisher. Now is the time to register the song if you haven't already done so. Go to your computer and type "copyright a song" in the search engine. There are one hundred forty-five million hits to choose from! One of the first will tell you what a deal it is to pay them $120 on top of the copyright fee to fill out your form. They say it would cost over $700 to get a lawyer to do it. You pay them the money, and then you do the work. You're prompted to fill in the blanks on the computer screen that will be the information on the copyright registration form and their job is to press the printer button.

If you want to register your songs with the Copyright Office, visit their Web site, www.copyright.gov. You now have three filing options: total and partial online filing and old-fashioned hard copy. If your song is not published, you can complete the whole process electronically by filling out the registration form, making your payment online, and sending in an "electronic deposit copy," a.k.a. an mp3 file of your song. You can also use totally electronic filing if your song is published only online. If your song is published in hard copy, you may either complete the registration online or print out a registration form and mail it in. In the latter two cases, a hard copy of your published work must be sent to the Registrar of Copyrights. It's easy to file a copyright registration. All the instructions are clearly explained on the site. Click on "Performing Arts" under the "How to Register a Work" heading on the Copyright Office's home page. Then follow the instructions for Form PA.

When your officially stamped copyright registration form returns months later, put it somewhere safe. It could be the foundation for the mansion of your dreams.

≡ 70 ≡

STAYING IN THE CLOSET
Don't be afraid to pitch or show your songs

Some songwriters fear being ripped off so much that they never actually show their songs. Other songwriters keep their songs secret because they are embarrassed or afraid of criticism or ridicule. If you're not showing anyone your songs, it's obvious that you're a closet songwriter.

You are not alone in the closet. You would be surprised how many people have written songs. Sometimes it seems to us that everyone in the world has a song stashed somewhere around the house.

We addressed the fear of being ripped off in chapter sixty-eight. Basically, you do not have to worry about people stealing your songs. Other writers are too busy writing, and legitimate music business people are far too inundated with great songs to risk their reputations and their legal fees to defend a copyright infringement suit.

Fear of ridicule is not so easily overcome. Unfortunately, our parents often invalidate our first attempts at creativity. "That's nice," they say, "but you can't make a living at it." Or they launch into a full-scale lecture on what makes a really good song and why ours isn't. The tender bud of our creativity is nipped off.

Some songwriters react by going underground. We continue to create but don't show anyone. Others of us shut down, stop creating, and eventually become convinced we're not creative. Some of us go on creating, even though the process is painful because the original external critic has now taken up residence in our own head. Therefore, we find ourselves constantly dissatisfied with what we're writing. No matter what form the damming of our creativity takes, it spells trouble in our lives.

The desire to write songs is a gift meant to be shared. When something happens that dams up the flow between the desire and the expression, the energy backfires. It gets diverted into activities that are not good for us. We find ourselves overeating, using drugs or alcohol, obsessing about sex, spending money compulsively, gambling, overworking, or being preoccupied with the past and future.

If we are lucky enough to wake up to what we're doing, we may still think we'd be fools to try songwriting. We buy into society's devaluation of creativity: We're too old, it's too late, we're not good enough, it's not practical.

All this results in either not writing at all, writing song fragments and never finishing anything, or writing complete songs but never really recognizing what we've done or showing it to anyone. The pain of the original blow to our budding creativity is awakened every time we approach the songwriting process. The pleasure that was the motivation for the original songwriting impulse has become inextricably entwined with pain.

If this sounds familiar to you, there is help. The A.R.T.S. program mentioned before deals with these very common experiences. Much of the healing available through this program comes from being in contact with other people who are experiencing the same problems. With this solid support base in the safety of a communal closet, every one of us can go out into the world with the courage to share our art.

Many of us were negatively conditioned in our childhood. Did you ever hear of Pavlov's dog? Pavlov discovered that if he rang a bell every time he fed a dog, eventually the dog would salivate at the sound of the bell. That's positive conditioning, because the dog got a reward when the bell sounded. Similar experiments have been done with negative conditioning. Suppose every time an animal heard the bell, a slight electrical shock was delivered to the floor of the cage. Eventually, the animal jumps when the bell sounds, with or without the shock.

The fear and shame that we feel about our creativity was learned. We were not born with it. Something shocking happened to us, probably thousands of times, in subtle ways we can't remember. Most of us grow up receiving constant messages from our family and from society at large that art is not an important and necessary part of life. Once we realize that we need to connect with our creativity to lead relatively sane lives, it's up to us to recondition ourselves. We need to teach ourselves that it is all right to be creative and share our songs. The first step is to share your song in a totally safe environment.

That's what A.R.T.S. provides. You only need two people to start your own A.R.T.S. meeting. Call (212) 873-7075 or visit www.artsanonymous.org for help. If that idea doesn't appeal to you, you can open the closet door a crack and let in one special person. Choose someone you know you can trust. Explain that you want to share a song and that you want positive support for it—no criticism! (This is part of the rule read at the beginning of each A.R.T.S. meeting.) If you have chosen your supporter correctly, you will experience the unconditional respect you need to take the next step.

For many of us, it's difficult or impossible to make the simple statement, "I'm a songwriter." We think we're frauds. We can't be songwriters because we are not getting rich from writing songs; in fact, we're spending money on it, not earning money from it. We aren't songwriters because no one will record our songs. We aren't songwriters because we don't deserve to live our dream.

Many of our recommendations in this book aer about getting your song out through established commercial methods. It's natural for songwriters to want to teach the world their songs. The reality is that our chances are slim. Songwriter Sue Schiffrin talked about this hard reality at a UCLA seminar on "Women in Songwriting": "There's a statistic and I'll tell it to you because I know it and I'm still writing songs in spite of the fact that I know it. They say that of all the songs that are written, 1 percent of those songs get recorded and 1 percent of that 1 percent get to be hits. The odds are against you."

Arthur Hamilton, who wrote "Cry Me a River," was moderating that seminar. He made the perfect rejoinder: "Never face the facts." Don't let the impossible odds get you down. You are still a songwriter even if you don't beat them. If you really want to make it as a full-time songwriter, you will need endless persistence. But your songwriting is just as valid if songwriting is not your career.

If you are currently a closet songwriter, gently recondition yourself over a period of time so that you can open the door wide and walk out into the sunshine. Then share your songs at every appropriate opportunity. You never know who could be in the audience.

Sting talked about the early days of The Police in an interview in *Rolling Stone*.

The group would play their hearts out no matter who did or didn't show up to listen. One night, there were only two people in the audience. The Police played as if they were in a packed stadium. It turned out that the two people were disc jockeys who got turned on to the group and promoted their music on their stations. The two-person audience turned into a major breakthrough for the group.

We decided to move to Nashville the second night of our first visit. We attended a "Pickin' Party" in a private home and experienced more than community; it was communion. Our idea of heaven on Earth is to be in a room where everyone loves songs and sings and plays along. It doesn't matter a bit whether the song ever gets heard beyond that room. We shared it and we were moved. Nashville makes being a songwriter doable, even though making a living as a songwriter is nearly impossible.

You need to know that the only requirement for being a songwriter is the desire to write songs. Songwriting is a tool for personal expression and growth. You need to let your songs out, and the world needs to hear them. This is as true for the one song you sang in the closet to your one friend as it is for the biggest-selling song in the world.

≡71≡

TO WHOM IT MAY CONCERN

*Don't send songs to a company
without a specific person's name*

You have a song you think would be great for a particular artist. You're a fan of that artist, and you have several of her albums at home. You see that the albums were on XYZ Records, so you pop your CD in an envelope and address it to A&R Department, XYZ Records. After all, the A&R staff at record labels helps artists find songs, so you think they will be kind enough to direct your CD to the appropriate person within the company. Think again.

First, that record company is probably getting one to three thousand CDs a week from unsolicited sources. By addressing your CD to an anonymous A&R person, you just qualified to be in that pile. Most likely there is a person hired just to sit all day and hit all those envelopes with a rubber stamp saying "Unsolicited Material—Refused Unopened."

Second, just because your artist has a couple of albums out on a certain label doesn't mean she is still recording on that label. Even if she is still on the label, she may be out on tour and won't be looking for songs until her next recording project is planned.

Third, A&R people at the major labels are the pared-down staff from the original label, which has since merged with other labels whose staff has been let go. So four people are doing the job formerly done by twelve or twenty. To survive the pressure, they have to limit their availability to known quantities; namely, publishers they already have relationships with.

Even publishers, who used to be approachable by songwriters, are getting harder and harder to access. But they are the first line of possible entry into the mainstream music market. So try approaching a publisher.

"How and who?" you ask. ASCAP, BMI, and SESAC help developing songwriters because they want you to join their respective organization and not the other one. If you can get to one of the music business centers (New York City, Nashville, Los Angeles), make an appointment to speak to a Membership Representative at each of the performance rights organizations. You can play them a song or two, and they may give you some names of publishers to contact.

Songwriters' organizations can also point you in the direction of publishers who might be open to meeting with you or listening to your songs.

Writer's Digest's *Songwriter's Market* is a good starting point for making connections. It can be purchased in any bookstore or from the Writer's Digest Web site (www.writersdigest.com). But don't just send your CD off to a company because it is listed in the book. Take the extra effort to make personal contact to be sure you're not wasting your time and money by sending the wrong song at the wrong time to the wrong person. To turn all those wrongs into rights, you need to communicate directly with the person (or her assistant) who—you hope—will love your song as much as you do. You can also do an Internet search for "music publishers," but the results are a mixed bag of legitimate publishers and song sharks. For more on this, see chapter ninety-eight, "Cyber Song Sharks."

When calling publishing companies, ask for the Creative Director or Creative Manager. That's the job title of the listeners in the larger companies. You probably won't get through to that person, but their assistant will do for this first call. If your CD package is going to be opened at all, you have to make phone contact with a real live, flesh-and-blood person who says, "Yes, send a CD." Get that person's name! It doesn't matter if it's someone's assistant. Getting one toe into that outer office is an inch closer to getting into the inner sanctum.

Once you get the go-ahead, ask your contact if there is something special you should write on the outside of the envelope. Companies often have a code so the people in the mailroom can distinguish between the unsolicited CDs and the CDs that have the secret password. Don't forget to say "Thank you." This could be the beginning of a long and profitable relationship between you and this person. A year and three pitches from now, your lower-level contact may just get a promotion. That's when your patient nurturing of this relationship can really pay off.

You're not pitching your song to some anonymous department at a publishing company. You're dealing with people who appreciate recognition and consideration as much as you do. It's up to you to show your awareness of this reality by taking the time to make person-to-person contact and find out what you can do to better your chances of having your song heard.

Relationship is the name of the game when it comes to making the connections that get your songs recorded. Songs sent through the mail rarely are recorded, although that's just what happened with our Patti LaBelle cut. Most songs get recorded through some personal contact, however farfetched. Steve Kipner, who wrote "Let's Get Physical," got his tape in the door while delivering sandwiches to make ends meet. Allan Rich, who co-wrote "I Don't Have the Heart," passed a tape to a producer when he sold him a pair of shoes on the Venice Beach boardwalk. Billy Steinberg's girlfriend's brother, a drummer for Linda Ronstadt, got Billy his first major cut. Al Kasha, Oscar-winning co-writer of "We May Never Love Like This Again" from *The Towering Inerno* and "The Morning After" from *The Poseidon Adventure*, shared a story in his workshop of how he got next to New York's *Late Show* producer by going to the same barber, among other things. Once they had several relationships in common, Al presented the producer with the idea for a new *Late Show* theme in a way that made money for both parties.

Music is a person-to-person business; so pick up your phone before you mail that CD.

ONE PITCH AT A TIME

*Don't pitch to only one potential
recording situation at a time*

Some songwriters who are new to the game believe they would be cheating somehow if they sent a particular song to more than one prospective user at a time. That's not the way it works. In the songwriting business, there are no limitations on how many people you can pitch your song to simultaneously.

What do you do if two or three of them respond at the same time and want to use the song? (We should have such problems!) In this case you will have to investigate the nature of each situation. Maybe one is just a publisher who likes the song and wants to give you a single song contract. The second may be a producer who wants to record the song with a new artist. The third may be a producer who wants to put a hold on the song for a major artist and wants to share in the publishing, too.

Publishers come in all shapes and sizes. There are one-man shows and multinational conglomerates. There are catalog collectors who are building up the size of their catalog, and there are active song pluggers. They offer single song publishing contracts ranging in length from one to twenty-five pages.

If a publisher contacts you, the first thing you want to do is review a copy of the single song contract they are offering. That will tell you a lot about the company. Check to see if they automatically insert a reversion clause. Consult with a music business attorney to get a full understanding of what the contract means. We recommend that you read Don Passman's book, *All You Need to Know About the Music Business* to get clear and easy explanations of the issues involved. There are good contracts and bad contracts, or contracts that are more or less favorable toward songwriters. Ask your attorney to tell you where this contract falls in the good/bad spectrum and why. You may decide to pass on a publisher on the strength (or weakness) of the contract alone.

That is not to say that you have to accept the first contract they send you. The publisher may or may not be willing to change the contract. You or your attorney should call the publisher to see if negotiation is possible. If the contract is unacceptable to you, and the publisher won't change it, notify the publisher that you aren't willing to sign the song under the terms of the contract. Chalk it up as another educational adventure in songwriting.

If the contract is acceptable or the publisher is willing to negotiate it into acceptable form, you still need to decide if you really want to sign it. If you pitched to the publisher because you saw the company name in some directory, but you don't know much about the company, now is the time to find out.

A visit to the ASCAP (www.ascap.com), BMI (www.bmi.com), and SESAC (www.sesac.com) Web sites to search for the publishing company name will confirm the publisher's membership in one of these organizations. Your local or national songwriters' organization may know something about the publishing company. Ask your contact at the publishing company to tell you about the company's catalog. Which writers do they work with and what songs have they published? Do this in a friendly, information-gathering manner, not as a suspicious challenge. You might ask how large the company is and if the person you are talking with will be the only one pitching the song. You are considering going into a business partnership with this person and this company. You have the right to know about your partner.

In the good old days when publishers nurtured and trained songwriters, paid for the recording of demos, and were songpluggers in a market in which artists were artists and writers were writers, the usual deal was 50/50. The songwriter would sign over ownership of the copyright to the publisher. The publisher would get as many artists as possible to record the song, collect all monies (except performance royalties, which go directly to the writer from the performance rights organizations, a.k.a. PROs), and then give 50 percent to the writer.

Today, the songwriter is expected to be self-nurtured and trained, demo producer, and songplugger. Sometimes, publishers just do the paperwork, which is called administration. Songwriters with track records (a history of hit songs) also have their own publishing companies and wield sufficient clout to maintain partial ownership of their copyrights, which means they collect more than 50 percent of the royalties. Top writers can maintain complete ownership and collect 100 percent.

Songwriters with no track record usually don't have the clout to participate in the publishing income. However, if you make the connection for the recording of a song, even if it's your first cut, you may be able to make a more favorable deal than the traditional 50/50. We do not recommend you do these delicate negotiations yourself. Unless you possess the knowledge and skills required, have your music business attorney cut the deal for you. See chapters seventy-four and seventy-five for more on how to handle your give and take with a publisher.

The second offer from the producer with the new artist holds some attraction. You never know; his artist may be the next big hit, and you'll be in on the ground floor if you go with this one. (Our friend

Jerry Vandiver had that experience when a song of his got on the first album of a then-unknown artist. Millions of sales later, he's glad he let that song get cut by Tim McGraw.) When you pitch directly to the producer or artist, you are your own publisher. You are entitled to two streams of income, one as publisher and another as songwriter. If this is a new producer with a new artist, they probably won't ask to share in your publisher income. At the very least, there's a potential for you to come out of this deal with nothing lost and a very good demo gained.

A producer with a lot of clout and an artist who is a proven success present a different set of variables. Often they will ask to have a hold on your song. That means they want to record it, but they won't be recording it for a while. They want you to refrain from pitching the song to anyone else in the meantime. For more on holds, see chapter seventy-seven, "Hold It, Hold It, Never Let it Go."

A producer with clout might also ask to share in the publishing income. Then it becomes a question of whether you want to share the publishing income, how much you'll share, and under what circumstances you'll share it. Again, if you are lucky enough to have these kinds of dilemmas, we recommend that you consult the best music business attorney available to you.

Pitch your songs to as many possible recording situations as you like. There is such a thing as going overboard, though. Read on to see what we mean.

73

SHOTGUN PITCHING

*Pinpoint your pitches; don't force the
wrong song on the right contact*

You think you've written a great song, and you want everyone in the world to hear it. So you get a music business directory: Writer's Digest's *Songwriter's Market* (www .writersdigest.com), *Music Registry* (www .musicregistry.com) and *Billboard's International Buyer's Guide* (www.billboard.com) are three very good ones. You can also buy a music business database to install in your computer. Then you can press a button, have your printer spit out labels for every name on the list, pay somebody to do high-speed CD duplication in bulk, and mail the CD to everyone.

There might be a good reason to do that, but pitching your song isn't it. If you want to get your song recorded, you need to aim it like a dart, straight at the bull's-eye of the artists most likely to record it. With shotgun pitching, you waste your time and money sending your CD to the wrong people, and you don't endear yourself to the listeners who waste their time dealing with your CD.

Aiming a song at an appropriate artist is called "casting" the song. Just as casting the actors in movies is an art that gets recognized in the credits, casting

your song to the right artists takes skill and creativity.

Each artist has an image, a personality they express as an artist. This may or may not exactly coincide with who they actually are. It isn't something accidental, though. Artists hire personal managers who advise them on focusing their image, among many other things. Included in the concept of image are the kinds of messages the artist will choose to express—and not to express.

A very young female artist won't sing a song about being married and divorced. A conservative country artist won't sing a song about cheating and getting drunk. A heavy metal artist won't sing a cute song about butterflies and puppies. A sophisticated jazz artist won't sing a song about trucks and honkytonks. It's pretty easy to imagine what a known artist would not want to sing, but it takes a bit of digging to hone in on that message the artist wants to sing next.

Many times we write with a particular artist in mind. But the creative process likes to surprise us; the direction of the song may take a U-turn in mid-writing.

Even if the finished product does seem to fall into the intended artist's ballpark, we have a casting session for each song after we finish writing it. The result is a list of artist names that is kept in the file with the song. The list grows as other names occur to us or are suggested to us.

The first question you need to ask yourself is, "Does the artist record songs written by outside songwriters?" For most artists on the pop charts, the answer to this question will be no. Don't waste your time and theirs pitching to these closed situations. If the answer is yes, proceed to research the approaches to that artist.

To cast your songs accurately, take time to study the artists you think might sing the message contained in your song. This is incredibly easy to do on the Internet. Just do a search on the artist's name. We just tried "Celine Dion," a well-known artist who records outside material. It yielded over twenty-seven million hits! The first page of these will keep you busy for a while. Read the bios, listen to the music, and think. Study the artist's last few albums. What sort of messages does this artist like to deliver? Where are the artist's vocal sweet spots? What song structures does the artist favor? Would your song fit in with them? Can you really envision that artist getting into singing your song? Can the song be demoed in that artist's style and feel? Project into the future: Where will the artist want to go creatively with her next album?

As TAXI screeners (www.taxi.com), we were once given the task of screening songs for Garth Brooks. After going through an entire box of tapes and CDs, we were in shock. Did those writers really think Garth Brooks would sing those songs? Had they ever listened to Garth Brooks? Our conclusion was that it should be mandatory for every songwriter to have the experience we just had. What an education! If you put yourself in the shoes of the listener who is dying to find just the right song for the artist, you won't waste your time with casual pitches to artists you haven't researched.

The artist is surrounded by people who give input on recording projects. The personal manager, the producer, the A&R person at the record label, and sometimes the agent and the attorney are among those who officially or semi-officially perform this function. Artists aren't recording all the time. Generally, they are out touring in the summer. They and their support staff are only looking for songs in the months before a recording session is planned. All of this information is available on their official Web sites or by searching for phrases like "Jane Doe's manager."

If one of your fantasies is to be a detective, you can live it out in aid of your songwriting. The artist also has an unofficial network for song input: hairdressers, doctors, dentists, band members, fitness instructors, roadies, second cousins, etc. If it's geographically feasible, any contact you can make with someone in this unofficial network may lead to the possibility of pitching directly to the artist.

If the artist is coming through your town on tour, make it a point to go to the concert and see if you can make contact with someone in the artist's entourage.

There is a difference between getting your CDs to as many potential outlets as possible and just sending them out helter-skelter. Carefully aim each one at a particular target. You may not hit the mark, but at least you tried and learned something in the process.

74

I'LL GIVE YOU EVERYTHING

Don't be willing to sign everything and anything away at the slightest interest by a publisher

You've done your homework. You've captured the idea and chipped away at it lyrically and musically, like Michelangelo uncovering the shape in the marble bit by bit. You've sought feedback and re-written. You've gone through the creative maze of the demo-making process. You've researched and made enough contacts to have the door open just wide enough for you to slip your CD in. Then one day, while you are sharpening your pencils, putting out the garbage, doing the dishes, anything but facing the endless challenge of songwriting, the phone rings. It's Joe Producer and he wants to record your song. What's your reaction?

When that call came to our house, it was from Philadelphia International, the label created by the songwriter-production team of Kenny Gamble and Leon Huff, Grammy-award winning writers of "If You Don't Know Me By Now." They said that Patti LaBelle wanted to record "Body Language," a song we had written with Harold Payne. We had pitched the song directly to them, doing business as Pea Pod Music. The caller wanted to know if their company could share in the publishing. Overcome with excitement, Pat blurted out, "Yes! Yes! Yes!" Wrong, wrong, wrong.

First of all, this was not a decision she could make on her own. That song is a piece of property created by three people, each of whom owns an equal share of it. No decision can be made on it unless and until all the owners agree. Second, as song-writers, we are not the best people to ne-gotiate these deals. We are victims of our eagerness to have our songs exposed. Fur-thermore, there are people who have been in the business end of music for a long time and know a lot more than we do about the small print that can mean big differences. We highly recommend that you have such deals negotiated by a lawyer who special-izes in the music business.

Your friendly local lawyer who helps you write your will and plan your estate will know nothing about this. Music busi-ness law has its own language, and you need someone who can speak it for you. You must go to a specialist for a deal as po-tentially important as a song being cut by Patti LaBelle. Our friend and collaborator Harold Payne is a wonderful artist (www .affinityrecords.com). When this offer came,

Harold was under contract to a personal manager. Since the manager was going to earn a percentage of whatever Harold earned while under contract, we turned the negotiation over to his manager. Although he isn't a lawyer, we knew he was a legitimate and honest person experienced in making these kinds of deals in the music business. And because of his relationship with Harold, he was motivated to make the best possible deal for us.

Why all this wheeling and dealing? Why isn't a simple "yes" or even an ecstatic "Yes! Yes! Yes!" the appropriate response to the situation? There are way too many variables for a simple answer to suffice. When you write a song, you create a copyright. Literally, that means the "right to copy." Actually, it's a bundle of rights that no one can touch without your permission. There's the right to make the first recording of the song and reproduce it mechanically via CD. There's the right to synchronize your song to a motion picture or a television show. There's the right to use a bit of it with different lyrics as a TV commercial, the right to put it in a musical teakettle, the right to print it up on sheet music and sheet music books. There's also the right to have it performed on the radio, on TV, in music videos, at ball games, and in elevators. Now there are the rights to have it downloaded, streamed, or offered in a music subscription service. What if an entirely new form of delivering music to consumers is invented next week? Your rights for the future need to be protected in the deals you make today.

(Almost twenty years after this deal was negotiated, we were called by Michael Ajakwe Jr., a playwright who loved that Patti LaBelle album so much he had written a musical around the songs and called it *Body Language*. Imagine our thrill to see singers and dancers performing "Body Language" on the stage of the historic Warner Theater in Washington, DC [www.bodylanguagethe play.com]! Are we glad that we maintained ownership of the copyright? Yes!)

Back to the discussion of rights. All of the rights we talked about above also hold for foreign markets. There's a great big world out there clamoring for American music. There's also a world of international copyright law and constant litigation going on to clarify the meaning of the laws. When we were editors of the California Copyright Conference (www.theccc.org) newsletter, we had the great opportunity of covering their monthly dinner meetings, at which panels of experts discuss the latest developments in matters affecting copyright. Copyright law is a universe of knowledge. If you learned everything you needed to know about this subject, you would have no time to write and record your songs.

This is not to say that you needn't bother your pretty little head about it. You do have to study the basics of the legal aspects of songwriting. You need to understand what you're signing, even though you've had your lawyer take care of it. An excellent source of information is Don Passman's *All You Need to Know About the Music Business*. Our friend John Braheny's book, *The Craft and Business of Songwriting* (Writer's Digest

Books), covers both the legal and creative aspects of songwriting in depth.

The contracts songwriters are very often offered are called "single song contracts." These usually come from publishers who want you to assign your bundle of rights to them. In return, they are supposed to pitch your song to recording situations and make money, half of which will eventually pass down to you as the writer. We are describing a very complex situation so simply that the description is barely accurate, but bear with us.

A publisher will often tell a writer that the single song contract is "standard." There is no such thing. We've seen single song contracts ranging in length from two to twenty-five pages. One of the first contracts we were offered was very long. We took it home and studied every dot and comma of it. We decided we needed to have a few small changes in the contract. We made an appointment with the publisher and showed her the changes we wanted. Her response was an attack: "I paid lawyers hundreds of dollars to write that contract! You don't know anything about this! I won't change a thing." We retreated to our closet and came out two or three months later.

One of the bottom-line changes we were asking for, and that we recommend writers insist upon, is a reversion clause. Without it, you have signed away your song for many, many years, during which time it may sit gathering dust in the publisher's file. When a publisher owns a lot of copyrights, it's called a catalog. Buying and selling catalogs is big business. It has

nothing to do with you and your precious song that you sweat blood over. A reversion clause is language in the contract that says, "If the publisher/producer fails to record a commercially released version of the song in x amount of time, ownership of the song reverts automatically back to the writer(s)." Don't get lost in the shuffle; make sure your songs come back to you if the publisher is not getting anywhere or doing anything with them.

We won't go into all the details of the single song contract, except to say that all of the various rights mentioned above can be dealt with separately, and deals can be structured to vary according to the status of the song on the recording. For example, you might agree that if the song becomes a single, the co-publisher can have 50 percent of the publisher's mechanical royalties (payment for the sales of CDs) on that single only, or on all future recordings of the song, or for the next five years. If the same song turns out to be just an album cut, the deal may stipulate that the co-publisher will receive 25 percent of the mechanicals. The point is, it takes experience to be able to sense the appropriate level of give and take between the two parties in the deal.

So when your phone rings and it's Mary Publisher, say to her, "I'm glad you're interested in the song. Why don't you send me a copy of your contract and I'll have my lawyer look at it." If it's Joe Producer, ask briefly about his intentions for the song, and then say, "Great, I'll have my lawyer/manager/co-publisher call you." Then sit back, relax, and enjoy the roller coaster ride.

≡ 75 ≡

ONE HUNDRED PERCENT OF NOTHING

Don't be inflexible in negotiating rights

At the opposite end of the songwriter pole from those who are ready to give away all their rights at the drop of a contract are the writers who insist on hanging on to everything, no matter what. These songwriters act as their own publishers and pitch their songs to artists, A&R people, or producers. When they get a nibble on a song, if they think even a little bit of their bait is going to be lost, they yank their lure right out of the water. Songwriters who have a lot of clout can pull this off. Most of us cannot afford to.

Inflexibility in negotiating shared rights and attendant royalties on a song is called the "100 percent of nothing" syndrome. Sadly, many decisions about whether to record a song are made not on the merits of the song but on the financial possibilities of the deal. If you are not willing to deal away some of your rights in the song, you will exclude your song from deals in which the users of the song insist on sharing the income of the song.

These users do have a point. Without the exposure they are willing to give the song, the song would make no income. True, you could find someone else to record the song who would not insist on sharing the publishing royalties, but you also might *not* find someone else.

If you take the song to a publisher, the publisher will definitely demand a percentage of the income on the song. The usual amount is 50 percent, but songwriters with clout can negotiate for some share in that publisher's half. If you think that the publisher can do something for your song that you cannot do, then it is worthwhile to share with the publisher. If you act as your own publisher, you give yourself additional pieces to play in the negotiation chess game. Some of these pieces need to be sacrificed in order to win the game.

These pieces are the various rights in the song: mechanical, performance, and sheet music royalties; synchronization fees; and other uses of the song. You can negotiate with the user of the song piece by piece, with percentages shared varying depending on the nature of the recording. (We say "you" here because you own the song. But because these negotiations are complicated, we advise that you hire someone experienced to conduct them for you.)

In the last chapter, we gave an example of piece-by-piece negotiations regarding the mechanical royalties. Here's a variation on that theme, using performance royalties: You could agree that the producer of the song gets 50 percent of the publisher's performance royalties for three years after the release of the song. Or you could agree that the producer of the record or the artist's publishing company get 100 percent of the publisher's performance royalties for the first year and 50 percent for the following two years.

Getting songs recorded is tough enough. Don't make it tougher on yourself by being inflexible in negotiating for royalty shares. This is called paying your dues. Getting your songs recorded is the name of the game. If your song is out there, you're a winner. Once you have a successful track record, you will have the clout to be more insistent and selective about the deals you make on your songs.

=76=

NO SIR, THAT'S MY BABY

*Don't be reluctant to let go of a song because
you're saving it for your "artist deal"*

For the songwriter who wants to be a performing artist, the moment of truth comes when someone else wants to record a song you're saving for yourself. Tom Kelly puts the question this way: "Is somebody else going to do this song better than I can or should I hang onto it myself?"

Billy Steinberg remembers when he answered that question incorrectly:

> I had a band called Billy Thermal and we were signed to Planet Records. At the same time, Kim Carnes and her producer, Val Garay, wanted to record a certain song of mine, "The Price I Pay." I made a decision that I was saving this song for my own record. My own record was never released and never came to anything. If I had agreed, the song would have been on the album with "Bette Davis Eyes." It would have made me some money and it would have been a feather in my cap at the time, but I chose not to give them the song.

If you are lucky enough to have interest in your songs, we think you should let them get out there and build your credibility. It is extremely difficult to get an artist deal with a record label, and it is wise to do anything you can to make it easier or to give yourself more clout in the negotiations. Having written hits for other artists is a bargaining chip. You have nothing to lose by letting your songs be recorded and much to gain.

Many artists we know today got their toes in the door by letting others record the songs they had written for themselves. And many songs are recorded several times before an artist makes the magic with it that shoots it up the charts. The first time your song is recorded is the only time you have the power to refuse permission. After that, anyone who wants to can record it without your permission, as long as they're willing to pay the statutory rate.

Unless you feel the recording will damage your song in some way, we say "Go for it!"

How could your song be damaged? How about the time when we were offered the opportunity to have a song of ours in a movie? Wow! We were excited by the prospect. Then we found out that the movie was about a serial killer Santa. In spite of the fact that the music supervisor was a friend of ours and told us we were stupid to say no, we stuck to our refusal. We were glad we did when the movie came out to resounding rejection.

Even with a hit song track record, a record deal may not be in your future. We know hit songwriters who have wanted to be artists for years. We're talking about major hit songwriters and many, many years. They might even get a recording contract from time to time, but not much comes of it. If they had held back their songs all that time, they'd be nowhere now. Instead, they're very successful as songwriters who have learned to live with the frustration of having *part* of their dream not come true. Better some than none.

Unless you are so far into a potential record deal that you are actually negotiating the deal based on the master demos on a particular set of songs, we think it's best to keep all your options open. Billy Steinberg agrees:

> If a really great singer wants to record that song or might if they had a chance to hear it, I think it's a major decision to decide not to even play it for them because you're going to save it for yourself. That's why writer artists have to take a careful look at where their real potential lies and not delude themselves.

It's a delusion to think that your career as an artist depends on keeping one particular song exclusively for yourself. As a songwriter, you learn with each song you write, so the next one will be better, and the one after that even better, and so on.

Breaking into songwriting is hard, but it's a featherbed compared to trying to make it as a recording artist.

The reason it is so difficult comes down to the bottom line: money. A record company is going to have to believe in you to the tune of spending about $250,000 to produce your first album and $500,000 on videos, radio promotion, and tour support. That's a fair amount of faith. Many artists don't sell enough records to pay back that investment on their first albums. Bruce Springsteen didn't until his third. The generally accepted estimate is that a label invests up to $1,000,000 in a new artist before they see a profit, and fewer than half of the artists make those costs back. These are very sketchy figures. The record company spends a great deal more money, and much of it, including the $500,000 in promotion, is recoupable. That means the artist will eventually pay for it out of future royalties. In an article on Salon.com, "Courtney Love Does the Math," Love gets to the bottom line on a million-selling record. "So [the record company] profit is $6.6 million; the band may as well be working at a 7-Eleven." These economics and the fact that the major record labels have conglomerated down to a total of four have led to a proliferation of independent labels of all sizes. For more on this, see chapter eighty-seven, "Independence Daze."

Clive Davis, who doles out recording contracts to *American Idol* winners, advises aspiring artists: "If you're college material and you want to be an artist, wait until you get your full education, because the chances of making it are not good. You should be prepared for alternative careers. But if you love music to the extent that you can't dream of anything other than that, you should pursue that career until you feel that you've taken it down the road and have gotten the best professional judgments." It's a good thing Jo Dee Messina didn't hear that before she packed up her car and came to Nashville at the age of nineteen with nothing but her determination to make her lifelong dream come true.

It seems to us that writing songs for hit recording artists is the next best alternative to being one, and it has the advantage of not destroying your privacy or disturbing your family life. Instead of saying, "No sir, that's my baby" when someone wants to record a song you wanted to record yourself, we recommend you try the time-honored phrase, "Take my wife, please!" with a new twist: "Take my baby, please!"

77

HOLD IT, HOLD IT, NEVER LET IT GO

Know how to deal with songs that
get stuck "on hold" with producers

This is a story about the time it can take to get a recording on a song. Once upon a time, a songwriter sent off a tape of a song. For two long years, the tape sat in a pile gathering dust. By this time, the songwriter, whose name is Allan Rich, had forgotten about sending off the tape. Then, one day, Allan got a call. It was James Ingram, saying, "I've been so busy. I've had these songs piled up in my house for years. I'm finally getting a chance to listen to them. This is the first song in the last two years that made me cry. I want you to know that I'm cutting this tune. I want you to put it on hold for me."

When an artist or a producer asks a writer to put a song on hold, they are asking the writer not to show it to anyone else because they intend to record it. This is usually done on the phone or in person. It is a verbal agreement. There is no compensation to the songwriter for tying up a song and no guarantee that the song will actually be recorded. Meanwhile, if the writer holds to the hold, other recording opportunities for the song may come and go. Allan's song was on hold for another year before the song came out and became

the number one hit "I Don't Have the Heart." That was a hold that paid off!

However, it is a common experience for songwriters to get burned by putting a song on hold. Many artists take holds very lightly, while the songwriters who are waiting for that elusive recognition are clinging to the hold for dear life. Another writer told us: "I had four of my best songs on hold for a year with an artist. I was having lunch with a bunch of music people and one of them said, 'Did you hear so-and-so's new album?' I almost freaked at the table. I had been keeping on top of the situation and, as far as I knew, my songs were going to be on that album. They weren't." In that case, the artist held the songs but did not record them. It often happens that the artist even goes so far as recording the song, but it gets bumped off the album after the fact. This is because many artists record more songs than they intend to release on the album, then pick the ten strongest from those.

If you are asked to put a song on hold, you have to judge for yourself how serious the artist or producer is about recording the song. If you feel secure that the artist and producer mean what they are saying and really will cut the song, try to get them to commit to taking action within a definite period of time. Follow up when that time has elapsed and then decide if it's still worth keeping your song out of circulation.

If you have reason to feel that they are less than 100 percent reliable, you can commit to an equivalent percentage of reliability in holding the song. When they first ask for a hold, you can tell them you have already sent it to other people. If you get a definite bite, talk to the first artist or his representative. Ask him if he is really going to record the song. Tell him you need to know because you have someone else who wants to cut it.

This can get very touchy. You can anger and alienate the first artist this way. It's always best to be as up-front as possible. This route can also lead to missed recording opportunities if the artist or producer doesn't like your attitude.

This is one you'll have to play by ear.

═ 78 ═

MAKE ME A STAR

*Don't think that someone is going
to "make you" a success*

Songwriters experience a lot of rejection, especially in the beginning. During this long time of knocking on doors and having them slammed in our faces, songwriters dream of a Prince Charming publisher, or a fairy godmother producer, or *anybody* who will make the magic happen.

We remember the first time we thought it was happening. We showed some songs to a publisher in a multinational corporation. We had other connections with him and regarded him as a friend. He listened to two songs with no great reaction. On the third song, he literally jumped up out of his chair and shouted, "This is a great song; I love it!" Pat remembers thinking, "This is it. This is my dream come true. This publisher is actually jumping up and down over one of our songs."

We left his office flying high and waited for fame and fortune to knock down our door. Two weeks later, when we had heard nothing further from the publisher, we called him and asked about the song. He had forgotten about it. So much for fairy tales.

This feeling that someone is going to "make us" leads us to stumble over our tongues and walk on eggshells around people we think can do the trick. These actions give the very people we want to impress the message that we are insecure and uncomfortable (especially with those eggshells all over our tongues). This discomfort is contagious and makes people not want to deal with us. We make our worst fears a reality by believing that we are weak and they are strong.

It is sad but true that songwriters are not appreciated or recognized in many ways. The general public has the impression that the artists write all the songs they sing. Record labels contribute to this impression by not giving writers credit on CD labels.

Organizations representing songwriters have to fight for our rights against encroachment by piracy, censorship, illegal downloading, and users who don't want to pay for the use of our songs. Often this fight takes place in courts and legislatures that are neither impressed nor inclined to help unless Dolly Parton comes in to speak for us. Before a recent election, we were invited to meet all the candidates for state representative in Tennessee, right here in Music City, USA. We asked several of them, "How much money do you think a songwriter makes on the sale of a record?" We were given blank expressions and wild guesses: One dollar? Five dollars? They were shocked to learn that the real figure, depending on who publishes and how many writers are involved, is a penny or two—by law! We were amazed that these folks, who should be representing us, didn't have a clue. This is in spite of the fact that the entertainment industry, especially the music industry, is one of the few U.S. industries with a positive balance of trade. Countries in Europe offer higher royalties and more protection for their songwriters and copyright owners.

Considering the institutionalized disregard for the value of songwriters and the constant rejection that is number one on our job description, it's no wonder we wish someone would take care of us. The good news is there is someone who can make you a star, someone who cares about you, knows your value, and will give you everything you need to achieve your dream. That someone is you.

As the slogan of the Nashville Songwriters Association International states, "It all begins with a song." Without a great song to sing, an artist is nowhere. Without an artist singing a great song, the record labels have nothing to sell and the radio stations have nothing to play. If you have written a great song, you are going to make the person who uses it very rich. They may be a vehicle for you to get where you want to go, but you are the source.

Now don't get all smug and uppity. That won't win you any friends. Just realize your worth and approach your pitching situations with both self-respect and a reasonable regard for the people you are dealing with. They are not gods; they are people like you who love songs. They want to love your song just as much as you want them to love it. Sometimes they do love a song of yours but still can't use it because it doesn't fit the project they're working on at the moment. This is a sugarcoated rejection, but still a rejection. (For more on rejection, see the next chapter.)

For now, remember that it's your belief in yourself as a songwriter that will "make" you. Your belief will make others into believers. When you walk into a publisher's or producer's office, hold your head up high and don't be afraid. You have nothing to lose and everything to gain. Your songwriting gift may or may not be the gift this person needs right now, but it is still a valuable gift that will find its proper outlet if you keep valuing it and offering it.

79

NEVER AGAIN
Don't give up after being rejected

A close cousin to the closet songwriter is the songwriter who shows songs to one or two—or even a hundred—publishers, gets rejected, and gives up. We know this feeling intimately. We could wallpaper several rooms with our accumulated rejection letters. It's all well and good to say, "Don't take it personally." Personally, there have been times when we've had such powerful emotional reactions that it feels like hitting a cinder block wall at seventy miles per hour on a motorcycle. Fun, it's not.

The temptation to chuck all this crazy songwriter stuff gets strong at times. What can we do with these feelings? Why, write a song about them, of course!

I'm Never Gonna Write Another Song Again

I'm never gonna write another song again
Everything I write down comes out wrong
I'm packing up my old guitar and pen
And putting them in the garbage where
they belong

Chorus:

I'm never gonna write another song again
It hurts too much to try to tell the truth

And then somebody listens in a big
glass tower
He says he likes it
But he ain't got no use for it
I'm never gonna write
I'm giving up this fight
I'm never gonna write another
song again
I'm never gonna write another
song again

I'm never gonna hum another tune again
Never gonna search my mind for words
I'm burnin' up my demo tapes and then
I'm gonna try my luck at something
less absurd

Chorus: repeat

I'm never gonna stay awake at night again
Dreamin' I'll be on the radio
I'm trading in my Teac for a tent
And driving out to the forest to hear the
wind blow

Chorus: repeat and add:

I'm never gonna write
I'm giving up the fight
I'm never gonna write another song again
This is the last one
I'm never gonna write another song again

© Pea Pod Music

211

Luckily, we're too foolish to take our own advice. How do we hang in there in spite of the incredibly bad odds and the constant rejection? You gotta be nuts—nuts about songwriting. That's the bottom line. If you won't take no for an answer, no matter how many people say no to you, you make your success inevitable. The game goes to those who are left standing after the rest have quit.

Johnny Cash told a wonderful story about his early experiences with rejection. He was backstage complaining about how hard the road to success was, and Gene Autry heard him. Autry gave him a pat on the back and said, "Hell, son. If it was easy, everybody would be doing it."

Richard Marx went through six or seven years of rejection before he got his chance that led him to the top of the charts with "Hold On to the Night" and "Satisfied." Julie Gold was writing songs for twenty years before "From a Distance" was recorded. That song won the Grammy for Song of the Year. Billy Steinberg couldn't give away his songs for many years. We were amazed when Sam & Annie Tate told us that "I've Had My Moments," the wonderful song they wrote with Dave Berg, was rejected for five years before Emerson Drive made it a hit. There are the occasional overnight successes, but 99 percent of songwriters experience rejection 99 percent of the time.

We heard of a well-adjusted person who greeted each rejection with enthusiasm. She figured that she would have to go through a hundred rejections before she had one acceptance. Each time she was rejected she said, "Great! That means I'm one closer to that acceptance."

It helps to know that there are more variables in choosing a song than are known in your philosophy, Horatio. Financial politics, for instance, influence the choice of songs. A little bit of fine print in most new artists' contracts, called the controlled composition clause, says that the record company only has to pay three-fourths of the going mechanical royalty rate for any song the artist writes, co-writes, or has any control over. If outside songs are chosen that have to be paid at the full rate, the artist has to pay the difference out of his or her own pocket. This situation forces artists to keep their projects closed to outside songs.

One quick study of the songs on the *Billboard* charts will verify that most songs are written either by the artists or their producers. Maybe 2 or 3 percent of the Top 100 pop songs came from outside writers. The field is a bit more open in country music, where there is more respect for songwriters and songs in general.

For a song to be chosen for a recording project, it has to be the right song for the right artist at the right time heard by the right person in the right mood. That's a lot of rights to line up in a row. It's practically a miracle it happens at all. Here's a story our friend Lisa Palas tells. She co-wrote a song with Bernie Nelson. Each of them had a publisher and neither publisher thought enough of the song to make a demo of it. Awhile later, Lisa's publisher had a pitching session coming up and asked his assistant to put a bunch of songs on a tape for it. At the meeting, the publisher played the tape and the artist passed on song after song. Then, the work tape of Lisa and Bernie's song began to play! The assistant had put it on the tape by mistake because it had the same word in the title as another song that the publisher had really wanted. The publisher apologized to the artist, "Sorry, that's on there in error," and reached over to skip it. But the artist said, "Wait a minute, I like that." That's how Lisa got a Randy Travis/Kris Kristofferson duet cut on her song "We All Have to Walk Our Own Road." Lisa adds, "Both of those publishers really did a lot for me and they were right more than they were wrong." This was a miracle that made a rare wrong right!

Miracles aside, the artist is usually not the first person to hear and love the song. Let's say the first person is the publisher. After that first person gets excited by the song, it has to be run through a gauntlet of ears: those of the producer, the artist, the A&R person at the record label, various assorted record executives, perhaps an attorney, and the artist's manager, hairdresser, and astrologer. The point is, this is not one person's decision, and timing is everything.

Songwriters who are making it in today's market are tough, hardworking, smart, and well connected. They're competing with you and with each other for those same two or three songs on the charts that are open to outside songs. They make it their business to know who is about to

record and who is looking for songs now. They don't have nine-to-five jobs to cope with; they're fulltime songwriters. They do their homework and aim their songs with pinpoint accuracy at particular artists. And they live with rejection every day.

It's one thing when you do your pitching and get your response in the mail. You can weep in the privacy of your own room when you open the envelope you hoped would contain a lifetime contract with a million-dollar advance that turns out to have a fifth-generation photocopy of a form rejection letter. It's another thing to deal with rejection face-to-face. If you have the opportunity to show your songs to a publisher or producer in her office (a very rare opportunity), it will not do to show any anger or pain when the listener turns your song down. You may feel like screaming, but restrain yourself.

It's hard for the listener, too. They may feel guilty about saying no, and it's up to you to put them at ease so they will want to see you again. Relationship is the name of the game. If you can find a common ground to share as one person to another, such as sports, children, or a joke, do it. Don't waste your listener's time. Be friendly, but be businesslike. Get to the point and pick up any pointers the listener is willing to pass along. Be sure to say "Thank you" when you go. Then go home and scream into your pillow.

It's important to express that disappointment appropriately. If you hit your listener with it, you may never see that person again. But if you don't let loose with it somehow, it will build up inside you as resentment and rage until you are immobilized.

Songwriter/vocalist Morgan Ames put it bluntly:

> Getting a thick skin and staying sensitive at the same time is a talent of its own. If you can't maintain your vulnerability while getting killed for lunch and breakfast, you really should not be in this business. I don't encourage anyone who isn't driven to do it to be in this business. If you do not have a built-in ability to not die when they kill you, you will be one of the bitter, defeated people of this business. My theory is that when they kill you, they don't mean anything by it. When they kill you and walk away, they look back and if you're picking yourself up, they take note of that as they move up.

Songwriter Sue Schiffrin was "killed" by a person she respected very much and the experience gave her something to live for:

> When I started writing, there was this wonderful man named Irwin Schuster, who was at Screen Gems Music. He was a great song man. This guy had ears; he could hear a song. In three seconds, he knew if it was a hit or not. He picked up all these great Barry Mann and Carole King songs.
>
> I went into his office and I had been writing for about six months or a year and I played him my songs. He said to me, "Sue, do yourself a favor. Get married and have kids." I was devastated. I said to him, "You know what, Irwin, you're going to eat those words one of these days." And that was the thing that inspired me to do the impossible. Every time I wrote a song, I thought, "I wonder what Irwin's going to think of this song."
>
> It was true, I was not a great natural immediate songwriter. I had to learn it and I didn't learn it by going to school. I learned it by doing it. I don't care what anybody tells you, if you really want it badly enough, if you care, if your heart's really in it, you'll do it and get better.
>
> Years later, I had lunch with him and he said, "I take it all back."

We heard of another story in which the same change of heart took place in less than a half hour. A songwriter in Nashville brought a song to an A&R person at a record company, who was not impressed. He said, "I don't hear it," which didn't mean he was hearing impaired; he just didn't like the song.

Many of the publishers and record companies are near each other in Nashville. The songwriter had an appointment with a publisher across the street immediately following this rejection. He played the same song. The publisher loved it. He said, "This would be great for Tammy Sue Doe. Let's go show it to her record label."

So they walked across the street, back into the same A&R person's office. The publisher played the song and the A&R

person said, "Yeah, that would be great for Tammy Sue." Go figure!

The secret of hanging in there as a songwriter is to keep saying yes to songwriting. Keep taking the next step. One step at a time. Write the song, make the demo, make connections, pitch songs, learn about the music business, and do that all over again a hundred times. Number 101 could be the one.

Even if it isn't, even if your number never comes up, aren't you doing this because you love it? No one can take that away from you. Songwriting is good for the soul, it's nonviolent, and it's not fattening. How many activities have all that going for them? Only you can prevent rejection burnout. *Never* say, "Never again."

80

BURNING BRIDGES
Don't leave a trail of enemies behind

Those who would rather fight than quit represent the other extreme reaction to the fierce competition and constant rejection of songwriting. We've heard of a songwriter who attacked a publisher with a chair because the publisher turned down his song. We've also heard of a big-name artist who starts out "wanting a piece of the song" in exchange for the favor of recording it and ends up claiming the entire song and all the writer's royalties. We know a manager who got an assignment for her songwriter client and then took it away from him because she decided she wanted to do it herself. All's fair on the songwriting battlefield and might makes right? Wrong!

It's a small world, and the music business world is even smaller. Everybody knows practically everybody else. When music business people gather to schmooze, they like to tell stories. Word got around about the violent songwriter, and all who heard refused to risk an appointment with him. Likewise, eventually no one wanted to deal with the artist, and his big name dwindled from household word to has-been. The manager lost her songwriting client and her credibility. The songwriter

went on to get a big writing/production deal and lived much more happily after breaking with her.

If you think you can afford to treat someone badly, think again. It's not just the bridge between you and a particular person that you are burning. You are scorching your reputation and damaging your credibility. The music business is like any other: There are many wonderful, honest business people whom you can trust absolutely, and there are also a lot of not-so-wonderful, not-so-honest people whom you can trust as far as you can throw. If you want to work with the good guys, you have to be a good guy yourself. They can afford to choose their contacts. If you look like trouble, they won't want to deal with you.

The music business is like life. Ideally, you don't do the right thing because you think you should or in order to impress others. You do it because it feels good to be totally honest in your dealings. That's the real payoff: that people will be attracted to you and want to work with you because they know they can trust you is just a beneficial side effect.

Let's assume that you're resolved not to be the perpetrator of the low blow. What can you do when someone else does you wrong? If copyright ownership, a contract or significant income is involved, it may be time to see a lawyer about your legal options. Often the money involved doesn't warrant an expensive legal proceeding. You need to examine the situation carefully. Didn't you have an uncomfortable feeling about how things were going? What made you think it was going to turn out all right despite your gut feeling about it? Could you have been indulging in some hopeful fantasy that clouded your instincts about this person? Why didn't you speak up earlier? If the bad ending was a total surprise, why didn't you see it coming?

These are questions we've asked ourselves when situations exploded in our faces. It's a healing and growing process to take responsibility for our own part in the bad things that happen to us. Each time we understand how we contributed to the situation, we get better at spotting the problems and avoiding them the next time. It is not healthy, however, to get into self-hate and blame or to obsess about the situation. Study it, learn from it, and move on.

Part of moving on is resolving not to bad-mouth the person who did you wrong. It doesn't make you look good, no matter how you look at it. Are you bragging that you got involved with someone that took advantage of you? Does someone you can trust tell tales on someone else behind their back? No.

Find a safe, personal place to express your anger and resentment. Then you are free to act in a businesslike way when it comes to dealing with people in the music business. Don't be fooled by the artistic nature of the product or the casual style of dress. Music business is big business. Look at every encounter as if it were a job interview. You wouldn't complain about how badly your last employer treated you. Not if you wanted the job.

If someone else burns the bridge between the two of you, forgive, for your sake, and remember. Remember to watch for the warning signals you missed. A friend explained this to us in a vivid image that has stayed for many years. Lessons in life are like bricks hurled at your face. You stand there and the bricks hit you square in the face several times, catching you totally by surprise. Then you begin to notice the bricks approaching just before they hit you. Twenty bricks or so later, you learn to duck so they miss you entirely. With a little practice, you can spot the not-so-honest people in the music business and gracefully avoid them.

Honesty is the best policy in every situation, including songwriting. The Golden Rule also applies in the music business. It feels good and it's good for your career to keep as many bridges intact as possible. A songwriting opportunity just may want to come across that bridge.

LET MIKEY DO IT

*Don't expect to sit back and let the
publisher or lawyer do all the work*

It's a great day when you sign your first single song contract with a publisher. By all means, break out the champagne or the sparkling cider and celebrate. Look back on all the effort that got you where you are. The dozens of rewrites, the hours in the studio, the hundreds of rejections, the contract offered, the lawyer consulted, the contract renegotiated—and now, the signature. This is a moment to savor. All you have to do now is sit back, let the publisher pitch your song to Madonna, and collect your royalties after she makes it a number one hit.

Would that it were so. The reality is that, even though you have a publisher supposedly working to get your song cut, you have no guarantee that the publisher will do anything. All you have is your reversion clause, which says you'll get the song back after a set period of time if the publisher does not cause a commercially released recording.

Even songwriters who are signed as staff writers can't depend on their publishers to work their songs. A staff writer is signed to a long-term contract. During the term of the contract, the publisher owns all the songs written by the staff writer, and the writer receives regular advances against royalties that her songs, the publisher hopes, will earn.

You would think that a publisher would be motivated to ensure the staff writer's songs are recorded and earn back those advances. That wasn't Sue Schiffrin's experience:

> They take a song, they don't even comment about whether they think the song is great or lousy or whether it's weak or whether it's strong. They pitch it to artists, but they put it on a CD and send it in the mail. At the record company, they've got a thousand CDs that came in that week. They all go in the garbage.

> You can't be just a songwriter anymore, you have to also be a publisher as well. Even though I have a publishing deal with the largest publishing company in the world, I still have to go out and get my own covers. Publishers have become collection agencies; they're banks. When I trust my publisher to go out and get me a cover, it doesn't happen. But when I make phone calls to

record companies and make relationships with people, I get more cuts.

So putting your signature on a publishing contract does not give you a license to sit back and relax. It just gives you another calling card and a little bit of clout, because it says someone else believes in the song besides you. You're in partnership with the publisher. Depending on the individual you're dealing with, you may find that the publisher would appreciate your input and willingness to expend some energy to push the song. Perhaps the publisher would be open to a casting session, in which both of you talk about which artists each of you has in mind for the song.

You might also find that the publisher wants nothing to do with you. If that is the case, think twice before signing another song to that publisher. Music is a person-to-person business. Find a person who will deal with you as a person. You can get abuse anywhere. You can always pitch the song yourself and not have to share the royalties with someone who won't give you the time of day.

Another person who will not "do it" for you is your attorney. Your attorney's job is to explain the situation to you and to advise you of the pros and cons of the various alternatives. Your attorney can tell you what the contract means, but it's up to you to understand it. You need to ask questions until you do understand it, because you are going to have to decide what to do. Your attorney cannot make decisions for you.

You are setting yourself up for some nasty surprises if you think your publisher or your attorney is going to take care of you. Only you have your best interests as the number-one priority. You may be high on your publisher's or attorney's list, but it's still a list to them. To you, it's your life. It is always going to be your responsibility to look out for yourself.

We don't mean that you should be hostile or demanding. But it is necessary to be assertive. Don't be afraid to ask questions. Get as many opinions and as much information as you can. Then use what you learn to take care of yourself.

82

READY OR NOT, HERE I COME!

Know what you're doing before you move to a music center

Thinking of moving to L.A.? Or Nashville? Or New York City? These are the Big Three when it comes to the business of music and writing songs. You can improve your writing skills and read the great selection of books on songwriting and the music business in your hometown. You can try to make connections for your songs through the mail and on the phone and the Internet. But you will be in competition with the songwriters physically present in the offices of the people to whom you are only an envelope among thousands of other envelopes.

Some people will tell you that you definitely must move to one of these cities if you want to make it as a songwriter. They have a point. If you're ultra-serious about being a songwriter, pack your bags. But don't make the leap until you take a look at what you'll be in for. At least, make a vacation/research trip to the music center you think might suit you best. How do you decide which city will be your new home?

Let's take a look at L.A. first. If you don't live in Los Angeles, you might have a romantic picture of the glamour capital of the world where the streets are paved

with stars. There are stars on the sidewalks of Hollywood, but they're hard to see through the dirt and smog. There are wonderful places to live on the beach and in canyons where you could almost forget that the city stretches for seventy miles in every direction but west—if you have lots and lots of money to rent them. Real estate prices in Los Angeles are sky-high. There is public transportation, but your music business appointments could be twenty miles apart, and it takes triple the time to get anywhere on a bus, so having a car and being willing to spend hours in it every day crawling in snail-paced traffic are practically mandatory. L.A. is huge. People who live here carry a two-hundred-page map book in their cars and have to use it all the time.

The music business is very large in L.A., which means that getting some kind of job in the field is not impossible. Barry Manilow started in the mailroom of a record label and so can you. L.A. and all the little cities that surround and are surrounded by L.A. also abound with employment opportunities of every description. The climate is mild, if you can stand the smog, and it never rains except for when it pours. And when you get your big recording, you can go to Disneyland to celebrate.

L.A. is the site of ASCAP's "I Create Music" EXPO and TAXI's Road Rally, two excellent educational opportunities. If you are considering a move to L.A., try a research trip in April or November timed to coincide with one of these two events. After the demise of the National Academy of Songwriters, grassroots groups came together to fill songwriters' constant need for information exchange. NSAI has a couple of regional workshops in the L.A. area, Just Plain Folks (www.jpfolks.com) has a chapter, the L.A. Songwriters Network (www.songnet.org), and Songsalive (www.songsalive.org) have regular gatherings. There's a veritable alphabet soup of organizations in town: ASCAP, BMI, SESAC, SGA (Songwriter's Guild of America), NARAS (The Recording Academy), CCC (California Copyright Conference), and LAWIM (L.A. WoMen in Music). All of them have educational and social events.

Thinking of moving to Nashville? You are not alone. Musicians and songwriters flock to Nashville every day. Having flown the L.A. coop for Nashville the day after our youngest left for college, we can speak from experience. You will be amazed how friendly the folks are in Nashville. It has been voted, and deservedly so, the friendliest city in the U.S. Every door is held open, drivers let you in the lanes, and people call you "Ma'am" and "Sir." We are grateful every day for being here. We are also concerned that the city's efforts

to attract major businesses (Nissan moved their U.S. headquarters here, for example) and the accompanying building boom and influx of people might ruin the small-town feel of Nashville. The good side of that boom is that the job market is growing with it.

The real estate market is also on the rise here, with people buying and selling lofts/condos for a profit before they're even built. There are good neighborhoods where you can buy a house for less than you'd pay for rent in L.A. It's also possible to find affordable places to rent in Nashville. Songwriters share the rentals of houses and apartments while they're working their "day jobs" and making songwriting connections at night.

Because of the glut of musicians and songwriters in Nashville, it's a tough town for making money in music. Hundreds of songwriters sing every night in dozens of clubs—all for free. Actually, it costs the songwriters the gas to get there and whatever they spend in the venue. If you're extra good at playing or singing, you could make thirty to fifty dollars a song working on demos. Unless you can stack up a lot of work, that's not going to pay your rent. And don't dream that your big break will set you up for life. Nashville is known as a "five-year" town, meaning it takes five years to get that break. And even a number one song won't keep you forever. A good friend of ours had one of those chart-topping songs not too long ago and still works as a plumber to make ends meet.

The major record labels and most of the major publishers' offices are concentrated within walking distance of each other in an area called Music Row. However, a car is needed to travel to your home base, since Nashville's public transportation will probably not serve your needs.

Nashville is Music City, USA; country is the main focus but not the only kind of music being made there today. The song is the thing in Nashville, and it has the reputation of being the ultimate songwriter's town. NSAI holds weekly workshops and special professional writers' events several times a year. The Songwriter's Guild has a Nashville office. Call ahead to these organizations to plan your research trip at a time when something special is happening for songwriters. Other organizations to visit in Nashville are the Recording Academy (NARAS), the Country Music Association, the Gospel Music Association, ASCAP, BMI, and SESAC. While you're in town, we hope you'll drop by our Sounding Board workshop, which is held every Monday night except for major holidays.

Looking to take a bite out of the Big Apple? Bring extra teeth! New York is a rough town. As native New Yorkers, we can tell you that there's an awful lot of cement in New York. The people move fast and talk even faster. We distinctly remember wondering why people talked about the weather when we were living there. We traveled in subways and walked through tunnels underground to work and never saw the sky. So what's the big deal about the weather? The forecast for New York: cold, slushy winters and hot, muggy summers.

Finding a place to live is difficult and very expensive, but public transportation is great. You don't need a car, and you probably wouldn't want one because there's no place to park it. Of course, New York is one of the major cities of the world, and jobs of all kinds are available for the quick and the persistent.

Numerous record and publishing companies have offices in New York, as do ASCAP, BMI, SESAC, the Recording Academy, and the Songwriters Guild. All of these organizations sponsor educational events of interest to songwriters. New York is home for all kinds of music, especially musical theatre and jazz. But your country songs won't find a home here in the concrete canyons.

The three big music centers are not your only options. Quite a few cities generate their own special forms of music: Austin, Dallas, and Houston; Atlanta; San Francisco and Bakersfield, California; Chicago; Detroit; Memphis; Miami; Minneapolis; Muscle Shoals, Alabama; Philadelphia; and Seattle. In addition, there are songwriter groups springing up everywhere. Do you know where your nearest songwriter group is?

Our advice is to research your destination music center. Take a two-week trip to explore the area, preferably timed with a songwriter-related event. Research your housing costs and employment options. If you have to work a day job just to pay the rent, you may be too exhausted at night to pursue your music career. Ask people who know the city about which areas are high in crime, or call the police station that services the neighborhood you are considering. Also research the songwriting community to see if you could happily become a part of it.

If you decide you want to move permanently, save up and have a three-month cushion of money after you've paid your first and last months' rent and the utility deposits. Then get yourself out there and meet as many people as you can. You came to the music center to make connections, so get out there and connect!

But what if your life won't let you pull up stakes so easily? You have a great job. Your spouse doesn't want to move. You don't want to disrupt your children's lives. Your aging parent needs you close by. Can you still be a songwriter if you don't live in a music business city? We'll answer that question in the next chapter.

≡ 83 ≡

DISTANT DREAMS

*Don't despair of being a songwriter
because you live in the middle of nowhere*

You have a great life! Good job, nice home, strong family ties; the roots that connect you to your community go deep. The trouble is, you have this burning need to write songs. And you've been told you can't really do that unless you move to a major music center. Well, that's true—and not!

Our thanks to Barbara Cloyd (www. barbaracloyd.com) for the title of this chapter. We attended the NSAI Songposium class she taught by that name, and much of the information we'll share with you here was gathered from her class. As hostess of the Monday night open mike at the world-famous Bluebird Café, Barbara meets countless songwriters who come from everywhere to line up for the opportunity to sing on the same spot Garth Brooks was "discovered." Everyone in the Songposium class (except us) was from out of town. They came to hear how they could realize their distant dreams. Barbara gave them a wake-up call. "Yes, if you really want to be a songwriter, you have to move to a music center." We don't think that's what they expected to hear!

But, as Barbara added, "Life changes. Businesses close. Kids graduate. People get divorced." The day may come when the move to a music center will be feasible. In the meantime, there's plenty to do. First and foremost, you can become a better songwriter. As we've said before, that's one of the great things about songwriting—it's a never-ending learning process. Lucky for all of us, educational opportunities abound. There are excellent books that cover all the songwriting bases. John Braheny's *The Craft and Business of Songwriting* is a veritable one-book encyclopedia on everything songwriting. There are books on melody writing, lyric writing, idea generating, demo production, making and selling your own CD—you name it. There are also CDs and DVDs on many songwriting subjects.

Then there's the Internet. You may not be able to be there in the flesh, but you can be there "virtually." Even if there isn't an NSAI regional workshop in your area (see chapter forty-four, "Diving In, Crawling Out," for how to start one), you should join NSAI because you'll benefit from attending their Thursday night workshops online at www.nashvillesongwriters.com. And don't worry if you're busy on Thursdays. Membership entitles you to access all of the archives, which go back several years. You'll find a parade of music publishers, hit songwriters, and songwriting teachers waiting to share their experiences and information with you.

Or, you may want to go to songwriting college online. Try SongU (www.songU .com/luboff) for free. Nashville's Danny Arena and Sara Light have done more than provide excellent courses you can take at your own pace and real-time cyber-classes; they've created a community that covers the earth. In one online "12 Steps to Building Better Songs" course, we collaborated on a song with twenty-five people who were scattered all over the United States and Canada, plus one writer in India who got up at three o'clock in the morning to be with us. We were able to talk with each other, read written suggestions, display a handout on a "white board," and call up other files and sites for everyone to see. It's truly amazing and wonderful.

The other highly respected source of online learning is Berklee College of Music, based in Boston (www.berkleemusic .com/school/courses/songwriting). Berklee offers top-notch teachers and courses, but a single course taken for credit can cost three times more than a full year's unlimited access to all of SongU's courses and services.

You might choose to get one-on-one songwriting coaching, a.k.a. song consultations. That's a service we offer (www.writesongs.com) and we know a number of other good people who do as well. For more on that subject, see chapter one hundred and one "Dollars and Nonsense."

Once you have your songs honed to perfection, you can pitch them from afar. TAXI (www.Taxi.com) is the A&R vehicle for you if you don't live in a music center. As screeners for TAXI, we can attest to the impeccable ethics of the TAXI organization. If TAXI forwards your song to a listing, it has a seal of approval that gives it a boost from the "unsolicited and unknown" pile of CDs to the "listen to this one" pile. Visit the TAXI Web site for success stories. SongU members can use their "Spin 'N' Pitch" opportunities to get their songs heard. You might want to invest in a good tip sheet. Row Fax (www.music row.com), Songlink International (www .songlink.com) and New on the Charts (www.notc.com) are three high-level tip sheets. These run $150–400 per year. Look for listings that accept songlinks and mp3 files. When your song arrives in their e-mail box, they won't be able to tell that you're not in a music center. The song's the thing!

Some songwriters make frequent trips to the music center of their choice. They get a cell phone number with the appropriate area code and a P.O. box to give the impression that they live in the city. Some of our friends have understanding spouses in distant cities who tolerate living without their songwriting mate.

There's lots of flying back and forth for conjugal visits.

We do recommend that you make the effort to make personal connections by actually visiting your music city-of-choice as much as possible. But it's just as important to look to your hometown for connections. If there is not already a songwriting community, build one. Songwriters will come.

The band you see playing in your local club may have the talent and drive to be the next big thing. And you'll have been there at the beginning. Other songwriters who live near you are great resources of information, talent, and commiseration. Seek them out and share your love of songwriting. There's no place like home.

84

POLITICALLY INCORRECT

*Don't think that politics have
nothing to do with songwriting*

Songwriting is an art of the heart. We flail around in the unknown trying to find the perfect word, the perfect note, the perfect chord. It's a spiritual experience! What's Washington, DC got to do with that?

On one level, the answer to that question is: "everything." For one thing, the Constitution of the United States, in Article One, Section 8, defines as one of Congress' basic powers "To promote the progress of science and useful arts, by securing for limited times to authors and inventors the exclusive right to their respective writings and discoveries ..." That power gave rise to the Copyright Law, a.k.a. U.S. Code Title 17 (www.copyright.gov/title17), which defines our rights as creators of the intellectual property we call songs. When was the last time you read the Copyright Law? If it weren't for the Copyright Law, you could write songs forever and never make a penny from them because you wouldn't be guaranteed ownership of your creations.

Well, some hardware manufacturers would like that to be the case. They want to sell CD players, mp3 players, iPods, and whatever else they come up with before you finish reading this sentence. They do not want to pay for the music that you can download onto those devices, and they don't want the consumer to pay either. They want the music to flow like water from a faucet. They're not interested in how much blood, sweat, and tears you put into the song or how much money you spent in the process.

The Copyright Law was originally written in 1909 and did not get a major overhaul until 1976. That was almost seventy years during which songwriters got paid the same amount of money for each record sold (two cents), while prices on everything else increased exponentially. What other worker in the United States has a maximum allowed payment set by Congress and doesn't get a raise for seventy years?

The Copyright Law is not carved in stone. It is the subject of a constant tug-of-war among various interested parties. Now, more than ever, a world-wide battle rages on as new technologies make it easy to capture perfect copies of digitally produced music. Visit www.copyright.gov/legislation. There you will find the most recent bills proposed and passed into law that change the details of the Copyright Law.

Those bills that may or may not become law are where the fight is fought.

One of the major champions of the songwriters' cause is the president of the Songwriters Guild of America, Rick Carnes. He fought for and won an unprecedented victory, a seat at the table for songwriters with record companies and publishers when decisions are being made about the division and distribution of digital income from songs. That proposal died before it was passed into law, but, as we write, Rick is lacing up his gloves for another round next year.

Rick challenges songwriters to get informed and get involved:

> Every once in a while, type in "copyright law," or "copyright congress" in some Internet search engine. Find out what issues are affecting songwriters. Go to the Songwriters Guild Web site (www.songwritersguild.com). Go to the ASCAP, BMI, and SESAC Web sites. Don't just read which stars are having what hits, look a little deeper into the Web site. Read what's happening politically, because nobody's immune to the Copyright Law. It affects every creator.
>
> If the quality of your government's protection of copyright is poor, you will have a poor life, regardless of how successful you are. If the quality of your government's protection of copyright is good, you can have a very good life even if you have an only mediocre career. The number one determiner of your success will be your government, not your output as a songwriter. If we

only got one-quarter of the earnings of the record, a mere 25 percent of the take, I would never have had to write another song after "Can't Even Get the Blues." But the fact that we got two cents of the sale at the time, and less than 1½ percent of the profits of radio and airplay, I got nothing. Radio got rich, the record labels got rich. That's because of the way the copyright law is set up. It allows that to happen. So the poor quality of protection of songwriters, of our earnings, has determined the quality of my life.

And it's not just the quality of your life as a songwriter. It's the quality of your children's lives and their children's lives. One of the changes in the Copyright Law made the duration of copyright protection "life, plus seventy years." That means you own the song as long as you live and your heirs own the song for seventy years after the last collaborator dies. If you write with a young collaborator who lives fifty years longer than you do, your heirs could be collecting royalties on your songs for 120 years.

It all comes down to people making decisions in Washington, DC. Who are they? What decisions are they making that will affect your family for generations? How can you have an impact on those decisions? Aren't you curious?

The answer to the question "Who are these people?" is easy to find on the Internet or in your phone book. The answer to "How can I have an impact?" is in the next chapter.

85

BOONDOCKS BLUES

Don't think you're not important to the songwriting world because you don't live in a music center

Whenever we conduct our collaboration workshops, whether we travel to a town far from Music City or writers come to Nashville for educational events like Songposium, we hear songwriters singing the same tune. It goes like this: "There are no songwriters where I live. I'm out in the middle of nowhere." If you're singing the boondocks blues, we have news for you: You may be more important to the songwriting cause than the biggest hit writer in a music center. According to Debi Cochran, NSAI's legislative director, "It couldn't be further from the truth that you have to be in a major music city in order for your congressman to be important."

Debi is talking about the fact that the major decisions in the ever-changing and ever-challenging world of laws that affect songwriters are being made by legislators who do *not* represent music centers. Do an Internet search for the following: House Ways and Means Committee, Senate Finance Committee, House Commerce Committee, Senate Commerce Committee, House Judiciary Committee, and Senate Judiciary Committee. Check out the member lists on these committees. It's

your representative from Iowa, Vermont, Oregon, and Idaho.

Here's what their decisions mean to songwriters. The Ways and Means/Finance committees deal with, among other things, how taxes are collected. What's that got to do with songwriters? Plenty. On May 17, 2006, after five years of intense effort by NSAI, which included individual songwriters carting their guitars up to Capitol Hill to serenade legislators, the Songwriters Capital Gains Tax Equity Act was signed into law. Prior to the passage of that change to the U.S. Tax Code, songwriters paid as much as 40 percent in individual income tax and self-employment taxes when they sold their catalogs. (This refers to the sale of the publishing on a large group of songs.) Today, songwriters and writers/artists pay a flat 15 percent tax rate, just like their corporate counterparts have always done. Debi says:

> The bill was sponsored in Congress by John Tanner from Tennessee, and by Ron Lewis from Bardstown, Kentucky. Bardstown is certainly not a major music center. But Ron Lewis was on the House Ways and Means Committee. And when we sat down and

told him that equal partners in a publishing company would pay different taxes on catalog sales if one of those equal partners happened to be the songwriter who created the songs, he just couldn't believe that it was even true. He said, "That's not fair." And we said, "That's what we think!" So here's a congressman from Bardstown, Kentucky who took on an age-old tax inequity and got it fixed." Successful songwriters who sell their catalogs will now save many thousands of dollars in taxes.

"But," you say, "I'm not a successful songwriter; what do I care?" How about your ability to post your songs on a Web site and collect money from the people who download them? You can do that from anywhere and there are lots of people who just love to build their own unique collections of songs and are happy to pay the dollar or so per song to do that. How much of that dollar will you get? How will you get it? Will you get it at all? The House and Senate Commerce Committees deal with all of the new technology areas affecting how songwriters' creative content is used and compensated. As of this writing, there are members on those committees from Nebraska, North Dakota, Michigan, and Ohio, among other places that we don't associate with the music business. But if you live there, you, as a constituent, have more power over that member than we do.

The House and Senate Judiciary Committees deal with what is legal and what is not legal. Debi gets emotional talking about this one:

Napster was one of the first companies to throw out the idea: 'If I can steal it, I have the right to.' And they tried to educate a whole generation of young people to demand that music should be free. Sorry, but you can't steal my intellectual property because it's convenient for you to do so and because you can make money off it!" It's not a new thing that people don't want to pay for the songs that shape their lives, but it is new that technological developments have made it easy to download perfect copies. The word copyright comes from the "right" to "copy." Intellectual property is just as real as any property. You wouldn't want someone to steal your car. Copying a song without the right to do so is stealing. It's a crime. We hope that you will live this truth and spread the message.

And just like you'd be wise to hook up with an up-and-coming artist in your hometown who has potential to hit the big time, it's smart to connect with your local politicians. Debi advises:

You need to be in touch with people who are running your city and county and state, because some of those people are going to go on to be national leaders. They need to be engaged right off the bat. Technology and the issues surrounding these changes in technology are important in every city in the world.

You can change your tune from the "Boondocks Blues" to "I Am Songwriter, Hear Me Roar."

PART 9

THE CD RELEASE PARTY'S OVER

Post-Record Release Problems

86

MAJOR LABEL MISHAPS

*The record deal rainbow does not
necessarily lead to a pot of gold*

There are songwriters who are also excellent performers. Many of these writers dream of lining their walls with their own gold records. It's a worthy dream, but getting there can be a nightmare.

If your goal is to get signed by a major record label, what does that mean to you as a songwriter? Some writers develop a case of tunnel vision, which leads to self-limiting decisions. Case in point, Billy Steinberg's illuminating story:

> I had a band and I kept doing these demos to try to get a deal as an artist. But all these A&R people would say, "We have such-and-such an artist on our label and we'd like to have him cut this song." I was always disappointed because I was calling up to hear them say, "We want to sign you to make a record." At a certain point, the light bulb went on. I realized I'm really not a great singer, but I am a good songwriter. I was very stubborn; I didn't want to see that.

Billy learned this lesson the hard way. Only after he began to concentrate on his strengths did he become an extremely successful songwriter. Take a good, honest look at yourself. If you're thinking about simultaneously wearing the distinctly different career hats of writer and artist, check out how they fit by looking in the mirror the world provides you. Ask yourself serious questions, such as:

Am I willing to live the lifestyle of a recording artist? Can you handle the inevitable rejection you will experience trying to get your career going? Can you handle long periods of separation from your spouse and family while you do a concert tour to promote your record?

Do I have an outstanding talent as an artist? If you're in this for the long run, you have to believe in yourself and your talent. You have to put that belief to the test by scrutinizing the truth about yourself. Discovering what your gift is and how you will give it to the world is an ongoing process of self-examination. Talent is not enough. It will take very hard work and dogged determination for you to hang in there and stand out from the crowd enough to attract a major label's attention.

Do I want to be a recording artist more than anything? You're going to need a real hunger for expressing yourself as an artist to make it through the obstacle course you're going to face. If you know in your heart that you couldn't stop it if you tried, you can surrender to your destiny gracefully. If you're being driven by the sheer pleasure of doing something you love, there is no way you can fail, no matter what level of fame and fortune you do or do not reach.

If the answer to any of these questions is *maybe*, you don't have to give up your dream of being an artist. You may want to put it on hold while you concentrate on your exquisite skill as a lyricist. When you become a successful songwriter, you will have credibility and be presented with opportunities to expose your previously hidden talent. Many publishing companies have production arms that embrace writers with artist potential. That's how Dierks Bentley, Lee Ann Womack, and Terri Clark got signed. Or read on to the next chapter about being an independent artist.

If you're still determined to be a recording superstar, you need to know that others who have pursued and captured that dream were in for some rude awakenings. We've heard story after story of artists who got signed and then put on the back burner because the record label lost interest. The label records songs with the artist from time to time over the course of several years, but nothing ever gets released. Or the label releases a record, but they decide not to promote it until it reaches a certain slot on the charts—but it never gets there because they didn't promote it. One duo we know of had a couple of singles released and a $750,000 investment by the label in recording an album and shooting videos. Imagine their chagrin when the label dropped them and took the loss rather than release the album. How about the writers/artists who had a song climbing the charts and got loans from the bank based on potential future ASCAP royalties? They're still paying off the interest years after the label dropped them. Then there are the artists who sell lots and lots of records but don't make any money because the record label recoups enormous expenses from the artists' royalties. And don't forget the artists who have to fight the record labels in court to get the money owed them.

How can you avoid major label mishaps? Maybe you can't, but it helps to have someone on your side. Tim McGraw spoke up for Jo Dee Messina when she got dropped from a label. They're big names now, but there was a time when they were young and struggling artists together. Martina McBride used to sell merchandise on Garth Brooks' tours. When she got signed, he went to her label and told the people there that they needed to get behind her; she was special. The moral of those stories is: Make friends wherever you go. You never know who will be your friend indeed when you're in need.

As an artist, you will need to surround yourself with people you can trust who will help your career. A key person is your manager. A strong manager can open doors for you at a record label and keep your relationship with the label positive. A producer could be the one who will make the connection for you. (Hint: Look for someone who is fairly well known but not too busy. Music business attorneys sometimes pitch artists to labels, too. At the level of the major labels, it's big business and you will need a team of folks who carry big sticks to go to bat for you.)

If you're batty enough to want to be a writer/artist, but you're not willing to do big-label battle, there is a way. Read on.

≡ 87 ≡

INDEPENDENCE DAZE

*Don't think your work is done
when you've produced your own CD*

Let's take up where we left off in the last chapter: You are one of those songwriters who is also an excellent performer. You've tried to break through to a major label deal with no success. Or you've made a conscious choice to eschew the big-business politics of the major labels and strike out on your own as an independent artist. Ain't technology grand? Now that you can fit what used to be a huge recording studio into your laptop, you can produce your very own CD. You can send it to a CD manufacturing service and get it wrapped nicely, just like the CDs they used to sell at Tower Records—before the Tower fell. Hmmm … if Tower couldn't sell enough CDs to stay afloat, how are you going to sell yours? Have you just invested several thousand dollars in high-tech wallpaper?

Almost everyone we know has a thousand CDs tucked away in a closet somewhere. While they were in the studio recording those CDs, dreams of sales danced in their heads. Sure, they sell one or two when they sing out at a club, but at that rate it'll take a decade to sell them. Meanwhile, they're not recouping the money they spent.

As screeners for TAXI and judges for Just Plain Folks, we've had the pleasure of listening to hundreds of these independently produced CDs. We are absolutely amazed at the wonderful music being produced by writers all over the country. So if they're not selling, it's not because the material isn't good. It must be because the writers didn't realize that producing and manufacturing the CD was just the beginning of the job.

It's great to be an independent artist and not have to deal with the politics and pressures we wrote about in the last chapter. But being your own record label means you are the one who has to do *all* the jobs. That means you do the radio, TV, and press promotion. You set up tours to promote the sale of your CD. You travel from town to town selling your music. You see to it that CDs are in the stores in the areas where you will be performing. You establish and maintain an Internet presence. According to the Songsalive! (www.songsalive.org) president and co-founder, gilli moon, it's a full-time job and then some. gilli says:

The Internet is the hugest tool of all for the independent artist. You want to draw fans to your Web site. Once there, fans should be able to get news about your activities, buy your music, sign up for mailings, read your blog, join your fan club—get everything they want. [See how she does it at www.gillimoon. com.] You need to create links to other sites. MySpace (www.myspace.com) is key for independent marketing because you can leave comments on different pages, or find new friends and new fans and generate a community fan database. It's a great networking tool. That also helps you book gigs because you can contact fans in the region you're going to go to and they can help with setting up and promoting your gigs. General Internet promotion includes participating in discussion groups, writing your own blog and getting on to other people's blogs.

You can offer your CDs on the Internet, either as hard copies or downloads. CD Baby (www.cdbaby.com) is an excellent place to accomplish both types of purchase possibilities. Broadjam (www.bro adjam.com) and iTunes (www.itunes. com) are also good sites, but only for downloads. Making your music available through sites like these and on your own site can generate some sales on the Internet. But if you really want to create a growing fan base, you'll have to hit the road, and you're going to have to hit it hard. As gilli put it, "I'm always on the road." We get e-mails containing long lists of dates and places from friends living the indie artist life. They're out there singing at clubs, events, and house concerts for months at a time. If you like being at home, this is not the life for you.

Happily, as an indie artist, you have more freedom of choice than a major label artist. When a big label spends a million dollars on your album, they're going to send you out on a national tour to support their release of your CD. As an indie artist, you can make the traveling life more manageable by touring one region of the country. gilli says, "You can set up gigs; make press, radio, and TV contacts for promotion; and locate stores that will sell your CD with two reference guides, *The Indie Bible* (www.indiebible .com/writes/) and *Musician's Atlas* (www .musiciansatlas.com). Have an electronic press kit (EPK) ready to e-mail to media and venues through Sonic Bids (www.son icbids.com)."

You do want to have a distributor in place before you set out on your CD promotional tour, but you don't want CDs in every store in the country. Here's gilli's take on that:

People think if they get a distribution deal and their CDs are shipped to the stores, that they've accomplished something, but they haven't. You have to promote the CD so people will know it's in the store. If the CD doesn't sell, then the artist is the one that has to pay the shipping return, not the label or the distributor. My thinking on that is have your CD in the system with a distributor but don't worry about having it on the shelves in the stores. It's easy to get a distributor online and any distributor will put it in the system. Then people anywhere can request the CD and get it from a store, even if it takes a couple of days.

When you're organizing a tour of a certain region of the country, contact the distributor and tell them, "Here are the places I'll be and I want five CDs in all of the stores in those areas." They'll do that for you. They have less of a risk because you're going there to promote it. I call that micromarketing.

It makes touring less daunting to take on a region at a time.

The amazing thing is that gilli not only does this for herself, she helps other artists do it through her Warrior Girl Music label (www.warriorgirlmusic.com).

If even this scaled-down version of being a writer/artist seems too much, you can still produce your CD, make a thousand copies, give them away to friends and family, and sell a few here and there. You may not recoup your expenses, but you'll have the satisfaction of holding your creation in your hand. And that's a good feeling.

═ 88 ═

IN IT FOR THE MONEY
Don't think you'll get rich quick on one lucky break

After paying years of dues and suffering the slings and arrows of thousands of rejections, you finally get a song recorded. It may even be by a major artist. You're in seventh heaven. Your dream is coming true, and you are going to become a millionaire. The truth is out; you were in it for the money all along. You're going to take the cash and run to the farthest tropical island and spend the rest of your life on the beach.

As they say in the biz, "Don't quit your day job." Unless your song is a major hit, you're not looking at retirement-sized income. With one other collaborator and a publisher involved, you might get one-half of one-half of 9.1 cents per CD sold, depending on the status of the artist's controlled composition clause. Income from CD sales, called mechanical royalties, would be $0.02275 per copy, or $22,750 if a million were sold. Your income on a million-seller would be $15,166 with a publisher and three writers involved.

If your song is an album cut, that is probably all you will see from that song. If the song gets played on the radio, you will be entitled to performance royalties from ASCAP, BMI, or SESAC. If it gets played on the radio a lot, it could mean a lot of money. In fact, there are songs that earn their writers a million dollars from performance royalties collected around the world. If this book helps you in any way to get to that point, there is a way to show your gratitude. You can fly us to Tahiti for an on-the-beach song consultation!

Performance rights organizations (PROs) collect money, a.k.a. license fees, from the users of music, such as radio and TV stations, sports stadiums, concert halls, and stores that use music to make their customers happy and more willing to buy. Then they distribute that money to their members using information they gather about airplay and song performance uses. Methods for gathering performance information keep improving as technology makes surveys of music uses more accurate.

Your decision about which PRO to join is one of the most crucial decisions you'll make as a songwriter. If you have a song that is going to be played on the radio on more than a one-shot basis, you must join a performance rights society in order to get paid your performance royalties. Each organization has a different way of figuring how much to pay its members, and we have learned from married collaborators, who joined separate organizations in order to compare the difference, that the amounts can vary widely.

No other country in the world has competing performance rights organizations. We have three: American Society of Composers, Authors and Publishers (www.ASCAP.com), Broadcast Music, Inc. (www.BMI.com), and SESAC (www.SESAC.com), which doesn't stand for anything in English; it was derived from a French organization with which it no longer has any connection.

Back to the big decision. We can't tell you which to join, but we can say that if you are about to get substantial airplay, you should thoroughly research all three organizations and seek professional advice on which would be your best choice.

One reason not to quit your day job is that this money takes a long time to come through the record company's and performance rights organization's accounting systems. Expect to wait at least a year for the first check to arrive in your mailbox and three years for foreign royalties. Performance rights organizations pay quarterly, and record companies pay your publisher, who holds the money awhile (collecting interest, of course) and then pays you at whatever frequency you agreed to in your contract.

Songwriting is not a get-rich-quick game. You probably have a better chance at winning the lottery. We've been told that you have a much better chance of being struck by lightning than getting a number one song. Yes, there are some top songwriters who do very well, even some millionaires. But they've been at it for twenty or thirty years, and they did it for love, not for money. The sad fact is that the average annual income of all songwriters, including those millionaires, is five thousand dollars. The love of songwriting is the only thing that will make you hang in there long enough to make the money possible.

Anyone want to chip in on a lottery ticket?

= 89 =

MY WAY OR THE HIGHWAY

Be willing to relinquish control over the finished product

You wrote the song, you own it, and no one can use it without your permission. Once you have given that first permission to record the song, others can record it without consulting you. But before that first recording, if you do not sign the song to a publisher, the song is totally yours to control. This sounds like a powerful position. You might get the impression that you had some say in how the song comes out. Forget it.

Unless you are the producer, or related by blood or marriage, you will not be invited to the recording session. You will have no say in the outcome and no opportunity to contribute to the arrangement or the artist's performance. This situation prompted Melanie (the single-named Woodstock performer) to write "Look What They've Done to My Song, Ma" in the sixties, and it's still true today.

You have to let go of the idea that you will have some say in how this song that you have so much power over will sound after someone else gets through with it. The best you can do to influence the situation is to make a great demo.

If your demo is hot, if it is rich with hooky riffs between the vocal lines, if the groove is undeniable and the tracks are right on the money, the producer will probably copy your demo. We've heard of producers who, after trying and failing to get the same feel as the demo, have fallen back on using the actual tracks from the demo. This is easy to do in this day of digitally encoded music information.

The fact that you have no control over the outcome of the recording of your song may give you the impression that you should be careful to the point of overprotection when giving that first permission. We don't think so. If the record turns out bad, probably no one will hear it. You still have your demo to pitch, so you haven't lost a thing.

Plenty of songs have been recorded several times before the version that hit came out. "From a Distance" is a very good example. That song was recorded by thirteen different artists, including Judy Collins, the Byrds, and Kathy Mattea, and in five languages before Bette Midler recorded the version that won Julie Gold the Song of the Year Grammy. This is not to imply that the pre-Midler recordings were not good; they just weren't the right artists at the right time.

As a songwriter trying to establish a track record, we recommend that you take any recordings you are lucky enough to get on your song. You never know who will hear the song and make the recording of it that hits. The head of Almo Irving Music, the publishing arm of A&M Records, signed Julie Gold to a publishing deal after hearing "From a Distance" performed in a German cabaret.

We used to hear Keith Anderson sing "Beer Run" at songwriter nights in Nashville back at the turn of the century. A year or so later, he sang the song with an introduction that told the story of a phone call he got. The caller said, "We got someone here who wants to cut your song, but he wants to change it." Keith said, "I think the song works. I don't want to change it." The caller said, "Well, it's Garth Brooks." Keith is no fool. He quickly replied, "Yeah, I was thinking about changing that song!" Keith and his collaborators all agreed. The song became "Beer Run (B Double E Double Are You In?)," a duet with Garth Brooks and George Jones. It came out around September 11, 2001 and Garth didn't want to release it as a single. He felt it was too much of a good-time song for the times. Even though the record didn't do as well as it might have, it opened the doors for Keith that led to his record deal and his career as a country artist with hit songs "Pickin' Wildflowers" and "Every Time I Hear Your Name."

The idea at first is to get your songs out there. When you have a sizable track record, you might be a little choosier about who gets to record your song. If the idea of letting go of the results of the recording session on your song is abhorrent to you, you might want to consider joining the growing ranks of songwriters/producers.

Getting a song recorded these days is like getting a camel through the eye of a needle. Many recording artists write their own material, and many others are permanently joined with songwriters/producers who supply them with songs. On the theory that if you can't beat them, you might as well join them, many songwriters are developing their demo production skills into expertise at producing the final project. With today's technology, the line between demo and finished product is blurring anyway.

The songwriter who presents a record label with a package ready to go—artist, song, and producer all in place—is giving them something they want … less work. If one of the demo singers you hire absolutely knocks you out and you enjoy working with each other, you might want to try joining forces to produce an artist master demo. That is two to four songs of almost master (commercial release) quality to use for label shopping (pitching the artist to record labels for a recording contract).

Your songs are like your children. At some point, they have to stand on their own two feet and live their own lives. Fortunately, you can go on making new songs forever without threatening the planet with a population explosion. Keeping the long view of yourself as an infinitely creative source will help you over the rough spots when one of your song children turns out badly.

90

WHAT THEY DON'T KNOW WILL HURT YOU

*Register a song that is getting airplay
with your performance rights organization*

Getting a song recorded is the songwriter's dream come true. It's especially dreamy when you make the connection yourself with the artist, which makes you the publisher. The record company will ask you to issue a mechanical license, so you will do some research and deliver the appropriate piece of paper to them. You're already a member of a performance rights organization, so you've got your bases covered.

Sorry, but you're way off base. Membership in a performance rights organization and five bucks will get you a cup of coffee. Your performance rights organization is not a guardian angel who watches over you and notes your successes on a golden scroll. If you don't tell them about your recording, they will never know. They won't look for it in their survey, and you won't get paid. But since no one will ask you to do this the way a record company asks for a mechanical license, you may not know that registering your song with your performance rights organization is a prerequisite to getting paid for any airplay.

Ask your performance rights organization how to register your song when airplay is imminent. All the PROs (ASCAP, BMI, and SESAC) have online title registration. Please note that this administrative work with the record company and the performance rights society needs to be done by you only if you do not have a publisher representing you on the song.

How about that mechanical license? Is there anyone you should inform about it? It is possible to have the record company pay you directly for sales of records. However, we recommend that you let the Harry Fox Agency in New York City collect mechanical royalties for you. Harry Fox, which is related to the National Music Publishers Association, collects mechanical royalties for many of the largest publishers in the world. They charge a small percentage of the royalties for the service and it is well worth it, as we will explain in chapter ninety-four, "Pennies from Heaven." When a recording you have made the connection for is about to be released, contact the Harry Fox Agency (www.harryfox.com).

After all you've been through to get this recording, don't keep it a secret from the organizations that are the conduits for your income stream from the song. In the end, the glamorous music business comes down to filling out forms, shuffling papers, and accounting for figures in a column. But the check won't be in the mail unless you let someone know they should be sending it.

91

ONCE IS ENOUGH

Join your PRO twice if you're self-publishing

When we had our first success with a song that we pitched directly to an artist, we made a mistake that cost us a substantial sum of money. We take solace in the fact that we can pass what we learned onto you so you will not make the same mistake. Since we had made the connection with the artist, we were the publishers of the song. We were already members of a performing rights organization, so we notified them of the recording. We figured we had done all we needed to do.

Ignorance is not bliss, we discovered. We did receive songwriting royalties from ASCAP in due time, a year to eighteen months after the release. But a couple of years later the light dawned: We saw we had not received royalties as the publishers of the song. We called ASCAP and explained that we had neglected to join as publishers and to notify them we were the publishers on the song, a process called title registration. Unfortunately, the recording was too old for them to make any payment on the performances. The result was that we had collected *half* of the performance royalties possible on that song.

If reading this makes you realize you have made the same mistake, it is possible to retrieve some back performance royalties. ASCAP will go back nine months from the current quarter. BMI is not obligated by its contract with its songwriter members to go back at all. However, as a courtesy to the writer and depending on the situation, they may go back as far as nine months from the current quarter. SESAC will go back a year. Any royalties from further back in time are lost.

It is not necessary, or advisable, to join a performance rights organization as a publisher unless you expect a song of yours to be recorded, released, and played on a substantial number of radio stations or on television. ASCAP doesn't charge any fees. BMI charges publishing members a one-time processing fee of $150 for individually owned publishing companies, or $250 for partnerships, corporations, and limited liability companies (LLCs). Both organizations require proof of your status as an active publisher with songs that qualify for performance income. Unlike the other two PROs, you can't just join SESAC. You have to apply and be accepted by a "selective process."

When the time is right, the first step in the process is to choose which organization you want to join. This is a major decision, and again, we recommend you research the organizations to see which will pay the best for the uses your songs are most likely to have. Each organization has its own way of determining payments for various uses. Ask specific questions; for example, "My album is going to have airplay on college stations across the country. Does your survey cover those stations?" or "What are your rates of payment for television show theme songs?" The publishing company must be in the same PRO as the songwriter. If you choose to be an ASCAP songwriter, then you will be an ASCAP publisher. In other words, you cannot choose to be an ASCAP writer and have your songs published by a BMI company.

Generally speaking, radio performance royalties are paid on the basis of a statistical survey. You are not paid every time your song is played, because no one can keep track of all that information. There are over nine thousand radio stations in the United States. If you figure that each station plays fifteen songs an hour, twenty-four hours a day, that's 3,240,000 airplays to keep track of every day. Systems being developed for use in the future can track airplay exactly. For now, they find out what's being played at

x number of stations and then extrapolate mathematically from the sample to determine their payment for radio airplay for the whole country.

Television music is reported more accurately and is paid for according to different formulas that depend on a number of variables, such as whether the music is featured—that is, a singer is center stage singing it—or just playing in the background. The amount of payment also depends on the length of time the song is heard during the television show. Performance royalties are not paid by movie theaters in the United States, but they are in Europe.

The next step is to choose a company name. First you will have to come up with three or four names and submit them to your chosen performance rights organization. They will tell you which names are available. (Check out the names you're thinking of on the three PROs' Web sites. All have search features for publisher names which you can use to eliminate from your wish list names that are already in use. Not all names are on the sites, so not finding it in the search is not a guarantee that the name is free. We had to go through eight names before we found one that wasn't already taken.) Then, each time you make the connection that means airplay for your songs, notify your performance royalty organization—twice.

We don't want you to have to learn this lesson the hard way, like we did.

92

NO PAPER TRAIL
Don't lose those contracts!

Congratulations! You pitched a song to a major publisher, were offered a contract and, after some negotiations to make the contract work for you, signed it. Not only that, the publisher actually succeeded in securing a commercially recorded release of your song with a somewhat successful artist. You actually start getting some checks in the mail from the publisher. How great is that?!

Life goes on and the checks stop coming. Then you hear about a re-release of the song on a "Best of ..." CD and you look forward to more checks. They don't come. Now what do you do? Some songwriters who are members of the Songwriters Guild will go to Rick Carnes, the Guild's first president from Nashville, and ask for help.

Rick says:

The first thing I ask is "Do you have the contract under which you were supposed to be paid, so we can look at what the remedies are in that contract?" The songwriters never, never have the contract. It makes it impossible for us to go after the publishers. It does no good to fight, fight, fight to negotiate the right

contract and then lose the contract. But that is what 99.999 percent of all songwriters will do. Don't lose your contract! Keep it in a lock box that will survive World War III.

Many songwriters don't know that thirty-five to forty years after you sign a song to a publisher, you have the right to terminate the contract. That is true even if the contract appears to be binding forever. There are complicated windows of time when you have to give notice and when you can reclaim the copyright, which are best handled by an expert in the field. But what you need to know is, time flies when you're having fun being a songwriter. Termination time will be here before you know it. And when it comes, you're going to need that contract to get your song back.

You're not only going to need that contract, you're going to need the signatures of all your collaborators. Rick advises:

When you co-write a song, get some way of identifying your co-writer that will allow you to find her forty years from the day that you're writing. People are loath to give out their Social Security numbers now, because of identity theft. But that number may be your only way of locating the writer in the far future. Put it on the lyric sheet when you file the lyric sheet away. Don't lose it. Because thirty-five or forty years from now, when you try to reclaim that song, you have to contact all the writers on the song and everybody has to sign on the same paper. It's particularly hard to find females when they've changed their names four times. Males are little bit easier but not that much easier.

Anybody trying to find Rick Carnes thirty years from now isn't going to find me because that isn't my legal name. Finding me personally or my heirs is going to be very difficult if they don't have my Social Security number.

Those pieces of paper you signed can mean many more pieces of paper (money, that is) in your bank account. Don't put them in your recycling, or your shredder, or line your bird cage with them. File them so you can find them.

93

IT OUGHTA BE IN PICTURES

Learn about the drawbacks of
writing songs for films and TV

Lights! Camera! Action! There's something special about having a song in a film. Seeing your name roll by on the end credits is a thrill. Many new songwriters see movies that feature songs and dream of that glorious day when they will be part of that glitter and glamour. The fact that the songwriters' credits are the last to roll by, all clumped together, long after the caterer and the drivers get single billings and the audience has left the theater, is telling. Very often, people who make movies throw in the music as an afterthought. When it comes to songs in movies, songwriters are on the bottom of a very big totem pole. It can really get you down.

People who make movies and people who make music are two different animals. They have trouble talking to each other because they don't understand each other's grunts and growls. Movie people think that because they are spending so many millions of dollars, they should call the shots on the music, even if they can't speak the language. They wait until the last minute and then give a music supervisor the impossible assignment of locating/recording the perfect songs for two or ten

spots in the film. The music supervisor has to act quickly. He can't wait to deal with songs that have more than one person to go through to secure permission.

Enter music libraries. These are companies that accumulate the film and TV synchronization rights on songs from the copyright owners. That means you, as the copyright owner/creator of your song, can sign away just those rights, and not the others, such as the mechanical license/right to make CD copies. The deal for this varies from a flat fee, to royalties if they're earned, or a combination. It is usually an exclusive deal, which means you can only sell those rights to one company. The libraries then promote their songs for use; a quick, easy, inexpensive solution for the film folks.

Our friend Terri Fricon of Fricon Entertainment is, among other things, a music supervisor for feature films and TV movies. She told us:

> TV projects usually have a pretty quick turnaround. I get to work on a lot of "microwave movies"—the ones that have no time at all to do the job. Certain movies I've worked on have used a great

number of songs but the producers are not terribly particular about what songs they are. They just want a certain style of sound in the background. In those cases, we use music libraries pretty much exclusively. When we're looking at a film where they want a featured piece of music, then we deal directly with the record company and the publisher.

TAXI (www.Taxi.com) offers an additional service for songwriters who can produce their own broadcast-ready songs. You need to own the master recording rights, meaning you either did it all or got releases from whomever you paid to work for you. All you need is a signature on a piece of paper stating that they recognize the recording was a "work for hire," and they have received all the payment due them at the time of the recording. Broadcast-ready is not necessarily a finished master. If it could sound okay in the background on TV, it's broadcast-ready. Sometimes referred to as broadcast-quality as well, it's not as hard to achieve as you might think. Plenty of people have made eight-track recordings from home studios that have been placed in TV shows and films. The cost of TAXI's Dispatch membership is prorated at less than fifty cents per day in addition to the TAXI regular membership.

Dispatch is used when the people seeking songs through TAXI need them in a hurry. It's not exclusively for film/TV songs, but they tend to be in the majority because of the last-minute nature of those projects. Dispatch members get daily e-mails of the listing companies' needs. They respond with mp3 files of their songs and, in a matter of days, they know if their songs have been chosen. If you own the master recordings and have a deep enough catalog, you can make money with Dispatch. See the TAXI site for the latest success stories.

How much money will you make? Not much. The rules of supply and demand hold for film and TV music. Now that it's so easy for so many people to produce high quality recordings in their home studios, the users have lots to choose from. Film Music (www.filmmusicworld.com) reports: "Song Licensing fees for film and television are declining for all but the most popular films/songs." Still, if it's your song and you make any money, you're probably going to be pleased.

If your song is chosen for a feature film, it is usually taken for granted that you will not participate in any of the publishing royalties. Unless the songs in question have already been published, only songwriters with major clout like Marilyn and Alan Bergman and Billy Steinberg and Tom Kelly can insist on participating in the publishing of their songs in movies. Even when written by major league songwriters, songs get lost in the Hollywood shuffle. Billy Steinberg says:

> Tom and I have had nothing but misfortune in the area of placing songs in films. For example, we wrote a song we were really proud of called "Listen To Your Heart" specifically for the *Karate Kid III* movie. The film company was saying,

"We need a hit with this film and we're going to push this song." The film company usually wants the song recorded by an artist from the roster of the company that has the soundtrack deal. That's what happened in this case. They wanted the Little River Band to record it. Even though I didn't feel that was the right group for our song, the Little River Band recorded it and it came out very poorly.

Income from songs in films basically comes from the synchronization license. An agreement is made between the film company and the owner of the copyright that the film company will pay a certain amount for the right to synchronize the song with the soundtrack of the movie. Major league songwriters can charge a hefty synch fee for a song in a movie. Minor league songwriters do it for considerably less. It is the rare soundtrack album that sells enough to be a significant source of income for the songwriter. There may be some performance income from foreign performance rights organizations if the film is released overseas. ASCAP, BMI, and SESAC do not pay for performances in movie theaters in the United States. And there will be a trickle of performance rights royalties for many years when the film gets aired repeatedly on network and cable TV.

We had a song in a movie starring John Travolta. The film was called *The Experts*, and our song, "Hometown, U.S.A.," was played twice in the movie and played a significant part in setting the scene. We were excited when this project came to us and couldn't wait until the movie came to our local theater so we could watch our names roll by on the big screen.

Unfortunately, this was the film just before Travolta made a big comeback in *Look Who's Talking*, and his popularity was at a low ebb. The film company did some kind of test marketing in ten theaters in Texas and decided the film wasn't strong enough to spend the promotion dollars it would take to release it nationally, so the film went straight to video release. Fortunately, they did release it on cable as well and it still plays from time to time. Many of our friends and relatives saw our names roll by and wrote to us about it on their Christmas cards. (We never knew so many people read those credits. We're usually the only ones hanging out in the theater watching for who wrote the songs.)

If you want your songs to be in pictures, the people you want to impress and endear yourself to are the music supervisors. Their names roll by on the credits, too. You can also approach music libraries, but do some research to find out which ones have a history of success. When movies are in the planning stages, they are listed in the trade papers, *Variety* and *Hollywood Reporter*. Both have online versions. Another source is IMDb, the Internet Movie Database, (www.imdb.com). You might have some luck contacting the production offices directly. If they like your songs, they could pass them on to the music supervisor.

Then, when you get the cue that your song is in a film, get ready to roll with the punches.

94

PENNIES FROM HEAVEN
Don't think your royalties will automatically come to you

You've made and corrected three zillion mistakes in the process of writing, rewriting, demoing, and pitching your songs. Having made every possible mistake, you have nothing left to do but the right thing. The song has been recorded by an artist of note. You are the publisher or copublisher. You've filed the proper forms with the Harry Fox Agency and your performance rights organization. You have negotiated the deal with professional help; the papers have been signed. You await with perfect serenity the arrival of the check in the mail.

You may be disappointed if you expect business to be taken care of just because it's supposed to be. Some people who are supposed to give you your money would much rather keep it for themselves, thank you very much. If you let them, they will. They will not volunteer to pay you. Instead of serenely collecting your check from your mailbox, you may have to work up a sweat going after money that is rightfully yours.

For instance, we were copublishers on a song that was quite successful. The other copublisher was an established company,

and the person we were dealing with there was well known to us professionally and socially. We decided the song would best be administered by a large international publishing company that would charge a small percentage for the service and then split the remaining income 50/50 and pass it on to us separately. The person at that publishing company was also well known to us. We spoke to him on the phone and he said (and we quote), "You and the other publisher will have the same deal."

We sat back and relaxed, waiting for the check to come in the mail. We were waiting and waiting and waiting. Good thing we didn't hold our breath. A year and a half rolled by and there was still no money in sight from this song. So we started calling around and found that, not only had the large administering publisher not given us the "same deal" as our copublisher, he had sent *our* royalties to that copublisher, who had been holding them for a year.

We then called the copublisher and said, "Hey, you've been sitting with our royalties in the bank for a year now; you owe us interest." He must have thought that was a mighty funny idea, from the way he laughed at us. We did finally get our royalties with a lesson attached: Don't expect the other guy to look out for your best interests.

Lesson number two in this department has to do with a practice in the record business called the 100 percent returns policy. The record business is unique in that stores can return 100 percent of the product if they don't sell it. A few years ago, you'd hear about records shipping platinum and returning gold. That means they would send out one million and half a million would come back. In today's tougher times, the record companies are more conservative about the amounts they ship. The result of this acceptance of returned goods policy is that the record companies won't pay until they see how many come back. They also like to stipulate that they won't pay for a certain percentage of records because they break in shipping, even though there are no such things as records anymore. Downloading should eliminate the returns and brea.k.a.ge policies. Do you get the feeling that the record companies would really rather not pay the publishers the mechanical royalties on the songs, which are the only things that give their product value? Without the songs, they'd be in the blank CD business. But they often don't act as though they know that's the case.

We just heard a true story. The names will not be mentioned to protect the guilty. One of the big four record companies sold almost a million CDs on a major recording artist. A publishing company that had a song on the album was looking forward to the money coming in. It was not a big company and needed the money for rent, salaries, and so on. When the money did not come in at the expected time, the publisher called the record label to ask why the check hadn't arrived. Their answer: "We don't have a license on the song." That means the publisher did not give them a mechanical license, a piece of paper that the record label should have requested but didn't. The publisher thought the copublisher on the song had taken care of that. But, when the whole truth came out, the record label had not requested *any* licenses for the entire album and was using that as an excuse to not pay *all* the publishers. Caught in the act of a major copyright infringement and threatened with a federal lawsuit in the morning, the record label cut a check the next day. It's a "come and get me" business, even at the top level.

Enter the Harry Fox Agency with lesson number three: You have grounds for your suspicions about record companies. Every so often, the Harry Fox Agency conducts audits on record companies. That means they go into the record company's files and check to see if the royalties paid match the records sold. Many times they find that the record companies owe publishers money. Recently, the Fox Agency found over a thousand dollars that a record label owed us for one moderately successful song. Can you imagine how much the record company owed the major worldwide publishers with hundreds of successful titles on their label? For the auditing alone, if you are your own publisher it is worth the percentage that the Fox Agency charges to collect your mechanical royalties. It would not be worth your time and money to do the audit independently. Also, when Harry Fox does your mechanical licensing, they don't allow record companies to withhold funds for those nonexistent broken records.

Don't count on your money showing up in your mailbox just because it's supposed to. Our stories are only a few examples of how your money can get lost in the shuffle. When it comes to the money owed to you, keep an eagle eye on your income sources and follow through to make sure your check actually makes it into your mailbox. Then you can sing all the way to the bank.

95

FALLING OFF THE MOUNTAIN

Cope with your success

You started out as low as you could go and made every mistake in the book, but your love of songwriting helped you hang in there through it all, right up to the top note. You wrote it, you pitched it, they recorded it, it went up the charts, it hit number one, and you even managed to get paid for it. You have finally reached the pot of gold at the end of the songwriting rainbow. Now your problems are over.

But wait, what's that on the horizon? A whole new set of problems. What a life! Thinking your problems will be over if only you could have a number one hit will give you even more problems in terms of frustration and disappointment when the road after success proves just as rocky as the one before it.

It's true, fellow travelers, on the songwriting road. We solve one set of problems only to be faced with another, perhaps more interesting, set. You may wonder what could possibly be a problem after you've written the number one song in the country. You imagine that if such good fortune should come to you, you would live the rest of your life with a smile on your face. We have several friends who

have reached those altitudes on the charts, and we'll tell you what they told us.

Once you have been on top, you have only one place to go, and that's down. You could stay on top, but no one does that. Your own success will be the hardest act for you to follow. You will wake up the next morning and be confronted with the same blank sheet of paper or computer screen that challenged you before the world recognized your talent. You will ask yourself, "Can I do it again?" And part of you may say, "No!"

Your success may attract many opportunities. People will want you to write songs for projects, songwriters will want to collaborate with you, songwriters' organizations will call on you to share your experience, and before you know it, you will be overwhelmed by the demands on your time. One friend of ours told us that he feels crazier than he ever did before his success, because he now has more in his life than he can handle. For him, the idea of success has progressed from "If I only had a cut" to "If I only had a hit" to "If I only had constant demand for my songs" to "If I only had peace of mind."

As time goes by, if you are not lucky enough to keep having major songwriting successes, maybe you'll just be a working songwriter. You'll be out there competing with all the other working songwriters and the new, hungry songwriters who hit town every day. You will have the challenge of making peace with the fact that you might never write a number one song again. You might be called upon to sing a "medley of your hit" for a songwriters' concert and listen as other songwriters dazzle you with their incredible string of standards.

Should you have the luck to continue to be a successful songwriter, you still face the stiff competition and all the music business practices that disregard and threaten songwriters. It will be in your best interest to get involved in fighting record piracy, illegal downloading, controlled composition clauses, omission of writers' credits on albums, censorship, attempts by users not to pay royalties, new technology that allows for the use of music without payment to its creators, and the list of concerns is constantly growing.

Most people who have attained success want to give something back, and you will probably want to get involved in a songwriting organization. You might serve on the board or help with events. It will be important to do this in a way that doesn't keep you from being a songwriter.

Your songs will still be rejected, recorded badly, put on hold for too long, recorded and not released, released but not promoted, put in films that don't make it to the theaters, bought and sold by publishers who could care less about them, and used in ways you won't like.

You can't get much more successful as a songwriter than Paul McCartney. He tells the story of a conversation between himself and Michael Jackson. Michael said something like, "Paul, I have all this money and I'm thinking of investing in a business. What do you suggest?" Paul said, "Music publishing is a good business and it's something you can relate to." So, Michael went out and bought ATV Music, which is the publishing company that owns all the early Beatles' hits. Shortly after, Paul heard one of his songs in an athletic shoe commercial, and he wished he hadn't been so free with his advice.

The ultimate success is to thoroughly enjoy the process of songwriting and disregard the results. Most assuredly, you have to make all the right moves to write the best of all possible songs and make the best of all possible pitches. But the only way to hold on to your peace of mind will be to stop trying to control the outcomes; give yourself credit for doing the best you can and move on to the next song.

You will still have to open up to your tenderest parts and risk exposing them and making a fool of yourself every time you write. For that reason, Paul Simon calls songwriting a dangerous profession. Songwriting is not something you do until you get it right. You never reach that point. Songwriting is a lifestyle of adventure and learning.

PART 10

WILD WEIRD WEB

Internet Entanglements

96

FEAR OF THE FUTURE

"… the only thing we have to fear is fear itself …"
—Franklin D. Roosevelt

Technology marches on. The impact of the Internet on songwriting has been enormous, to put it mildly. Some writers are afraid they've been left out of the newest game in town because they're not technologically inclined. Some fear the way the Internet makes stealing songs so easy. We're here to tell you, "Fear not."

First of all, if people are going to steal your songs on the Internet, you have to get them up there first. That requires making digital files of your songs and uploading them to a site. For the folks who suffer from fear of computer programs, help is on the way. The programs themselves are becoming easier to work with. Most can be picked up intuitively if you (like Pat) have manualophobia (that's fear of reading the manual). And you don't have to do it alone. Tech support is a beautiful thing when it works well. Before you purchase a songwriting-related program, check to see that tech support is included, with a phone number to call a real live person. It's more fun if you can find a songwriter who knows the program and is willing to share the knowledge person-to-person. If you are one of the shrinking minority not yet inter-acting with the Internet (we do know a few of you), take courage. You can do it. You can put your songs on the Internet where the whole world can hear them, on your very own site or any of the music posting sites (see chapter eight-seven, "Independence Daze"). You can do this, even if you don't personally own a computer. Many writers we know use their local library's computers for all their Internet activities. And the library comes with built-in tech support, your friendly librarian.

And yes, the Internet is a hotbed of song piracy. 2.5 billion song files are downloaded illegally each month. If you don't want your songs stolen, you need to make sure they can only be listened to, not downloaded. Some writers feel it's good to give away a song or two in the hopes that the listener will buy others. Some only post a portion of each song to tempt the buyer. The point is, there *are* buyers. There are music collectors who troll the Internet making purchases. If you want to make money on your songs, they have to be out there for the collectors to find. Ironically, what has been music's greatest threat could also be its greatest opportunity.

In his remarks at the annual National Music Publishers Association, president and CEO, David Israelite, said:

> … The time we are in is truly the dawn of a new era in the world of music. It is an era that presents enormous challenges. It is an area that offers vast opportunities. …The next five years will be the most important period in the history of music publishing.
>
> This is a bold and amazing statement for an industry that is over one hundred years old … In the next five years, many battles will be fought. I believe the results of those battles will determine the future of the music publishing industry … We will experience an exponential growth in technology that challenges every previous notion of how creators are compensated for their art … we can adapt to the digital revolution and thrive in it.

Songwriters, too, will thrive in the new era. Brian Austin Whitney (Just Plain Folks) foresees a world in which many more writer/artists will be able to live out their dreams and live on their artistic expressions:

> With all the music that's out there on the Internet and all the ways there are to find music and buy music, there will be a larger number of people finding a smaller but passionate audience for their music, and finding a way to make a living doing that. The next wave will be people who make forty to seventy thousand dollars a year as very successful artists playing to ten or twenty thousand people who are spread around the world. You really only need ten thousand fans to make a great full-time living. If you can get ten thousand fans to give you twenty dollars a year for all the creative output that you give them, that's an incredible living.

So, venture fearlessly into the brave new world of songwriting in the Internet age.

97

JUST A CLICK AWAY
Be careful what you click for on the Internet

Late one night, Pat was surfing the Internet looking for a book. She found it on Amazon.com. She clicked on more information, other books like it, other sites to compare prices, and so on and so forth, until she was dizzy. Finally she decided to buy it from Amazon and clicked something on their site, expecting to get a screen where she would view and approve the order. Instead, she got a "Thank you for your order"-type message. Ooops! She bought it and couldn't figure out how to undo the order. Some time in the past she had entered our address and credit card information and, since they had that in their computer, they ran with it.

What's that got to do with songwriting? It's just as easy to click away rights to your songs. Just Plain Folks founder Brian Austin Whitney alerted us to this situation. Songwriters seeking exposure for their songs may enter phrases like "Web sites that allow free song postings" in a search engine and proceed to follow the links. Somewhere in there, they could be asked to accept or decline a long scrolling patch of legalese. Who reads all this stuff? Not them! They click "accept" and move on to the posting place. They don't realize that when they clicked on "accept" they entered into a contract that says somewhere in the fine print, "We can use your songs forever for free." The contract was probably written by a lawyer who doesn't understand the music business. The site owners who hired the lawyer may be good guys who just wanted to cover their bases; they don't mean to own your song forever. But the guys they sell the site to may not be so scrupulous with all the contracts that come as part of the deal. Clicker beware!

Should that put you off exploring the brave new cyberworld? No. Today's songwriter cannot afford to be Web-ignorant. The uses for the Internet are literally limitless. But, as is usually the case, where there are uses, there are abuses. It's up to you to tell them apart.

How can you use the Internet? It's impossible to count the ways. For starters, you can search for collaborators, songwriting organizations, places to perform, radio stations in particular areas, songwriter expos, songwriting contests, songwriting retreats, recording artist bios, touring information, recording equipment deals, demo studios, songwriting books, songwriting online courses, song consultations, CD distribution and promotion—you get the idea. Whatever you can think of can be typed into the search engine and you will be amazed at how many sites will come up. You could go on forever wandering among the sites. While you're wandering, keep track of where you've been. Don't just throw everything on your "favorites" list. Make folders for the categories to make it easier for you to find your way back to the sites that gave you what you needed.

Time is of the essence. On the one hand, you need to commit to some regular time periods to do this wandering, or you won't learn the routes. On the other hand, you need to limit that time, because it can suck you in until you're lost. So spend a little time and no money while you explore the songwriting-related sites. There's tons of free information to be had.

Your abuse radar should go up when they ask you for money. There are good reasons to give away your money (see chapter one hundred and one, "Dollars and Nonsense"), and no-good reasons. The amount of money you could spend is as unlimited as the Internet. But we're betting you don't have unlimited money. So before you click away your life savings, check out the site. Don't do business with any site that does not provide a physical address and a contact telephone number for customers. Ask other songwriters; the Just Plain Folks (www.justplainfolks.org) forums are a great place to get free advice from those who have traveled these roads

before you. Check with the Songwriters Guild or the Nashville Songwriters Association about the site. As you will read in chapter one hundred, "Fame Calling," one phone call to check the references of an Internet contact can save you thousands of dollars and a lot of time kicking yourself.

You can check companies with the Better Business Bureau (BBB) online (www.bbb.org). Follow the link to local BBBs and put in the city and state or zip code, then click on "Check on a Company." A search for a well-known cyber song shark (see chapter ninety-eight) shows a phone number—something that is not on their site—and seven complaints in the last thirty-six months. Only seven in thirty-six months and all resolved; that's not too bad, is it? Yes, it is, when you check out a bunch of other legitimate companies and find zero complaints, and when you think about all the songwriters who got burned and didn't file BBB complaints.

The difficulty with writing about the Internet is that it is growing and changing so fast that anything we say will be out of date before we're finished saying it. The few sites we mention in this book are either people we know personally who are highly ethical or well-established businesses we know you can trust. If a site is not mentioned, that doesn't mean it's not legitimate.

We often say to new writers who ask us where to begin, "Try the first dozen links on our site (www.writesongs.com). That will keep you busy for a long time."

Happy wandering!

98

CYBER SONG SHARKS

*Steer clear of companies that advertise
they are "looking for hit songs"*

When we began our update of this book, we put out a call on all the major songwriting sites for Internet horror stories. These messages reached over fifty thousand songwriters. We got one reply about a problem with a collaborator. "Wow!" we thought. "Songwriters these days are too smart to be taken in by cyber song sharks. How great is that?"

Would that it were so. Perhaps the songwriters savvy enough to be using the major songwriting sites also know to avoid the companies that gladly promise fame and fortune tomorrow for a bunch of your money today. But new songwriters, who don't know any better, are still being bitten by cyber song sharks every day.

As the universe would have it, just when we were wondering who was falling for the cyber song sharks' pitches, we got a phone call from a fledgling songwriter who lives in a small town out west. She told us she typed "songwriter" in a search engine and right up there on top of the results was a company announcing its search for hit songs. She clicked on the link and found a beautiful site with lots of pictures of big record companies'

buildings and other music industry landmarks. She sent them a couple of lyrics and they wrote back saying the lyrics were good, that she had ability, and that she should enter their contest. Then they said she *won* the contest. They would send her a contract. They would put her song on a CD and send it to radio stations and record companies. She was thrilled.

We tried to tell her many times during this conversation that the legitimate music business doesn't work that way. No legitimate music publisher or record label ever advertises that they are seeking hit songs. They don't have to. They are being inundated constantly with hit (and miss) songs. Notice the heading "Sponsored Links." That company is on the top of the search results page because they paid to be there and not way back among the other 11,600,000 songwriting-related Web sites. Does that mean that every sponsored link is suspect? No, because there's TAXI right up there on top, too, and TAXI is super-legitimate. How does a songwriter separate the truth from the lies?

One red flag is an offer to set your lyrics to music, either for a fee or free if you pay them to make a demo of your song. There isn't a single legitimate music publisher or record label that will consider lyrics only. They can afford to be choosy, since the number of wonderfully written songs that come to them through their personal and professional contacts is far greater than the number of songs they can use. If you are a lyricist, you need to find a composer on your own. (See chapter forty-four, "Diving In, Crawling Out," for tips on how to do this.) You will work together to make the best possible song and you won't pay each other for the privilege. Then you can present a complete song to legitimate music companies.

Red flag number two is their promise to promote your song, for a fee or for the cost of a demo. These guys churn out demos assembly-line style. You're not going to get a demo that will compete with those done in legitimate studios where they take their time to show the song in its best light. Yes, song sharks send out compilation CDs, so they keep to the letter of their promises, but the people who receive them throw them immediately into the trash.

Another twist on this twisted tale is the fact that copyrights are matters of public record. That means anyone can search the records and find out who registered a song for copyright. You don't have to search the Internet for these sharks; they're searching for you. Some songwriter friends have told us they were approached by song sharks before they even got their registrations back in the mail.

Meanwhile, our songwriter out west kept insisting that she was happy with the results. We could not convince her otherwise. She said, "They sent me a contract." We asked her to fax the contract to us. What we saw was a contract for *her* to pay *them*. A real contract from a music publisher may be long or short, but it's all about how *they* are going to pay *you*!

We decided to test the song shark waters ourselves. We invented a name and an e-mail address for that name and submitted a lyric to one of these sites. Now, the lyric was actually written by a group of six-year-olds we taught songwriting to (we'll never forget how free and imaginative they were). Here's some of that lyric:

I'm Different

I'm different every day
Every day I grow
My hair gets longer
And my teeth fall out
And that makes me happy
So, so, so, so, so, so
I'm different

I'm different every day
My nose is on my hand
I walk on my eyes
My tongue is on my knee
My ears are on my back
Now you can understand
I'm different

Here's the response we got:

> The review staff has looked over your material and forwarded their response

to me. "I'm Different" was an outstanding lyric! There's a really great message behind this submission. Cacthy [their spelling] as well! You write very professionally, the words flow together well, and the idea comes through clearly. With a professional production, this could be an incredible song.

We're interested in working with your material, so please view the following special web page with information on how to get started with us.

The link led to choices of how much money we were going to send them.

Now can you tell the difference between what's real and what's fake? Which way is the money flowing? Does that mean that anyone asking for money is a fake? Things should be so simple. The truth is, in the beginning, you'll spend lots more money on your songwriting than you'll make. We'll cover the many ways it's okay to spend money in chapter one hundred and one, "Dollars and Nonsense."

99

NO CONTEST

There are "contests" and there are real contests—choose wisely

How would you like to win one million dollars in a songwriting contest? Who wouldn't? So you open your favorite Internet search site and type in "songwriting contests." Sure enough, right at the top there's something under the heading of "Songwriting Contests" about winning a one-million-dollar prize. And you can enter for free! Well, click away on that link. Huh? It's the Publishers Clearing House! Remember the TV ads of Ed McMahon knocking on people's doors to present big checks to the winners? What does this have to do with songwriting? Nothing. There's no place to enter a song on this Web site, just blanks for your personal information and a magazine subscription order form.

Other sites, not so obviously bogus, tout their contests and their prizes. They mention past prize winners and song titles. They say the songwriter won prizes worth *x* dollars, which included a certain amount of cash and a demo. Hmmm, the demo took almost 80 percent of the *x* dollars, so the writer got 20 percent of the eye-catching prize amount. What's wrong with this picture?

What's missing? The judge's names and qualifications, the contest sponsor names, the history of the contest, and links to the songs that won. Legitimate contests have pictures, bios, and links to their judges so you can judge for yourself if they're qualified. Legitimate contests are sponsored or given a stamp of approval by recognizable high-level music business companies or organizations. They provide links to the sponsors' sites, so you can find out more about who is behind the contest. Perhaps most important to potential winners, the best songwriting contests post extensive promotion of songwriters who win. There are photographs, bios, and links to the writers' sites and songs. As a winner, you can use these to promote yourself. Every little bit helps.

Some of the big songwriting contests that have been around awhile and do all the right things are the Billboard Songwriting contest, the CMT/NSAI Song Contest, the International Songwriting Competition (ISC), the John Lennon Songwriting Contest, the USA Songwriting Competition, and the Unisong International Songwriting Contest. Some songwriters complain that the big contests are like lotteries; the chances of winning decrease as the number of songs in the competition increase. The big-name judges do judge, but they only listen to the cream that has been skimmed off the top by worker-bee-type judges. So that photo in the contest promotion of the big star who's judging is far from a guarantee that said star will hear your song. Still, being a winner in one of those is a significant accomplishment that you may be able to parlay into a leap forward in your songwriting career.

But the big contests are just the tip of a titanic iceberg. There are dozens of big, medium-sized, and little contests to choose from. Songwriter info sites, such as www.musesmuse.com and www.music newsnashville.com have lists of them, with descriptions and links. Many of these contests are honestly run by good folks. You may have a good chance at winning the smaller contests with fewer entries. Some contests raise funds for local songwriter groups. If you don't win one of those, at least you contributed to a worthy cause. If a contest offers feedback on your songs, that may be worth the entry fee to you.

Some contests don't charge an entry fee. The most notable of these is the Just Plain Folks Music Awards(www.jpfolks. com), run by the indefatigable creator of JPF, Brian Austin Whitley. Entries for the JPF Music Awards arrive in the hundreds of thousands from all over the world and awards are given in over sixty genres. Judging is done by pros and peers, with the directive to choose the songs that "move *you* the most." Our experience as judges in this contest has been awesome. We are awestruck by the depth and range of the talent and creativity represented. The awards are celebrated in a theater in the L.A. area on a date close to the TAXI Road Rally in November, and the winners are posted permanently on the Just Plain Folks site.

Broadjam (www.Broadjam.com) runs regular contests with free entries for those dues paying members at the highest level, and varying entry fees for other levels of membership and non-members.

Most contests charge a twenty- to forty-dollar entry fee. If you enter several contests, that can add up. Would you be better off spending that money on some good songwriting books, courses at SongU, membership in NSAI, or a trip to a music center—all of which would help you to improve your writing? In our book, which you are reading, anything that helps you to be a better songwriter makes you a winner.

100

FAME CALLING

Be wary of the caller who says,
"I'm gonna make you a star."

An artist friend of ours told us this true story. She has been making a good living touring for years and had just produced her second independent CD. She was ready to advance to the next step in her career. One day, she got a phone call from someone who said he had heard her music on her Web site and exclaimed, "This album needs to be signed. It's excellent!" He rattled off the names of record labels he was meeting with. He said, "Let me book you; let me promote your CD."

She was thrilled! She had others praising her talent, so she had reason to believe that he could be excited to work with her. He dropped names of people she knew and with whom she had some connections. She visited his Web site. There was just enough truth in what he talked about to make her believe. That's how she learned the hard way that the Internet is not only a great place for you to find out about everything; it's also useful for people who want to find out about you.

He started booking gigs for her and taking a commission. Trouble is, they were gigs she had already set up herself. So he was making money using her connections.

After a year of this, she began to investigate. She had never met him face-to-face, so she searched the Internet but couldn't find a photograph of him. His Web site had disappeared. She found his name on other people's sites and discovered he was bragging about his connection to her to lure other people into dealing with him. She phoned some major labels and found they didn't know him. With twenty-twenty hindsight, she wonders, "Why didn't I do that first?"

He would promise big things and deliver just enough to keep her hooked and hoping. He got a song placed with another indie artist, made a contact for her with a semi-big-name group—as she said, "There were some legit things, but it still wasn't legit." The bottom line is, she wound up giving him ten thousand dollars and never got a record deal. She did not feel any better when she found another artist he had talked out of thirty thousand dollars. She laments:

> I was so disheartened. I felt so stupid. I called NSAI and they didn't know him. He hit me at a time in my life when I

had spent all this money on my new CD and the distributor had gone bankrupt. When they can research you on the Internet and they know a little bit about the music business, they can use that information to fool you.

Here's the lesson she learned:

> I'm a singer, I don't play guitar. People who have great voices are a dime a dozen. I have to work really hard. Illegitimate people can prey on that by promising to make the connections you crave for your career. You have to ask yourself honestly, 'What is this person's motive?' If they believed in you they would be busting their ass to get you a deal; they wouldn't be charging you money.

This is not to say that all phone calls are phony. Recently, we were in a Nashville publisher's office. The company is huge, with decades of connections to the top songwriters and artists. The gentleman we were visiting played us a few songs by a new female songwriter/artist he was courting. His plans are to sign her as a writer to his publishing company and have a producer work with her to cut some songs to shop her to labels. Her voice and her writing were outstanding. We asked where he found her. She's very young and from a very small town. She had won a regional talent contest, the winners of which had their performances posted on an Internet site. He heard her, was impressed, and called the local radio station in Alabama that had broadcast the contest to tell them of his interest. They got the message to her. So, okay, she made the phone call, but the plot is the same.

Except this time, the caller is a good guy. He won't be asking her for money. In fact, he'll be giving her money in advance royalties. He'll be setting up meetings with her and the publishing company staff, the label executives, and other songwriters. We asked him why no one had already signed her. He said, "I guess she's been offered deals, but she's been smart enough not to sign them."

So, it really could be fame calling, but fame won't be asking you for money!

101

DOLLARS AND NONSENSE

*Make careful choices about where
you spend your money on songwriting*

Now that you know not to send your hard-earned money to cyber song sharks, bogus contests, and slick promoters via the Internet, you're ready to read about the right places to invest to further your songwriting dreams. Let's face it, we're all dreamers. The odds are heavily against us making any money at songwriting. While some of your money will still be spent in the old-fashioned, over-the-counter way, perhaps even more will be sent over the Internet.

We have a friend who says, "If you can throw money at it, it's not a problem." That does work for most things, but the problem of how to achieve a songwriting dream is not one of them. Here are some of the ways besides song sharks that you can throw away your money: paying someone to collaborate with you, paying thousands of dollars to demo a song, making a demo of every song you write, copyrighting each song individually, buying a big collection of songwriting books you never read, sending out a bunch of unsolicited demos, making a lot of inappropriate pitches, and entering every song contest there is. Since

time is money, you've not only depleted your bank account (or, as some songwriters told us, they have gone more than ten thousand dollars into debt), you've wasted your precious time.

Most of us will spend more money on songwriting than we will make from it. The trick is to spend the money where it will do us the most good. We are driven to write songs and, if we have any sense, we're driven to grow as songwriters. And growing is what keeps the dream alive that someday we'll put some black ink in our songwriting account. Growing costs money.

Or not.

Thanks to the Internet and the library, there's a whole universe of free information on songwriting at our fingertips. When brand-new writers contact us, we send them to the links page on our site. The first half-dozen links there will keep you busy for a long, long time without spending a dime. All the major songwriting sites have ever-growing archives of articles on every aspect of songwriting. You don't even have to pay for the Internet connection if your library has one available for you to use. Many libraries do.

Speaking of the library and the Internet, our Nashville library now allows us to search their catalog via the Internet, find the book we desire in any library in the system, and have them deliver it to our local library for pick-up. Many cities have this kind of system. If your search for songwriting books at your library yields no results, speak to your librarian about how to put in a request.

Break out your cash and credit cards; we're about to start spending some money. By far the most important area of expense in the early stages of your growth as a songwriter is education. There are so many books, CDs, and DVDs available on every aspect of the craft and business of songwriting, you could run out of money before you finished collecting them. But a lot of books on a shelf does not an educated songwriter make. You really need to study the books. We're delighted when we see writers who have the earlier edition of this book and have highlighted, underlined, and scribbled notes throughout. Try buying one book or other songwriting educational media at a time and fully digesting it before you buy the next.

Assuming you already have this book, and you only have money to buy one more, the one to get is John Braheny's *The Craft and Business of Songwriting* at your local bookstore or from Writer's Digest online (www.writersdigest.com). We're not just saying this because John is our good friend and Writer's Digest is our publisher. John's tome covers every aspect of songwriting in great detail. The second book we recommend is our own *12 Steps to Building Better Songs*. It's less than thirty pages long, but it is all meat and no potatoes. It takes you through the thought process of writing a song from start to finish. It's a great tool for collaborating to get all the writers on the same page. It also helps you get all the voices in your head to agree. This book is only available from our Web site (www.writesongs.com).

Once you've read John's book and worked with ours, you can start researching other literature. Do an Internet search for reviews on the titles and see if you can find the books in your local bookstore and scan them for content and style. Only buy the books you really feel you'll read.

We offer a number of workshop subjects to songwriting groups around the country. But more often than not, the groups will choose a "how do I get my songs cut" subject over a "how do I write strong songs," because they are laboring under the delusion that they already know how to write songs. *The song is the thing*. Never give up on your quest for information on how to write better songs. That means you will research online courses, video courses, workshops, conventions and expos, and memberships in songwriter organizations. Take your time to decide which will work best for you.

Another educational option is the personal songwriting consultant. That is someone who will work one-on-one with you to improve your writing. Just as a coach works with an Olympic athlete, songwriting consultants help you emphasize your strengths and eliminate your weaknesses. We have this service and we know of at least a dozen others who also offer it. You can find us by searching online for "songwriting instruction" or "songwriting consultation." Each has his or her own way of working with writers. If this service is something you're interested in, research each Web site carefully and then call the person to see if you feel you can work with her. Be wary of people who try to force you into a long-term contract commitment. Some people pose as consultants and offer you "feedback" on your songs (which will be glowing), but what they really want you to do is send them money for second-rate demos. A real songwriting consultant will probably find some areas in your song that could use improvement. Check the person out with NSAI or the Songwriters Guild before you spend your money.

The tools of songwriting are another area of expense. They can be as simple as a pencil and a piece of paper or as complex as a computer-driven recording studio. You need a rhyming dictionary and a thesaurus. Both of those come in handy, but you don't need to buy the actual books if you write on your computer and your computer is hooked up to the Internet where sites such as Rhymezone. com will feed your need for rhyming lines. You don't need to buy a Martin guitar or a Steinway piano. Any instrument that keeps in tune will do. You might profit from buying an inexpensive synthesizer. The built-in rhythms and one-finger chording they offer can be useful writing tools. Some people find songwriting software such as MasterWriter (www.master writer.com) helpful. Others don't. You can find out for yourself which of these groups you fall into by trying it out free for thirty days. The best songwriting products on the Internet will offer free trials or money-back guarantees.

Of course, you will spend money on demos, and our chapters on that subject will help you do that wisely. Once you have your demos, you'll want to find the connections to pitch them to. You could invest in a membership in TAXI, the purchase of a good music business directory, or a subscription to a high-level tip sheet. Then you'll have to put together your submission packages. That means buying blank CDs, jewel cases, mailing envelopes and postage, or the gas to drive around dropping off your CDs. All these purchases can be researched on the Internet. Often you can find better deals online than at your local stores.

Keep track of all the money you spend. If you're lucky, you may generate income from your songwriting. Then you'll need those receipts for your tax deductions.

AFTERWORD

"The fundamental things apply as time goes by ..."

—Herman Hupfeld

Music is a worldwide industry that generates billions of dollars and, as the NSAI slogan goes, "It all starts with a song." And that song starts with us. We make the biggest mistake of all when we don't realize our worth.

As we sit alone, or with one or two other songwriters, and search our hearts and the ether for the perfect way to express our emotions, tell our stories, and teach what we've learned, we are doing our right work. We can feel this in our bones. This love of songs is a gift we have been given and must share. We can't keep quiet; we must make music.

So, regardless of the technology storm in the world outside, back in our writers' room, it's still the same old story. We're still having fun looking for the missing chord. We're trying to connect our hearts to our minds and make them work together to create a song that no one can deny. ASCAP's Ralph Murphy writes an annual analysis of the anatomy of all the number one songs, called "Murphy's Law." At NSAI's Songposium we heard Ralph's report. Seventy percent of number one songs use the pronouns "you" and "I." They get to the hook in 60 seconds. The average intro is 13.2 seconds. Since the deregulation of radio, commercial time has increased from 11½ minutes to 28 minutes per hour. That puts a bigger burden on a song to hold the listeners' attention from one commercial to the other. Now song structures are morphing, new hybrid forms appearing, choruses are changing—all to meet radio's need for revenue. Is this what we're writing for? Yes.

And no.

Musical wallpaper has its uses. Songs as background noise in movies are fine. But, as for us, we serve the song. We dream of creating what used to be called a standard. That's a song so universal that it moves many singers to sing it and the whole world to sing along—a song like "As Time Goes By," which has been recorded hundreds of times by many different artists. Here's a short list of artists who recorded it: Merle Haggard, Natalie Cole, Rod Stewart, Frank Sinatra, Barbra Streisand, the Norman Luboff Choir (that's Pete's dad), Neil Diamond, Willie Nelson, and Tony Bennett. And it's probably being recorded somewhere, in some language, even as you read this. We'll drink to that!

Take up your club soda or champagne and let's have a toast! Here's to connecting with our songwriting community, fighting for our songwriter's rights, and living the songwriting life. But, most of all, as time goes by, here's to writing songs. The world needs all of our songs.

Write on,

Pat & Pete Luboff

INDEX